'Tony Breslin's highly readable and engaging book works on three levels. First, it offers a comprehensive chronicle of the impact of lockdown on our education system. Through clarity of narrative and the voices of a wide range of participants, we are reminded of the multi-layered and capricious events of spring and summer 2020. I have a strong sense that those interested in education will return to these pages for many years to come.

But *Lessons from Lockdown* provides much more than a captivating narrative of schooling during the pandemic. Breslin is a knowledgeable and experienced educator and articulates several decades of change within education, thus contextualizing the various responses to the closure of schools across the UK.

Finally, and most powerfully, the book makes a series of clear-eyed, well-balanced recommendations. These stimulating suggestions will, unquestionably, be discussed in staffrooms across the nation and, if we are to have the future we desire for our children, by those in power.'

Daniel Coyle, head teacher, Newman Catholic College, Brent

'This book captures a vital moment in time and offers a highly readable and engaging account of what happened when education was thrust into lockdown early in 2020.

But it goes further than that, placing the decisions taken in a broader context of educational policy and practice. Therefore, it should not be a surprise that it tells a tale of how many individual schools and teachers were left largely alone to make the best of the situation. In many ways *Lessons from Lockdown* demonstrates how the pandemic has shone a light on the injustices, inequities and poor political leadership that are endemic in our education system.

Tony Breslin's extensive research, drawing on the immediate experiences of a range of key players in the education sector, does us all a service in making sure that those decisions, actions and consequences are not all left to be reimagined with the benefit of hindsight, but chronicled here and now.

As we see the longer-term impact of lockdown on our children, our schools and on the wider educational community, researchers of the future will be intensely grateful for this book's ability to present a broad and deep narrative of what the lockdown of the first part of 2020 felt like to those involved.

The arguments that Breslin marshals from these experiences to challenge us all to reimagine what our education system should seek to achieve and how it should be structured are provocative and engaging.'

Nick Johnson, chief executive, British Educational
Research Association

'A lesson or class is a structured period of time where learning is intended to occur. *Lessons from Lockdown: The Educational Legacy of COVID-19* opens wide many doors to learning at the same time: principals' and policymakers' office doors, staffroom and classroom doors and, in particular, the doors to pupils' homes.

Drawing on extensive discussion and research, Dr Tony Breslin argues that one impact of COVID-19 lies in the way that the resultant lockdowns have challenged the success of traditional educational practice. As such, there are opportunities for change in every classroom, every school and every schooling system, and in local and regional agencies.

Lessons from Lockdown provides an immediate provocation of the work to be done while at the same time acknowledging the critical driver of such change: the collective capacity of all of those involved in supporting young people to thrive.

Breslin calls for direct engagement between policymakers and experienced educators, and identifies opportunities for change that span parental engagement, family learning, the development of schools as community hubs, the need for a stronger social curriculum, the well-being of both students and staff, and the growth of digital literacy, and offers detailed recommendations on each.

This book will help us to achieve the educational outcomes that we all hope for. If acted on, its recommendations have the power to create a new culture of schooling, a culture where "flourishing" is a regular descriptor of not only the experience of students, but of staff, schools and their communities.'

Ross Dean, teacher educator, school leadership, school improvement and adolescent well-being consultant; researcher, learning focused communities; and founder, Victorian Educational Leadership Consortium, Australian Education Union, Melbourne, Australia

'This book arrives just in time, as a new school year begins – albeit haltingly – under the continuing threat of the COVID-19 virus which, only a few months ago, abruptly interrupted educational systems around the world and created unprecedented chaos in the teaching and learning process.

In exploring the implications of this health crisis, Tony Breslin focuses on the interrelatedness of factors that exert a collective and profound effect on all aspects of the educational system. As such, the book includes both a retrospective analysis of specific policies that shaped the pre-COVID-19 educational system and a rich description of the ways in which a broad cross-section of stakeholders experienced the recent school closures and ensuing confusion associated with the virus. This is followed by a thoughtful examination of the inequities inherent in the current educational system that have been laid bare by the pandemic. Readers are asked to consider the significant and potentially permanent nature of societal changes associated with this and future global health crises, and to resist the compulsion to return to the familiar. They are urged, instead, to view the crisis as an auspicious opportunity for re-thinking taken-for-granted educational policies and practices and collaborating with all relevant stakeholders, for the purpose of creating a more equitable education for all.

Although this ground-breaking book focuses on a specific national context, the themes that emerge from this work are remarkably similar to those that are surfacing in schools across the globe, making *Lessons from Lockdown* a particularly informative and valuable book for all those concerned with schooling, regardless of the country in which they live.'

Betty Merchant PhD, Henrietta Frances Zezula Lowak endowed distinguished professor, Department of Educational Leadership and Policy Studies, College of Education and Human Development, University of Texas at San Antonio

'Schooling in England needed a reset before anyone had heard of COVID-19, but that ongoing crisis has also shone an unforgiving light on the limitations of the system. In this incisive and timely piece of research and analysis Tony Breslin makes a powerful case for us to use the experience of crisis to pursue reform in areas ranging from school governance, to parental engagement to social inclusion.'

Matthew Taylor, chief executive, Royal Society for Arts, Manufactures and Commerce (RSA)

'It has become somewhat fashionable to talk about building a better and a different education system following the pandemic. The fact that Tony Breslin has already written an informative and challenging book on the subject is evidence that he has been thinking of these things long before the recent difficulties caused others to also do so.

This is, therefore, a well-thought-out account of some of the questions we need to address and a good guide as to how to begin to put them into action. Tony Breslin's experience and commitment to children and young people, as ever, underpins everything that he writes.'

Estelle Morris, Baroness Morris of Yardley, former secretary of state for education

'In the rush to reopen schools after lockdown, the temptation to "get back to normal" and simply catch up on the months of lost learning appears to be overwhelming.

Tony Breslin argues this must be resisted. Instead, now is the time to rethink the entire system, from the starting age of formal education to the currently limited opportunities to learn in later life, to what is taught, how and why. For too long, changes to the education system have been driven by political considerations, short-term difficulties and even, at times, nostalgia. *Lessons from Lockdown* sets out why this piecemeal approach to reform needs to stop and provides an invaluable contribution to the debate that now must take place.'

Rosemary Bennett, former education editor, *The Times*

Lessons from Lockdown

Lessons from Lockdown explores the impact of COVID-19 on our schooling systems, on the young people and families that they serve and on all who work in – and with – our schools, and asks what the long-term ramifications of the pandemic might be for the pedagogy and purpose of formal education. Drawing on the voices of more than a hundred pupils, parents and professionals, it reveals how teachers and learners are adapting practice in areas such as curriculum modelling, parental engagement, assessment and evaluation and blended and online learning.

In this timely new book, Tony Breslin draws on his experience as a teacher, researcher, examiner, school governor and policy influencer to assess what the educational legacy of COVID-19 could be, and the potential that it offers for reframing how we 'do' schooling.

Whatever your place in this landscape, *Lessons from Lockdown* is a must-read for all concerned about the shape and purpose of schooling systems in mature economies – schooling systems and economies set on recovering from the kind of 'system shock' that the pandemic has delivered.

Dr Tony Breslin, a former chief examiner and local authority school improvement adviser, is a public policy analyst, educational commentator, curriculum development specialist and governance trainer. Director at Breslin Public Policy Limited and formerly chief executive at the Citizenship Foundation, he is chair of the governing board at Bushey Primary Education Federation and a trustee at Adoption UK.

Lessons from Lockdown

The Educational Legacy of COVID-19

TONY BRESLIN

Routledge
Taylor & Francis Group

LONDON AND NEW YORK

First published 2021
by Routledge
2 Park Square, Milton Park, Abingdon, Oxon OX14 4RN

and by Routledge
52 Vanderbilt Avenue, New York, NY 10017

Routledge is an imprint of the Taylor & Francis Group, an informa business

© 2021 Tony Breslin

British Library Cataloguing-in-Publication Data
A catalogue record for this book is available from the British Library

Library of Congress Cataloging-in-Publication Data
Names: Breslin, Tony, 1962– author.
Title: Lessons from lockdown : the educational
legacy of COVID-19 / Tony Breslin.
Description: Abingdon, Oxon ; New York, NY : Routledge, 2021. |
Includes bibliographical references and index. |
Identifiers: LCCN 2020043743 | ISBN 9780367639266 (hardback) |
ISBN 9780367639297 (paperback) | ISBN 9781003121343 (ebook)
Subjects: LCSH: Educational planning–Great Britain. |
Educational change–Great Britain. |
COVID-19 (Disease)–Great Britain. |
Community and school–Great Britain.
Classification: LCC LB2806 .B725 2021 | DDC 370.941–dc23
LC record available at https://lccn.loc.gov/2020043743

ISBN: 978-0-367-63926-6 (hbk)
ISBN: 978-0-367-63929-7 (pbk)
ISBN: 978-1-003-12134-3 (ebk)

Typeset in Dante and Avenir
by Newgen Publishing UK

This book is dedicated to my late parents,
Daniel and Catherine Breslin.
Their love, their values and their passion for
education remains inspiring.

Contents

Figures

Preface

The extent to which we draw on the lessons from lockdown in reconstructing our education and training systems, in the UK and elsewhere, is, of course, in our hands. This book seeks to collate and curate these lessons and poses at its heart one question: what kind of schooling do we want and need as we move forward from the experience of recent months?

The starting point for the text is straightforward and threefold: first, that COVID-19 has delivered a shock to our education and training systems, in the UK and beyond, which has the potential to be, and *ought* to be, long-standing; second, that this shock has ramifications for the pedagogy and purpose of education, the *what, how,* and *why* of learning; third, that this shock extends across, and has implications for, *every* kind of educational setting, from preschool to university, from adult and community learning to professional and vocational training – whether the provider is the state, the voluntary sector or private business – and young people in primary and secondary education.

Against this background, although the main focus in this text is on schools, the arguments and evidence set out in the pages that follow are about much more than what happens in our schools, vital though this is. While we concentrate on the statutory years, the perspective taken is one that understands the need for learning to be both life*long* and life-*wide*, that schools have a pivotal role to play in creating an appetite and capacity for learning and that they are a part of every individual's learning journey, not a precursor to it. Too often, books and papers that purport to be about education are actually about *schooling* and, quite specifically, the schooling of children and young people. I want to avoid this ambiguity from the outset: the

statutory schooling years are vital in laying the foundations for the fulfil-
ment of potential in adulthood, but education, unlike statutory schooling,
has no endpoint. And the need to both *reschool* society and *reskill* individuals,
of all ages, in light of the virus underlines this point.

In this context, three aspects of the lockdown are likely to prove especially pertinent for its legacy: first, the partial closure of schools, colleges,
universities and training facilities during lockdown has created, for at least
some practitioners and system leaders, a pause in the activity that they are
usually involved in and may, therefore, have created the space for the kind
of professional reflection rarely afforded to those engaged in teaching and
educational leadership – day in, day out; second, the suspension of various
stalwarts of the educational infra-structure – such as various inspectorates,
the testing of children towards the close of primary school, the cancellation
of the written papers that are usually central to public examinations and
performance tables in various settings – may allow us to assess the impact
of their absence, and, therefore, the extent to which their reinstatement is
either urgent or unnecessary; third, the rapid emergence of new pedagogies
in areas such as assessment, home learning and online and blended learning
might offer pointers to the educational and training strategies and facilities
of tomorrow.

There will be a strong desire to 'get back to normal', to reinstate life as was
(and not just in education), but I want to contend that we should resist this.
I have spent a professional lifetime arguing that educational institutions – in
common with, for instance, hospitals, the military, prisons, the police, care
settings, and the bureaucracies of the state and the corporate sector – are
relatively *total* institutions (Goffman, 1956), that is they are (often necessarily) highly structured with tightly defined roles and responsibilities and
a range of clearly set out procedural protocols and regulations. Thus, they
have a strong tendency to both reproduce and self-justify their practice
across generations. As such, our schools, colleges and universities maximise the feeling of change while minimising its impact, reproducing curricular and other long-standing pedagogic practices, rather than responding
to emergent need (Breslin, 2008). The kind of system shock delivered by
COVID-19 has the potential to fling us from these comfort zones, to make
us reassess our practice, to prompt us to ask if things could and should be
different and what could 'different' mean? Might 'thinking different' offer us
solutions to some of the recurrent challenges at the heart of our education
systems, challenges (notably those around inequalities of opportunity and
outcome) that, hitherto, have endured in spite of a plethora of educational
reforms, especially in the schooling sector?

In addressing these and related questions, the research that has laid the foundations for this text, carried out across ten weeks in June, July and August 2020, has involved more than a hundred participants, including those teaching, or involved in supporting teaching, in the primary and secondary phases; those involved in meeting the needs of children and young people with special educational needs and disabilities; those working in a range of alternative provision settings; school leaders and those involved in school governance, either as governors or trustees; parents, guardians and carers; those teaching in various parts of the independent sector; a range of policy influencers, policy shapers and policymakers, including those based in teachers' professional associations and in regulatory bodies; and, of course, children and young people in our primary and secondary schools.

All of our research participants have been engaged virtually, utilising a range of technologies as new to the author as they have been for most of those taking part, all of whom have been measured but candid in their responses, and generous and warm in their spirit, whether they have made their contribution through a series of ten focus group conversations, a set of sixteen one-to-one research interviews, or, for those unable to get to the virtual sessions, a small set of written submissions and extended telephone conversations. Unusually, as we outline in Appendix A, this research has been carried out largely *during* the writing phase, feeding the script as it progressed.

Each of these conversations has explored a range of themes identified as important by the participants but framed in research terms across three strands that might be termed, at their most simple, as 'before', 'during' and 'after'. Thus, in each conversation we started by exploring the nature of schooling across the UK, and sometimes beyond, immediately *prior* to the virus, noting some variations in the different national systems but focusing on a set of key commonalities; for instance, the different status accorded to academic and vocational learning, the common use of a range of quantitative performance measures to assess the success of individual learners *and* the educational settings in which formal learning takes place, the system-wide tension between attainment and inclusion and the tendency to marginalise the social and emotional aspects of learning in favour of more instrumental and measurable approaches. Readers from other jurisdictions will find varying degrees of similarity with educational and training systems in their own countries.

The second part of these conversations explored the different and nuanced *experiences* of lockdown, or rather the different *phases* of lockdown as our focus groups increasingly framed it, for the research participants, notably teachers and trainers and learners and their families. As we work through the chapters that follow, we will see how the sheer variety of experience belied the simple media headlines that spoke of a singular experience of lockdown and universal, usually catastrophic, outcomes, especially for those in the most disadvantaged settings. This is not to deny the impact of lockdown on these individuals or others, but it is to suggest that the reality is, and was, much more complex and that any responses to this reality will need to be sophisticated and carefully targeted.

Finally, we asked our discussants to reflect on their experiences and those revealed in a wider range of data to crystalise the lessons from lockdown, especially those that *cannot* be ignored, and to paint a picture of what schooling could (and possibly *should*) be like after the virus has passed.

Resultantly, and in light of the lessons learned and the visions offered, we offer, at the close of each of our ten chapters, a set of five recommendations – fifty across the text – for policymakers to ponder as we seek to secure a positive educational legacy from the chaos and tragedy that has been, and continues to be, COVID-19. We propose these tentatively and with humility, not least because with a publishing deadline that falls on 1 September 2020 (the day on which national governments in England, Wales and Northern Ireland intend that schools will reopen fully, three weeks after their reopening in Scotland), we know that this is a drama that has many acts yet to play and that by the time you read this our 'solutions' will span a continuum that runs from *obsolete* to *embedded*.

We also know that the years immediately following the arrival of the virus on these shores may prove to be more challenging than the period of the lockdown itself; nonetheless, we look to a legacy that has already impacted on how we value education, and on how we deliver it, how we think of those who work within it, how we deal with persistent inequalities of outcome that the virus has not created but has stripped bare and how we work with parents, carers and communities to do so.

Those involved in public-speaking coaching frequently talk about the 'power of the pause', the contrived but effective technique that provides emphasis through silence and allows audiences the space to ponder and (perhaps) applaud. The enforced pause of the lockdown has been far more impactful, the lessons for learners, educators and many others more powerful, although it is not a pause that has brought any *rest* for any of these actors, just a pause from the foregoing reality. We have an opportunity to show that this pause has been far from silent, that educators have been busily innovating and remodelling, recasting the nature of the total institutions in which they work as they do so. Necessity has been the mother of invention, of innovation, of creativity, emerging as toothpaste that we implore policymakers not to seek to force back into the tube, but to capture, welcome and embrace.

This book is an attempt to give voice to this welter of creative activity, an attempt to ensure that the lessons from lockdown are captured for the benefit of learners everywhere, an attempt to ensure that, from a *societal* and *educational* standpoint, post-virus rehabilitation is not about how quickly we can get back to where we were. Nor is it about reconstituting our schools in the image of 'crammer' colleges, obsessed by catch-up and so-called *curriculum* recovery, as if all the last few months have left us with is a shortcoming in *knowledge* and a loss of *coverage*.

Rather, it is about how far we can travel in light of our shared experience, and the different educational and training needs that will surely manifest themselves in the years ahead. It is also about acknowledging those long-standing shortcomings at the heart of our schooling and education systems, around the persistent inequalities of outcome noted above, around the need to build inclusion and attainment alongside each other rather than posing them as different and sometimes conflicting opposites and around attending to the well-being of children, their families and all who support their learning – as if we could build a sustainable education system without doing this, even if, prior to the virus, this is *exactly* how some practitioner-commentators might describe our efforts. As the leader of one of the country's larger academy groups tweeted as the proposed September 'reopening' of schools approached:

> There are far more creative, innovative, risk proof and productive ways to plan for the return to full-time, engaging education for all children next term, than simply forcing them all back to the classroom at the same time – let's think differently, reset rather than simply reopen!
> (Steve Chalke, founder and chair, Oasis Community Learning,
> @stevechalke, 2 August 2020)

If the enforced pause of an unwanted virus enables us to press 'reset' in just this way, to ponder these questions and to begin to frame our answers, it may be that some good will come of all of this yet.

Tony Breslin
September 2020
Hertfordshire, UK

Acknowledgements

I am grateful to the many people who have contributed to the writing of this book. Chief among these is Ryan McMahon who has served as researcher on the *Lessons from Lockdown* project. When the incredibly supportive Annamarie Kino, my editor at Routledge, commissioned my proposal for the book in June 2020, we agreed the gloriously ridiculous deadline of mid-August for the submission of the draft. I felt that I could drive the project forward and, at a stretch, get the 60,000 words drafted in this timescale, but I knew that I could not gather and sift through the range of news coverage and official reports, collate the research references or organise the range of interviews and focus groups that we both felt were vital if the book was to give voice to others and not just to its author. In this context, Ryan's contribution has been vital and immeasurable. And as somebody who had elected to pursue a career in teaching just before he was engaged to work on *Lessons from Lockdown*, I am relieved that this remains his ambition upon the project's completion. He will make a fine addition to this, the finest of professions.

Of course, great thanks are also due to Annamarie, Molly Selby the editorial assistant and their colleagues at Routledge, for their encouragement and patience. When I don my school governor or charity trustee hat, or when I train these noble volunteers, I talk about getting the balance between support and challenge right; Annamarie and Molly have done so with aplomb.

This book has its origins in a set of blogs that I posted early in lockdown. I am especially grateful to those who commissioned these pieces, especially Rachel O'Brien at the Royal Society for Arts, Manufactures and Commerce

(RSA) (the resultant blog gave this book its title) and Gerry Cernziawski at the British Educational Research Association (BERA), and to those who reposted these and other blogs, notably Marios Georgiou at Step Teachers, a former A level sociology student of mine. Others, including Frank Bennett and Helen Michaels at Digi-Board Education and Cosette Reczek at the Better Governance Commission, have allowed me to drop everything to concentrate on researching and writing these pages.

Special thanks are also due to more than a hundred individuals – pupils, parents, teachers, school senior leaders and support staff in primary, secondary and special schools in the state and independent sectors, youth workers, those working in alternative provision settings, school governors and trustees, teacher educators, educational researchers and policy shapers – from the UK and elsewhere who contributed to our ten focus groups or our series of one-to-one interviews and small group sessions. Thanks also goes to those who let us sit in on other projects and meetings, notably my colleagues in the Fabian Society Education Group, Alex Bell of Leadership Lemonade and Danny Coyle, head at Newman Catholic College, which, as Cardinal Hinsley High School, had been the secondary school that I had attended in Harlesden, North West London, the place it all began.

All of our research participants are listed separately in Appendix B. I am thankful not just for the time that every one of these individuals gave us, but the spirit in which they gave this time: openly and open-mindedly, generous with both their time and their ideas, insightful and, in spite of what was often near exhaustion, essentially optimistically, driven by a belief that in among the tragedy of the virus and the reality of lockdown might lie the seeds of innovation and opportunity. In terms of convening the focus groups, Ryan and I are especially grateful to Professor Rachel Lofthouse at Leeds Beckett University for helping us to convene the teacher education focus group and also David Miller, head at Pebble Brook School, for doing likewise with regard to the special education and alternative provision focus group.

My colleagues on the governing board at Bushey Primary Education Federation and on the board of trustees at Adoption UK, the senior staff in each of these organisations and my many friends across the school and third-sector governance communities deserve my gratitude and thanks. I am also indebted to those who have worked with me in a plethora of roles across a working lifetime in education, especially my tutors, Barry Dufour and the late Doug Holly at the University of Leicester School of Education and Denis Lawton and Paddy Walsh at the University of London Institute of Education, my many colleagues in the Association for Citizenship Teaching and the Association for the Teaching of the Social Sciences and the friends I have worked with at Langleybury School in Hertfordshire, the School of St David and St Katharine in Haringey, the London Borough of Enfield School Improvement Service, the Citizenship Foundation and Breslin Public Policy Limited. All have played their part in enabling me to understand how our schools work and why education matters. In among these, the late Terry Farrell will always deserve a special word, a London head who gave his career to working with young people from often disadvantaged homes and to moulding young teachers so that *we* could go on to do likewise.

Throughout the writing period a range of individuals have been incredibly helpful and have met with me to explore the issues at hand, while others have simply kept me going with their insights, their toleration (of my inability to discuss anything else) and their sense of humour. Notable among these are Mike Moores, my long-term friend and collaborator at Breslin Public Policy; Phil Bowen at Pigeon Penguin who augmented his enduring and patient support for all of my online efforts with introductions to a number of key research participants; Mick Callanan, delivery director at the Orwell Youth Prize; another long-term friend, Paddy O'Leary, who was always up for a mid-morning, socially distanced coffee in the garden once the regulations allowed us; Cosette Reczek, who read through the final text, offering forensic, incisive and supportive feedback that I hope I have done justice to; Sophie McMahon who drafted the diagrams; Richard O'Sullivan for his vital input to the final cover design; Sarah Green, Project Manager at Newgen Publishing; Kelly Derrick who copy-edited the text; and Mary Ann Cooper, inspirational head teacher at Bushey Primary Education Federation, where I am privileged to be chair of governors.

Finally, I want to thank my wife, Ann Bowen-Breslin, another inspirational head teacher (at Hillingdon Primary School in West London) and much, much more, and our two boys for their unstinting support. Their inspiration, patience, toleration and insight gets me up in the morning and, more importantly, reminds me why this stuff matters. My study has been their home classroom and their company my daily fuel.

Needless to say, while the input of those above, and many others, has been invaluable – and for this reason I invoke 'we' rather than 'I' for the greater part of the book – I remain responsible for what is written in these pages, warts and all.

About the author

Dr Tony Breslin is an adviser, writer, media commentator and public policy analyst specialising in education and participation.

His reports, *A Place for Learning: Putting Learning at the Heart of Citizenship, Civic Identity and Community Life* (RSA, 2016) and *Who Governs Our Schools? Trends, Tensions and Opportunities* (RSA, 2017), have made important contributions to the debates about the role of adult and community learning and further and higher education in a post-industrial age and the nature of school governance in a new landscape of academies, federations and multi-academy trusts.

Tony's experience in governance and as a senior leader in education and the voluntary sector is extensive. A teacher by profession and a curriculum development specialist, he is currently chair at Bushey Primary Education Federation and a trustee of Adoption UK. Previously, he has served as chair of the awarding organisation Industry Qualifications, the public-speaking social enterprise Speakers Bank and the educational charities and membership associations Human Scale Education and the Association for the Teaching of the Social Sciences.

A former local authority school improvement adviser, a chief examiner at GCSE and a principal examiner at A level, he is best known for his work as chief executive at the Citizenship Foundation (2001–2010) – the influential education and participation charity now known as Young Citizens – where he developed the concept of the citizenship-rich school and also for his work in the governance arena, where his recent engagement as a consultant trainer at Herts for Learning was, prior to COVID-19, taking him into primary, secondary and special schools several times a week.

Tony is a champion of the social curriculum, professional and vocational education, community engagement and lifelong learning, themes that are common in a wide-ranging publications list featuring more than a hundred articles, papers and texts, and in the work of the successful social impact consultancy that he leads, Breslin Public Policy Limited.

About the researcher

Ryan McMahon is in his final socially distanced year reading theology, religion and philosophy of religion at Girton College, Cambridge and intends to graduate in summer 2021. He is planning to enter the teaching profession and has been offered a place on the Teach First programme. Prior to university, Ryan, who grew up in Cambridge, attended Arbury Primary School, Chesterton Community College and Hills Road Sixth Form College, where his A level studies spanned English, history and religious studies.

Schools during lockdown 1

The debate during the later stages of lockdown about schools 'reopening' brought a wry smile to the faces of many in the school workforce. Why? Because, for the most part, schools across the UK did not close. Throughout lockdown they had remained physically open to the children of key workers and those deemed 'vulnerable', and not just during term time, but across the Easter and half-term breaks and, in many cases, on bank holidays.

They had also remained open, or rather had opened, as *virtual* institutions, issuing assignments to students online and delivering teaching and tutoring so as to support home-schooling, not in the conventional sense of the term but as the means of delivering an education to all of those not on the school site.

Prior to this, 'home-schooling' had been the preserve of a small (albeit growing) minority of parents. Some of these families had grown exasperated with a system that had failed to address a particular need, perhaps around attachment or autism; others saw it as an only option after exclusion or as a remedy to 'school refusal'; still others simply rejected (on behalf of their children) the nature of the schooling that they saw before them, judging it variously as impersonal, industrialised, authoritarian and overly structured. Their critics wondered about the capability of some self-selected members of the home-schooling community to deliver an education for their children and more broadly about what they saw as the enforced loneliness of the home-schooled child – the 'self-isolation', if we might borrow a phrase from the lockdown toolbox.

There is not space here to explore, on either side, these critiques but the point is that home-schooling was a minority pursuit, even if a wider group often speculated on what it might be like to join this community of self-educators. Lockdown changed all that. Lockdown redefined and reappropriated home-schooling for the mainstream. The implications of this appropriation are likely to be profound and long term, with the probability that a minority of those who have 'discovered' home-schooling during the lockdown are unlikely to return to mainstream schooling, even if *mass* home-schooling during lockdown is a dilution of such practice pre-lockdown (Fenshaw-Smith, 2020). One experienced former head teacher and local authority-based school improvement specialist observed: 'We've already got an increase in elective, home education referrals, and we are one of the three or four counties with the highest percentages of home-schooling in the country' (Graeme Plunkett, senior school effectiveness officer, Cornwall Council, focus group – secondary education, 15 July 2020). As if by way of explanation, one of the parents who spoke to us put it this way:

> We've been in a fortunate position where my wife was previously a (primary school) teacher and she's taken it upon herself to teach our younger two (primary age) children. She's put aside the work that's been emailed to us (by the school) and come up with her own schemes of work. She's staying up late, preparing what's going to be done for the rest of the week … and she's enjoyed it. The children have enjoyed it to the point, actually, where we're discussing what we're going to do in September. And should we actually continue home-schooling? Or should we send the younger two back?
>
> (Parent and education professional, focus group – secondary education, 15 July 2020)

Of course, only a minority of children and young people have the benefit of having a parent who is a qualified teacher and, in any case, many other parents approached the prospect of schools reopening, in either June 2020 or August or September 2020, depending on the year group their child or children belonged to and whether they were based in Scotland or elsewhere in the UK, with a yearning for some kind of restored normality, newly clear about the challenges teachers embrace daily. This kind of comment from the parent of a Year 6 child who returned to school on 1 June, and who happened to work as a member of the support staff at their school, was not uncommon: 'When they went back to school, it was just such a relief for me as a parent, but it was good for the children too, to see the kids talking to their friends and playing together' (Parent, focus group – parents, guardians and carers, 22 June 2020).

And while some families enjoyed the greater time together that lock-down afforded them, the need to balance the demands of home and, for those working at home, those of an employer or those of a business operating from home, was always a challenge, as this professional, a qualified teacher and company secretary reveals:

> Some parents wanted to be excited about helping their children with virtual learning, but were challenged to do so as they were working in demanding full-time jobs (albeit from home). Whilst there was understanding for virtual meetings interrupted by children, in the end, many parents felt that it was difficult to be everything: parent, worker and teacher, especially in instances where the parent is stale in their knowledge or unfamiliar with the subject – or the technology.
> (Parent, written submission, 31 August 2020)

The point is that there are no standardised tales of lockdown, just a multitude of experiences, patterned as always by factors such as social class, ethnicity, family structure, parental occupation, mode of employment and so on.

Early experiences of lockdown

If there was a commonality of experience, it was that of those working in schools during the early weeks of lockdown. For this was a system-wide shock, not the single school shock of, say, an unexpectedly poor inspection result, a disappointing set of performance data or the departure of a popular head or principal.

As February gave way to March, and news of the struggles to contain the virus in Italy began to dominate UK press coverage, the view that COVID-19 was merely another far-off concern began to wilt. Some parents started to withdraw their children from school, teacher absence rose as members of staff took on shielding responsibilities or became fearful for their own vulnerability, long-planned and richly anticipated school trips planned for the summer and autumn were postponed, as were parents' evenings and school-based training sessions for school governors; and the teacher union conferences, a long-standing feature of the Easter break, were cancelled. The headline of a *Daily Telegraph* piece on 14 March 2020, penned by the paper's education editor Camilla Turner four days before the closure of schools was announced and as the Easter holiday approached, gave an early hint of the juggernaut that was about to hurtle around the bend: 'Extended Easter school holidays on the agenda as heads meet ministers' (Turner, 2020b). The impending closedown would certainly produce more than an extended holiday break. The following Wednesday, 18 March, the closure

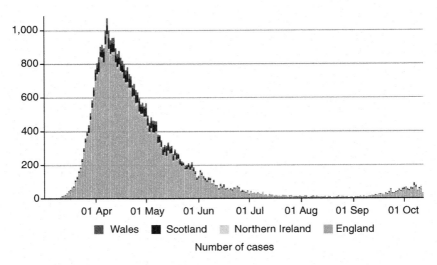

Figure 1.1 The pattern of deaths from the virus across lockdown.
Source: Department of Health and Social Care (2020b).

of schools and the cancellation of written public examination papers was confirmed and pupils, parents and teachers, especially those children and young people about to transition to junior or secondary school or into further or higher education said tentative goodbyes, unsure whether this was merely an interruption or the closure of this phase of their education. For some, it would turn out to be the latter. By this point, recorded UK deaths from the virus had reached 104, while the number of confirmed cases stood at 2,626. As this book goes to press the number of deaths from the virus is, albeit gradually, approaching (and *after* a downward recalculation during August), 42,000.

Figure 1.1 makes clear this reality and shows the pattern of deaths across the lockdown, while Figure 1.2 shows how the number of confirmed cases (in part a product of the scale of testing) changed across this period. Figure 1.3 reveals the level of hospital admissions, an indicator of the seriousness of the illness suffered.

At a human level, the following account from an experienced primary school deputy head, who was required to self-isolate just before the closure of schools was confirmed, is instructive:

> He [the head teacher] called me in and said, 'Diane, I've got to tell you something, I need to send you home!' Well, I said the most bad swear word, the worst ever swear word, that I've ever said in his office!

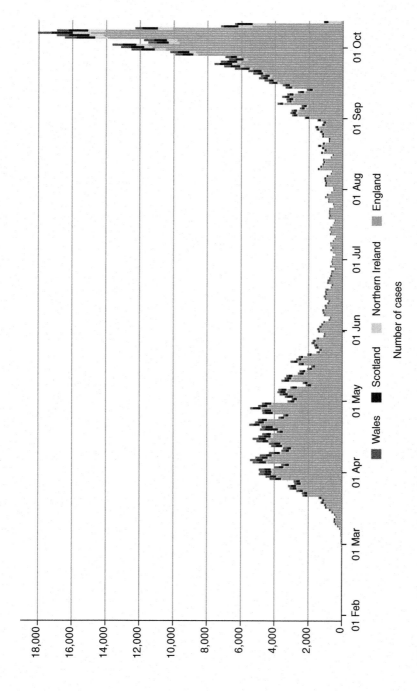

Figure 1.2 The pattern of recorded infection across lockdown.
Source: Department of Health and Social Care (2020a).

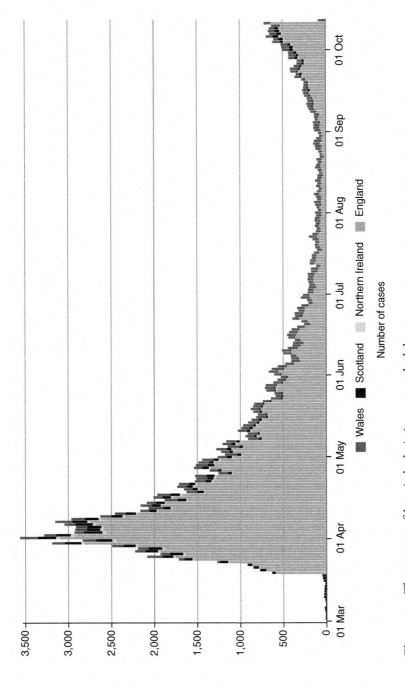

Figure 1.3 The pattern of hospital admissions across lockdown.
Source: Department of Health and Social Care (2020c).

Because I'm on that, you know, I'm on the, the list, the vulnerable group, the listed flu jab people. And I was absolutely furious. There were three other senior managers who he had to have that same conversation with, and we all picked up our belongings and our Surface Pro and we schlepped out of the school. For me, those initial days, knowing that closure was coming very shortly – well, I felt really, I didn't want to be feeling as useless as I was feeling; 'cause I felt that you feel a bit of a sense of responsibility, you know.

(Diane Rawlins, senior deputy, Arbury Primary School, Cambridge, focus group – primary education, 14 July 2020)

Rawlins continues:

There were just lots of different emotions that we went through in those early days. I was answering emails at the speed of light. I was juggling everything all at once. I was anxious that what if somebody needed me? Normally they'd just drop into my office and, of course, that couldn't happen anymore. So, I needed people to know that I was there for them. I might not be in the building. But it was really quite strange for me.

And for children and young people, the experience was just as disconcerting:

With the situation changing so rapidly, the announcement on Wednesday 18 March that schools would be closing and our examinations cancelled came as a shock: although exams are far from a pleasant experience, I did not experience relief in response to the news. Rather, I feared for the future, for what would become of my university offer for the following academic year; I grieved the loss of the final months at my sixth form, and I struggled through the hasty goodbyes. I recall one of my closest friends and I agreeing that 'it wasn't supposed to end like this'.

(Amy, Year 13 student, Hertfordshire, written submission, 27 August 2020)

A teacher, reflecting on how sudden the experience was for highly motivated students in examination groups in schools with a strong focus on academic success, offered this stark comparison: 'If this were drug therapy, this was [as] violently "cold turkey" as it gets' (head of department, East of England, research interview, summer 2020). Another of our interviewees, Nick Johnson, who is a parent, vice chair of his children's school governing board and chief executive at the British Educational Research Association (BERA), notes that there were other poignant reminders of what we, our children and our communities were missing during lockdown:

> My phone is synched to the school calendar and it pings daily with alerts for all of [the] things that aren't now happening ... parents' evenings, performances, transition meetings – these are the things that make the school what it is.
>
> (Nick Johnson, chief executive, BERA, research interview, 13 August 2020)

Many of us will have had similar alerts throughout lockdown. Partly because these alerts often go across year groups, they are also a reminder of something else – just how much schools and all who work in them do for our children, just how many meetings and gatherings schools convene and how many relationships they nurture and mediate; again, one of our research participants puts it better than any paragraphs of explanation we can offer: 'What is a school if it is not a complex set of relationships?' (Philip Preston, school governance trainer, Herts for Learning, focus group – primary education, 14 July 2020). Our policymakers would do well to take note: post-lockdown, the challenge is not simply to reinstate systems and address gaps in learning (vital though this is), it is about enabling the rebuilding of the relationships that make these systems work, and that enable our children not just to succeed, but to flourish.

Scaling-up schooling

The initial attempts by policymakers to 'get children back to school' will go down as a case study in how not to 'do' public policy. On Wednesday 18 March, at one of the daily news briefings that became a part of the typical lockdown day for the avid news watchers among us, Prime Minister Boris Johnson had announced: 'After schools shut their gates on Friday afternoon, they will remain closed for the vast majority of pupils, until further notice'. Schools had closed a week or so ahead of the start of an Easter break that policymakers had hitherto been holding out for; with this, and given the prime minister's words, many presumed that the closure would either be relatively short, perhaps through to the close of April, or, conversely, that schools might not be back until September. Whitehall sources suggesting in early May that primary schools would reopen to all on 1 June, the first Monday after the annual Whitsun half-term break, alarmed the profession, or at least its trade union leaders, and they initially performed (as deemed by the *Daily Mail*) to type, with the largest teaching union, the National Education Union, initially instructing its members not to 'engage' with heads and senior leadership teams (SLTs) in the quest to open, declaring: 'While we all want to see a return to some sort of normality, the NEU [National Education Union] believes it's really premature to talk about a June return date' (cited in Adams, 2020b). Within a week or so, the government's plans had moderated and envisaged a phased return that would see all primary-aged pupils make some kind of return to school by the end of the summer, but Courtney remained unimpressed:

> It's reckless, it's irresponsible. Mary [Bousted, with whom he co-leads the union] and I wrote to the government on May 1 asking them to talk with us before making any announcement, to get the science out there where people can see it, peer reviewed, about whether this would be safe or not.
>
> (Courtney, cited in Ridler, 2020)

This time Courtney's comments were echoed by Paul Whiteman, general secretary of the National Association of Head Teachers (NAHT):

> Based on the current trajectory it seems wildly optimistic, to the point of being irresponsible, to suggest that we will be in a position to return all primary children to school within the next seven weeks. This will give false hope to families and parents that we are further along the road to recovery than we actually are.
>
> (Whiteman, cited in Ridler, 2020)

In short, the government had brought the professional associations representing school leaders and classroom practitioners on to the same hymn sheet, even if the *Daily Mail*'s front-page response, citing the reopening of schools in twenty-two European Union countries, was predictable and aimed, again, at the teaching unions, screaming 'When Will They Learn?'

Unions aside though, there were other stakeholders in this: parents and their children, school governing boards, multi-academy trusts and local authorities. The safety concerns expressed by the teaching unions, and briefly endorsed by the British Medical Association, were increasingly raised by these players. Thus, the question was less and less one of 'When will the unions allow the schools reopen?' and more and more one of 'Will parents send their children in when they do so?' The initial binary presentation of 'goodies' and 'baddies' was simply unsustainable.

Clearly, there was significant concern among parents about the safety of a June return to school. Back in December, as we watched early news reports about the emergence of the virus in China, we had assured ourselves that a lockdown could not work in the 'free' West, that this was an obedient people rolling over in the face of a state with a long history of oppression. By April, our own streets were close to a similar silence, with our biggest city centres empty, our air clean and the birdsong a revelation for many. The lockdown had succeeded, albeit because of fear rather than deferential compliance. With another of the three-part slogans beloved of the prime minister's sidekick, Dominic Cummings, 'Stay at Home, Stop the Virus, Save the NHS', the streets were quiet. Indeed, when Boris Johnson announced its moderation in England in early May to the softer and more ambiguous 'Stay Alert, Control the Virus, Save Lives', he drew widespread criticism, notably from his counterparts in Wales, Scotland and Northern Ireland who failed to follow suit, revealing the first cracks in what had been a hitherto UK-wide approach to the virus.

Another lesson from lockdown had emerged: you may be able to flip a slogan with the click of a graphic designer's mouse (or a spin doctor's passive-aggressive insistence) but you can't turn fear on and off like a tap, especially the fear of parents for the safety of their youngest children and especially against the backdrop of a risk-averse culture that had been twenty years in the making.

By this stage, the sense of shared enterprise and common cause that had characterised the early weeks of lockdown had begun to fragment. Scroll forward another couple of months to July 2020 and the four UK jurisdictions found themselves midway through a clumsy, clunky and tentative exit from lockdown; less in lockstep and more like a group of first-time dancers struggling to find a shared rhythm, with the political consensus that had characterised both relations between the main parties *within* Westminster and *between* Westminster and the devolved administrations in Scotland, Wales and Northern Ireland fast disappearing in the rear-view mirror.

Moreover, throughout the crisis, the Westminster government in particular had attracted criticism for an approach to exiting lockdown that appeared to be based on the maxim 'announce first, worry about the detail later'. Nowhere did this approach have more impact than in schools.

Perhaps for this reason, the prime minister's pledge of a '£1 billion school rebuilding programme for England' (Proctor and Adams, 2020), announced in mid-June in the midst of the uneven school return recorded here, got barely a morning's headlines. If this was an attempt to 'bury bad news', it had failed. Maybe, a politician that some had considered a master at generating a spirit of optimism, whatever the reality, was losing his touch.

Towards September

As the academic year that never was morphed into the formal summer break that didn't feel like one and lockdown eased beyond the school gates, most believed that a full September reopening was inevitable. Even some of the most enthusiastic first-time home educators were growing weary of what, a couple of months earlier, had seemed like a new vocation, as this participant in our parents' focus group conceded:

> [At the start] I sort of flew into my old youth worker days and went 'this will be fun', I'll make-up some activities, twinkle registration and other things ... My husband wanted it to be creative as well. So, we had a theme each week and, you know we made a timetable, and probably for the first two or three weeks, we had quite a lot of fun ... We managed to split the home learning between us, and we were ... quite enthusiastic and energetic about it, and, you know, we'd do our Joe Wicks every morning. And, but, but yeah, the novelty certainly wore off pretty quickly.
>
> (Ruth Dwight, parent, focus group – parents, guardians and carers, 22 July 2020)

Moreover, as the lockdown wore on the differences in the *experience* of virtual and home-schooling, for children and their parents, became more visible, revealed sometimes through informal conversations across extended families and friendship groups. Some schools and teachers were more adept at providing appropriate work, some young people lacked the equipment to access the virtual provision, whatever its quality (a point we expand on in Chapters 2 and 10), some equipment faltered at either end of the home–school connection – sometimes because of a failure to understand how to use it, rather than a fault with the equipment itself – some battled with limited and crowded home spaces and others battled with the balance between working from home and supporting the learning of their child or children.

However, it soon became clear that the road from the pandemic was far less predictable than the road to it. The road to it, through January and February, had been characterised by an initially gradual growth in deaths attributed to the virus, crossing gradually into double and then triple figures and then stories of horror, notably from Italy, of what might be in store. The exponential acceleration in UK deaths through April and early May confirmed the worst of fears, first in hospitals and then in care homes, about the potency of the virus.

In contrast, the road from the pandemic – and it may yet prove presumptuous to talk about a road *from* COVID-19 – has been much less predictable or linear, with the government seeming to be under pressure from at least six forces to *ease* the lockdown:

1. The fear of economic Armageddon, with a spate of high-profile job losses and business closures from big brand employers during July and August 2020 substantiating this.
2. Particular concerns about the *survival* of specific sectors, notably in the retailing, hospitality and travel sectors.
3. The upcoming removal of the safety net of the furlough, and the apparent implausibility of extending it given the fear of the future state of the public finances.
4. Growing concerns (addressed substantively elsewhere in this text) of the impact of sustained school closures in the upcoming academic year on children's learning (Sharp et al., 2020) and on their mental health.
5. The apparently stark differences in learning lost between different social groups and between the state and independent sectors.
6. A general feeling that people had 'had enough' of the isolation of lockdown, and wanted to get back to some sort of normality, 'however' defined.

But the pressure the government faced was by no means in one direction; thus, this road to normality was strewn with hold-ups and detours not predicted when the easing process had first begun several months previous. Notably, policymakers faced the following:

1. Renewed surges in the virus across the UK, notably among some of our most disadvantaged black, Asian and minority ethnic (BAME) communities, especially but not exclusively in former mill towns in the Midlands, the North and the North-West, such that by mid-August, the *Sun* reported that a further twenty areas had followed the city of Leicester into some form of local lockdown and that another twenty-eight areas remained on the 'watch list' maintained by NHS officials for potential lockdowns (Fiorillo and Fuller, 2020).
2. Spikes in the virus in a number of popular UK tourist destinations, leading to hastily announced and near-instantly implemented quarantine arrangements for those returning from what they had considered to be post-lockdown holidays.
3. Spikes in a number of countries that were among those most heavily praised for what had appeared to be their near-eradication of the virus first time around, notably Germany and Australia.

4. Continued question marks over the effectiveness of the UK government's track and trace system and the failure to deliver a smartphone app to support this.
5. Similar question marks over when a vaccine might be available, how quickly it might be rolled out and how effective it might be.

These counter pressures inevitably clashed with an early summer narrative that presumed a straighter road to normality and with the reopening of schools as a signature landmark along this road. Instead, it was suggested that a road that was proving long and winding might be navigated by the opening and closing of different sectors, so as to maintain only a certain level of 'openness' in society at a particular point in time:

> We all know that what we have to try and do is to get to the absolute edge of what we can do in terms of opening up society and the economy without getting to the point where the virus starts to take off again … We have probably reached near the limits, or the limits, of what we can do in terms of opening up society.
> (Professor Chris Whitty, chief medical officer, 31 July 2020)

These counter pressures, and the choices they imply about the opening and closing of different sectors, led the children's commissioner, Anne Longfield, to issue a briefing paper setting out ten principles that ought to protect children's interests in future lockdowns, local or national. The second and third principles were explicit:

*   Children's perspectives must be better reflected in scientific and public health advice. Any measures implemented must take into account children's needs and circumstances where they differ from those of adults.
*   Education should be prioritised over other sectors: first to open, last to close. When only a limited amount of social interaction is feasible, the amount accounted for by education must be protected – at the expense of other sectors (and) activities.
> (Ann Longfield, children's commissioner, policy briefing
> 'Putting Children First in Future Lockdowns', August 2020)

The subsequent press reports that dominated the first week of August homed in on the choices that this might involve, and inevitably returned to a choice initially posed by Sage member Professor Graham Medley (which we cite elsewhere in these pages), a week earlier: pubs or schools?

The prime minister, who a month or so earlier had suggested that normality would be re-established by late autumn, weighed in with an interview published in the *Mail on Sunday*, widely cited in other newspapers and media outlets, acknowledging the reality of these hard choices, but notably without *directly* or *personally* raising the spectre of closures in particular sectors: 'Keeping our schools closed a moment longer than absolutely necessary is socially intolerable, economically unsustainable, and morally indefensible' (Boris Johnson, cited in Shipman et al., 2020).

The 'pubs versus schools' conundrum makes for good headlines, and did so for ten or more days in early August, but there are problems with such play-offs, three of which politicians and commentators consistently ignored in these exchanges:

1. Although society is organised in sectors, and various outcomes are measured by sector, individuals live their lives *across* sectors – they use pubs and schools, and playing one sector off against another ignores this.
2. If the price of opening schools is the closure of other sectors (not just pubs and restaurants but retailing and a range of service-based activities), the economic impact of this may accentuate job losses in these sectors and among those losing their jobs will be parents with children in the schooling system – and parental unemployment is causally linked with poor educational outcomes.
3. Seeking to convince parents and teachers that it is safe for children to return to school is likely to be doubly difficult if policymakers are tightening or reasserting lockdown in other sectors at the same time – however compelling the science may be on the inability of children to carry and transmit the virus to each other or to others in the school community, or the risk to teachers from the virus.

And so the build-up to the planned return to school in September played out, most of this quietly ignoring the logistic concerns around the practicality of delivering effective on-site, face-to-face schooling for all while maintaining social distancing, teaching in smaller groups and operating with staff teams that may still include colleagues who are shielding, in quarantine or who simply share the anxieties that some parents may still maintain.

Guided by science?

With such anxieties appearing to re-emerge, and local lockdowns growing in number, the risk of a less than smooth full reopening of schools appeared to remain on the cards and a different kind of intervention seemed called for.

It duly came, ten days before reopening schools in England, Wales and Northern Ireland and two weeks after their reopening in Scotland. With the English secretary of state for education, Gavin Williamson, and his schools minister, Nick Gibb, visibly shaken by what even the most measured of broadcasters and pundits were framing as the 'exam grading fiasco' (which we discuss in Chapter 5) and the minister responsible for apprenticeships and skills (a brief that includes further education colleges), Gillian Keegan, quarantining after returning from a holiday in the French Alps and Prime Minister Boris Johnson returning from a gap of several weeks allegedly spent holidaying in a tent in the Scottish highlands, it fell to the UK's chief medical officers and their deputies to reassure parents that schools would be a relatively safe space come the close of the month, even if mask wearing remained the norm beyond the school gates:

> We are confident that multiple sources of evidence show that a lack of schooling increases inequalities, reduces the life chances of children and can exacerbate physical and mental health issues. School improves health, learning, socialisation and opportunities throughout the life course including employment … We are confident in the extensive evidence that there is an exceptionally small risk of children of primary or secondary school age dying from COVID-19. The infection fatality rate (proportion of those who are infected who die) for those aged 5 to 14 is estimated at 14 per million, lower than for most seasonal flu infections … Our overall consensus is that, compared to adults, children may have a lower risk of catching COVID-19 (lowest in younger children), definitely have a much lower rate of hospitalisation and severe disease, and an exceptionally low risk of dying from COVID-19. Very few, if any, children or teenagers will come to long-term harm from COVID-19 due solely to attending school. This has to be set against a certainty of long-term harm to many children and young people from not attending school.
>
> (Department of Health and Social Care, 2020d)

And, turning to the safety of staff and parents, the medical experts continue:

> Transmission of COVID-19 to staff members in school does occur, and data from UK and international studies suggest it may largely be staff to staff (like other workplaces) rather than pupil to staff. This reinforces the need to maintain social distancing and good infection

control inside and outside classroom settings, particularly between staff members and between older children and adults. If teachers, other school staff, parents or wider family catch COVID-19 their risks of severe illness are similar to those of other adults of the same age, ethnicity and health status.

(Department of Health and Social Care, 2020d)

But they concede, alluding again to the 'pubs or schools' conundrum discussed earlier:

Because schools connect households it is likely opening schools will put some upward pressure on transmission more widely and therefore increase R. We have confidence in the current evidence that schools are much less important in the transmission of COVID-19 than for influenza or some other respiratory infections … [but] it is possible that opening schools will provide enough upward pressure on R that it goes above 1 having previously been below it, at least in some local areas. This will require local action and could mean societal choices that weigh up the implications of imposing limitations on different parts of the community and the economy.

(Department of Health and Social Care, 2020d)

This had been the most comprehensive statement – from politician, educationalist or scientist – yet issued on the risks (or otherwise) of fully reopening schools. For some, the scientists had, deliberately or not, rushed to the side of their beleaguered political masters; for others, they had shown their exasperation with these masters through issuing such a statement. The return to schools in Scotland had gone reasonably well, with attendance rates approaching normal in the circumstances. Only time would tell whether the response of parents UK-wide would mirror that of their Scottish peers, or whether the intervention of the medical experts would have a significant impact on their chosen course of action. For much of the lockdown, the politicians had claimed that they would 'follow' (or at least 'be guided by') 'the science'. Whether parents would remained to be seen.

Certainly, the Westminster government did little to quell parental or staff anxieties, decreeing a week or so before schools were due to reopen that those in secondary schools in lockdown areas would be required to wear masks in corridors and issuing, to wide-scale ridicule, new guidance to secondary heads over the August bank holiday weekend, with most schools due to reopen the following week.

Summary and key messages

An ongoing narrative around schools being 'closed' masks the amount of work undertaken by schools and teachers throughout the lockdown. 'Normal' schooling may have been put on hold, which has allowed for some reflection on normal practice, but this has been a busy and testing time for all involved in the education of our children and hasn't always been recognised as such.

Key operational decisions about precisely when and how to reopen schools need to rest with local leaders – head teachers and governing boards – given the rich understanding of facilities, resources and communities that they hold, but local leaders need clear and timely guidance. At times, the absence of a grasp of local school and community detail – and sometimes a simple understanding of *how* schools work – has revealed itself in the inappropriateness of the guidance provided.

Although many local authorities, multi-academy trusts and the various bodies that support schools in the independent sector have provided vital support for local leaders during an incredibly stressful period, attempts to micro-manage school openings from afar have, on occasions, produced stress and delay on all sides. These local system leaders have not been helped by mixed messages in the guidance issued by those in central government or by the lateness with which this guidance has been issued.

Local, regional and national lockdowns are likely to remain a possibility for some years to come and may – in the age of the supervirus – become a permanent feature of our existence. The multiple lessons learned, in the UK and elsewhere, about how schooling systems react to the announcement of lockdown needs to be captured and shared.

Policymakers need to work with the profession, and with system and school leaders in particular, to develop strategies for the opening and closing of schools that are clearly understood, easily communicable, credible and straightforward to implement with reasonable speed system-wide.

Recommendations

1.1 There needs to be greater cooperation between policymakers, system leaders and schools to collectively respond to the multiple impacts of COVID-19.

1.2 The Department for Education should urgently provide legal advice on the respective responsibilities of heads, governing boards, trustee boards and local authorities in the event of a future suspension of schooling.

1.3 Plans should be put in place for the possibility of future local lockdowns or school closures at the earliest opportunity.

1.4 There must be much greater recognition of, and sensitivity to, how policy announcements impact on capacity and confidence across the education sector.

1.5 Policymakers must find far more effective ways to directly engage with, and respond to, the experiences of practitioners.

Parental engagement and the experience of learning at home

2

The level of parental engagement in the schooling system and the range of new technologically enabled forms that this has taken offer a key legacy of COVID-19 and one that should not be ignored. Post-virus, a return to parents' evenings in crowded halls or as a room-to-room dash along unknown corridors for rushed appointments can never hope to satisfy the spirit of genuine parental *engagement* that has emerged in some schools during lockdown. For some, the option of online parental consultations may sit easier with work and family commitments. The potential richness of this new relationship between parents and teachers is highlighted by head teacher, David Miller:

> We now know that parents can do an awful lot more than we allow them to, and they realise how much we do as teachers to support their children – that's really huge. In the past, our parents have lacked the confidence to get involved; they've grown in confidence throughout this period, and we must build on that.
>
> (David Miller, head teacher, Pebble Brook School, focus group –
> special education and alternative provision, 8 July 2020)

Of course, some parents might argue that schools shouldn't be in the business of 'allowing' parental engagement, that it should be an implicit and explicit aspect of the relationship between any parent and any school and that it takes on additional importance in special education settings, or as one parent of a child (currently in Year 6) with special needs put it to us: 'I know from my own experience that a significant number of parents with SEN [special educational needs] children have been screaming to be heard, and that the school has been ignoring them' (Parent, written submission, 30 August 2020). Perhaps, in the shifts in systems and in thinking being spurred by the pandemic, there is a chance that, post-lockdown, such parents will feel listened to and *understood*.

Towards a new empathy?

And, of course, the foundation on which David Miller, who leads a school for children with severe learning difficulties, proposes to build isn't simply a new technique or technology, although lockdown has generated much in that regard. Rather, it is the potential for a new empathy between parents and teachers that emerged during lockdown that Miller wants to nurture and build on; a head teacher colleague of his concurs, highlighting the new two-way visibility between the home and the school:

> We have had a lot of feedback from parents saying, 'Oh, this is great. I can actually access my child and their level much better by seeing more of their work [and] by seeing how they interact with different types of work', [and we can see] how our staff are interacting with their children as well.
>
> (Neil Strain, head teacher, Stony Dean School, focus group – special education and alternative provision, 8 July 2020)

Like the virus itself, this empathy emerges from an intrusion, on both sides, into the lives of teachers and students; the poverty that some of our young people and their families contend with on a daily basis is stripped bare in the backdrops that shared screens make visible, as is the comparative advantage of some of their peers, not to mention the food runs that a number of schools in our most deprived communities have been making during the pandemic. And this isn't the spurious 'poverty porn' voyeurism of 'reality' television shows like *Benefits Street* and *Rich House, Poor House*; it is the lived experience of the children who sat in our classrooms, pre-lockdown.

Moreover, as another of Miller's colleagues reflects, the new modes of connection and communication – that have made this inequality *so* transparent and *so* undeniable – that some schools are now embracing may prove more inclusive than those that we have become used to: 'Technology has bridged a gap in our liaison with parents that we didn't realise was there' (Claire Smart, head teacher, PACE Centre, focus group – special education and alternative provision, 8 July 2020). Rebecca Brooks, a parent and an experienced secondary schoolteacher and home educator who has written a series of influential reports for the charity Adoption UK, a membership body for adoptees, adoptive families and adoption professionals, including one exploring the experiences of adoptive families in early lockdown (Brooks, 2020a), captures the way in which lockdown may have laid the foundation for a new relationship between parents and teachers:

> One parent spoke to me about how, as a result of trying to do some work with his children – both of whom have got special educational needs and are in an inclusion facility on the side of a mainstream school – his eyes had been opened to the way his children approach doing their schoolwork in a way that he'd not really seen before. It gave him a much greater appreciation of what the teachers were doing with his children at school.
>
> (Rebecca Brooks, education policy adviser, Adoption UK, focus group – special education and alternative provision, 8 July 2020)

Brooks continues:

> This was a new perspective for [this parent], that, having sat down and tried to do these activities with his children, he understood, to a greater level, the quality of work that teachers were doing with [his children] every day at school … and he also felt, as a parent, that he … had a much better understanding now of what was expected of [his children], so that he felt he could be more supportive to them. And so, the thing that he … he really wanted to continue after [lockdown] was … [that this] free communication [between parents and schools] be maintained, so that this understanding between schools and parents can be improved. Sitting in the middle, as I do, between parents and carers and educators, sometimes there's an enormous gulf of understanding where difficulties arise that don't really need to be there, but because of the [lack of] understanding of each other's role – parents don't always understand what teachers are having to do and … the procedures that they have to follow, and just how it all works in school.

Brooks's point is echoed by Amanda Spielman, the chief inspector of schools:

> I think lockdown has given parents a new-found respect for the job that teachers do … it's been hard for parents to keep children motivated and provide a structure to their learning, which teachers do so well …

many parents are going to be really glad to hand teaching back to the professionals.

(Spielman, cited in Griffiths, 2020b)

Ted Hartley, a long-standing advocate of, and authority on, adult, community and family learning makes a similar point, and suggests a policy response – a new focus on enabling parents to support their children's learning: 'Parents now know how difficult it is to teach children effectively and how helpful courses around home learning would have been and will continue to be' (Ted Hartley, 'Involuntary Adult Learning in the Time of COVID-19', written submission, 26 August 2020). A parent who spoke to us concurs with the sentiments expressed – from their very different starting points – by Brooks, Spielman and Hartley and reflects on the broader and unexpected benefits of lockdown, before concluding that there were also downsides:

> It's been alright, it's been good, I've seen much more of my son, I am here at dinner time, when [prior to lockdown] I'd have got in much later; I'm here all the time now – and the school has been great, and he's taken part in it all, done the work, kept in touch with his friends. But, still, I sense you can only do this for so long, you need to interact, you need to talk to more than a screen, that's me and him!
>
> (Participant, focus group – parents, guardians and carers, 23 July 2020)

This empathy extended to a recognition of the difficulty of some of the tasks that teachers were asked to undertake during lockdown, such as the regular phone calls that many schools required staff to undertake to check on pupil and family well-being, Interestingly, the empathy comes here from an educational professional and former teacher:

> Teachers would make quite regular calls … you know, they had to make a call at least once a week to, to connect with, with children and, and just sort of see where they are. And, and I was very struck by how they just weren't equipped to make those calls … [If it were me,] I would ask completely the wrong question, 'Are you okay?'
>
> (Manjit Shellis, assistant director for wider learning, Birmingham Education Business Partnership, focus group – parents, guardians and carers, 23 July 2020)

These comments are echoed in the words of another parent, whose daughter has an education and health care plan (EHCP). She is empathetic with regard to the teacher's task and thankful for their long-standing relationship, but acknowledges that these were not easy discussions on either side:

> I adore the deputy head of year who has been [my daughter's] supporter and protector ever since she started at secondary school, [and we tried] speaking once a week, but it was just mortifyingly embarrassing and ended up being a conversation. I mean, it was literally just, 'Are you okay?' 'Oh, I've just taken the dog for a walk.' I mean, it was, it was kind of that. So I, I just, it was just, just to concur with what [Manjit was] saying that [the teacher] was utterly unequipped, and [my daughter] was cripplingly embarrassed by the whole thing. And it … I mean, apart from the fact of establishing that she was still alive, it didn't really add anything to our week really.
>
> (Participant, focus group – parents, guardians and carers, 23 July 2020)

Of course, from a safeguarding point of view, checking that children are alive and well is a vital and often an intrinsically challenging task, but it does suggest that if we are to deliver learning that is more personalised, bespoke and *personable* post-lockdown, then enabling education professionals to have difficult conversations ought to be a more important ingredient in the initial training of teachers (and others who work in schools) *and* in their ongoing development.

Whatever the challenges, though, the tone taken by many schools at the start of lockdown, and their willingness to have such conversations, was welcomed by parents:

> I have to say that the message from the school as soon as lockdown happened was, you know, very, very much one of just don't worry about the work – it's their emotional health and well-being that really matters … just do whatever you have to do to keep yourselves and your children and your family happy. There are no expectations from us about you doing any work. If you want to send things in, then you can, and we'll try and have a look (at them) and give you feedback. So that, that came through loud and clear throughout the whole of lockdown.
>
> (Fiona Ellis, independent consultant, focus group – parents, guardians and carers, 23 July 2020)

And there was praise for teachers too from those whose children attended school during lockdown, often in mixed age groups, such as this from a National Health Service (NHS) key worker, the mother of a Year 6 pupil:

> I think particularly for David … the bit that … changed him is the way his language changed, the way he's grown up; he had to start to grow up, I think more in a different way, faster than he was … I mean, he's always been good with … children but, as I say, this ability to form bonds with children right across the years from reception up … There was very little falling out in those groups. I don't think there [was] any falling out actually, and that richness of the mixture of the ages, that stuff … I think that was a really positive thing.
>
> (Parent, research interview, 12 August 2020)

This is not to say that parents had a universally positive experience in terms of engagement with schools. A minority of parents who spoke to us, with children in both independent and state schools, had not had a single phone call, and some had waited several weeks for the arrival of the first home-learning assignments. The approaches taken by schools varied across sectors, across schools within sectors and within local areas, as this comment from David Miller, illustrates:

> I'm not naming schools, but a colleague of ours … has two boys. One's at one of the big secondary schools nearby, and one's at the other. And [their] experiences [have been] completely different. [They've been] getting an input from one school [and this] was, I would say, quite strong. And the input from the other was incredibly weak. It's interesting. I don't know whether that's common across the board, but that's certainly something that we've found.
>
> (David Miller, head teacher, Pebble Brook School, focus group – special education and alternative provision, 8 July 2020)

This difference in experience was not uncommon: those who spoke to us through focus groups, in one-to-one conversations and in unplanned exchanges gave very different accounts of their experiences, with the parents' focus group tending to be more critical than those in focus groups dominated by education professionals, some of whom were, of course, parents as well.

Brooks, drawing on her work with Adoption UK, recognises the challenge with which both parents and schools were dealing: parents were seeking to 'become' teachers, while schools were seeking to support children through technologies with which they were unfamiliar and at arm's length; it didn't always work and communication was key:

This transition to the role of parent as teacher was extremely difficult for some families to manage, and they really appreciated the school's understanding that they were doing their best and [the school's support] in getting their children to do this work by being in regular communication about the work and most importantly, providing feedback on the work. One of the biggest things that parents said was demotivating for children was [that] if their children had done the work online … but then they didn't hear back from the teacher … they wouldn't be motivated to have another go at it.

(Rebecca Brooks, education policy adviser, Adoption UK, focus group – special education and alternative provision, 8 July 2020)

And more of the parents who spoke to us concurred, especially where they felt the home-learning activities offered by schools were targeted at young people of a particular ability level:

My 14-year-old who is Year 9, he's not an academic, he does enjoy bits of school, he does enjoy [certain] school subjects, but he has to be at school [and] made to sit down in a classroom environment – he can't just pick up a laptop and start carrying on his work. It just didn't happen. He might've done some bits now and again … the 11-year-old? Yes, he's better – the way he would sit down. And for the first two weeks, we did two hours a day [but] that dropped quickly to one.

(Participant, focus group – parents, guardians and carers, 23 July 2020)

This parent continues, picking out patches of enjoyment, but also acknowledging their struggles with certain kinds of work:

We did the maths; so, I learned how to do fractions again, which is good for me. The maths was easier because it was either right or wrong, you know, you know: add, take away, fractions, multiply. I quite enjoyed it in the end, and he enjoyed it. But you know … the English was more difficult for me. It brought back all those horrible comprehension (activities), honestly, you know, write something about …

And so to their third child and, again, the teacher empathy resurfaces:

And yeah, the 8-year-old did a couple of Zooms [online sessions] with their classroom teacher. I watched them, and they were hit and miss. I mean, it's difficult for the teachers – they were in completely uncharted areas, waters. And it's just not the same as being at school. And I think (somebody else) said, you know it, and it's not anyone's fault, but it's geared to whole learning, [it's] geared up for the kid that might be 'expected progress' or 'greater depth' [two descriptors commonly used in English primary education].

Another parent, an education professional, describes how she progressively cast aside the home-learning activities set by the school and substituted alternatives:

Very, very quickly into lockdown, I stopped looking at what had to be done in terms of home educating [set by the school] and took a very different view; it was an opportunity to do something different, to learn some different stuff. And maybe this was an opportunity to reconnect as a family, to you know, to learn to cook, you know, and things like that, to have a go, [to] talk to me, [to] talk to other people about food and about culture and about, you know, what could we do around that.

(Participant, focus group – parents, guardians and carers, 23 July 2020)

And sometimes schools struggled to get the balance right between 'do what you can, don't worry', while sending out sets of materials that were sometimes suggesting the opposite, as Fiona Ellis noted:

There was a tension because, of course, they were also sending a lot of teaching materials and work to their children to do. So on the one hand, they were saying, don't worry about it all. And on the other, they were saying that if you want to [do it], then, here's loads of stuff.

In short, for Ellis – and she says this as a parent – the school couldn't do right for doing wrong:

I could hear from communications going back and forth – school newsletters and updates and [other] things that we got – that some parents were wholly underwhelmed by what the school was providing and really angry, and I think quite abusive because we did get a message home saying, 'Please, can you remember all of our teachers are human beings and they have children and health issues and things going on at home – they're doing their best'. And then other families feeling that ... there just sort of was too much stuff being sent home; it was either too much or too little. So, I felt for the school that day, you could, you could tell from them that they felt like they couldn't please everybody.

The fact that critical voices were more likely to arise from the parents who spoke to us may be down to the intrinsic selection bias that is likely to occur when such approaches are applied. We had neither the time nor the funding to randomly construct the groups in the way that, for instance, a polling organisation might; rather, we exploited our contacts and networks and aligned this with participation appeals on social media. The outcome? We were more likely to attract professionals proud to showcase excellent work, and informed, knowledgeable and largely graduate parents who, in some cases, had had their high expectations disappointed.

Nonetheless, even among these critical parent voices, the level of parental empathy for the scale of the task facing schools and the newness of many teachers to the technology concerned – a technology also new to some in the parents' group, but a daily workhorse for others – shone through, as the diversity of the following comments illustrate:

> The first thing is to get tech sorted in schools ... There is no one in my daughter's school who seems to know how to explain Google classroom to a parent. They don't understand it themselves.
>
> (Participant, focus group – parents, guardians and carers, 23 July 2020)

> Okay. Just to build on the idea of, of technology. I think what's really come out of, this is the extent of digital poverty. We've talked about the clunkiness of getting things through email. So now imagine if you have no laptop at all, you have a phone as a parent, one phone and a number of children. And we know the extent of the problem.
>
> (Manjit Shellis, assistant director for wider learning, Birmingham Education Business Partnership, focus group – parents, guardians and carers, 23 July 2020)

> I've got the three kids – they're all very different – and there was that kind of assumption [that they'd] just pick up the laptop. First of all, it was difficult with laptops because my wife's got a laptop. She works from home, but she was going to work at the time as well [and taking it with her]. So that's one laptop left [and], you know, I need it for work just to pick up an email now and again, but it's one between three and

it was difficult. You can't go out and buy a £1,000 Apple Mac, 'cause you couldn't even get to the shops.

(Participant, focus group – parents, guardians and carers, 23 July 2020)

We'll pick up these themes in Chapter 10, as we explore how technology might augment, complement and enhance existing practice, and the glimpses of its potential that COVID-19 has provided.

We also return to the issue of school–family relationships in our discussion of school leadership and the experience of school leaders during lockdown in Chapter 9, and with a sense of optimism: this has been an excruciatingly difficult time for all concerned, but we may have laid some foundations worth building on.

Summary and key messages

Lockdown has produced some stunning examples of successful parent engagement and, more broadly, a growth in empathy between parents and schools. A new transparency between the home and the school has been at the root of this growth and the new relationship that it promises; openness should be the watchword for this new technologically enabled relationship.

Post-COVID-19, schools ought to explore how relations with parents can be more agile, dynamic and affirmative, and digital access is likely to have a role here. The traditional parents' evening may still work for some schools and some parents, but it is unlikely to be sufficient for many.

Recommendations

2.1 Schools ought to be encouraged to periodically reassess the multiple ways in which they can build parental engagement.
2.2 Engagement with parents on pupil progress and attainment should go beyond parents' evenings and attainment updates.
2.3 Schools should endeavour to place the principles of family learning at the heart of their work with parents.
2.4 Online engagement ought to be a part of the parental engagement mix.
2.5 Schools should endeavour to facilitate and improve vehicles for parental voice.

Economics, education and inequalities   **3**

At the heart of the debate about the closing and opening of schools in light of the pandemic lies the interplay between education, economics and inequalities, and in particular, the impact of school closures on the most disadvantaged children and young people. We address issues about the examining arrangements, learning loss and psychological recovery in detail in the three chapters that follow this, but it is necessary to explore the concerns about the impact of closure on different student cohorts at this stage.

We do so in the knowledge that, as schools across the UK prepared to reopen in late summer 2020, the economic impact of COVID-19, especially on employment levels, became increasingly clear. As many looked nervously forward to the end of the publicly funded Furlough scheme, a month or so hence, which had kept to so many businesses and families economically afloat during lockdown, heads and governing boards were growing increasingly concerned about funding in the state sector and the decline of fee income in the private sector, and that the comparative impact of the pandemic was exposing the very different levels of apparently 'lost' learning experienced by children educated in each sector, as revealed in a major National Foundation for Educational Research study published on the day that the manuscript for this book was submitted to the publisher (Sharp et. al., 2020).

In the discussion with which we closed our opening chapter the concerns of the children's commissioner and the prime minister were clear about what they saw as the impact of closure, and the societal choices that might be faced given the need to re-establish full-time schooling; these concerns are shared among various players beyond the political sphere:

What is already clear is that the drastic losses in learning will have profound impacts on the lives of many children and young people. Every extra week away from face-to-face teaching adds to the cumulative damage over a lifetime. We need to assess the short-term risks of containing the virus against the longer term, but in many ways more profound, risks of damaging the prospects for a whole generation.

(Lee Elliot Major, professor of social mobility, University of Exeter, cited in Henry, 2020)

Natalie Perera, executive director at the Education Policy Institute, cited in the same article in the *Mail on Sunday*, concurs:

Pupils across the country have suffered huge learning loss since the lockdown began, with the most disadvantaged and vulnerable pupils hit the hardest by school closures. The period of disruption faced by schools is likely to have increased the achievement gap between the poorest pupils and the rest, which is already eighteen months of learning by the end of compulsory education.

And in the same newspaper and on the same day, a prominent columnist captured the political dimension to the inequality issue for a party elected to government after a successful appeal to former Labour voters in disadvantaged communities, notably in the Midlands and the North of England, with the following headline: 'For Boris's new working-class voters, getting schools back is now as vital as Brexit once was' (Hodges, 2020). These statements, framed by an article in a Sunday newspaper that is clearly positioned on the political spectrum, do not, however, give the full picture, which we argue in subsequent chapters is much more nuanced and differentiated than that screamed from newspaper pages or captured in the statements of politicians or others speaking from a clear standpoint in the educational or political landscape.

Nonetheless, influenza and viruses of any form, and their consequences, do *not* affect everybody equally, and even if they *can* be caught by anybody (as both the prime minister and the health secretary found out within days of each other), they are far more *likely* to be caught by some than by others. The truth is that, as decades of research in the respective sociologies of health and education reveal, illness, well-being and educational outcomes are all closely intertwined with socio-economic status, gender, ethnicity, age, disability and a range of sometimes less visible patterns of stratification and differentiation. The differential impact of COVID-19 on those already in poor health (who are over-represented in the most disadvantaged groups), those who work in lower-paid jobs, those from black and other minority ethnic communities and the elderly underlines just how discriminatory illness is. The prime minister's illness fed the myth that illnesses are universal in their distribution and impact; they are not, and never have been.

The world over, the poor experience poorer health, access poorer public services (in those settings where these exist) and live shorter lives. They are more likely to undertake physically demanding work, often during less hospitable hours, more likely to have few, if any, educational qualifications, more likely to suffer from low levels of literacy and numeracy, more likely to be the victims of crime, more likely to be incarcerated and more likely to come from minority communities.

The difference in life chances across a few stops on London's Central Line, between the city and the boroughs to its eastern edge that its towers overshadow and increasingly encroach on, is measured in years, not months or days. So it is, with the impact of COVID-19.

Schooling as an economic, social and childcare necessity

Those of us who work in education have always tended to bridle at the idea that schools are for anything but learning, whether that is through early phonics or A level physics, off-site visits or in-school assemblies. Those 'snow day' television news packages that inevitably reflect the frustrations of working parents who can't get to their place of employment, not because of the snow but because 'there's nobody to look after the kids' are a source of particular irritation; our silent, subliminal reply often being something like, 'I'm not here to look after your children, I'm here to *teach* them'.

It is the healthy reply of any educational professional but we've always known that there's a kind of reality denial about it; our schooling system has its roots in the factory system bequeathed to us by the first industrial revolution, as the form of our schools, especially our secondary schools, reflects: mass production for pedagogical purpose, a clear division of labour based mainly on subject specialism, the separation of learning into the neat boxes laid out on the timetable, strict division by age and sometimes by claimed ability and a clear sense of hierarchy reflected across the organisation.

And while some educational progressives have been routinely critical of what they see as industrialised or 'factory' schooling, and such modeling drives others to home-school in the pre-COVID-19 sense of the term, whatever its current form, a vital purpose of those early schools was to release their parents, and the older children who shared childcare responsibilities with them, to work in the factories. So it remains, a fact that COVID-19 made abundantly clear.

Of course, the mounting calls for schools to 'reopen' were and are, in part, educationally driven (a point that we explore in detail in other chapters), but concerns for the economy and enabling parents to 'get back to work' were and remain key, a point not missed on a teaching community with a passion to do more than *look after* children:

> The thing is that we've got an idealised notion that every interaction with a child is somehow about enabling them to maximise their potential. Of course, we know it's not quite like that, that we get paid to perform this role with various purposes, and one is childcare, but the idealism keeps us going at certain points. It's why we teach.
>
> (Michael Callanan, teacher of English, Parmiter's School, Hertfordshire)

Perhaps one way to address such a sub-surface reality is to embrace a more holistic approach, one that acknowledges this broader social and socio-economic function of schooling, rather than denies it. As a colleague, who later became one of our research participants, observed as the prospect of lockdown morphed into reality:

> Tony, this makes clear to me the sheer range of our work that goes way beyond the educational; we're the ones that end up doing it, so maybe the system needs to acknowledge that. We do this stuff and, if we didn't, who else would?
>
> (Daniel Coyle, head teacher, Newman Catholic College, Brent)

Thus, might our experience of lockdown serve as a positive reminder of the social value of schools – as hubs of education, yes, but also as places for children to meet and interact and as childcare facilities that enable parents to work and society to function? And if we're going to acknowledge these *multiple* purposes of schooling, can we, beyond COVID-19, begin to judge school performance (not unreasonable in such an important publicly funded service), across a wider scorecard, one that engages educators in the process and one that has greater empathy for these educators?

The persistence of educational inequalities

Inequalities of outcome have been a challenge for education systems the world over since the inception of mass schooling. This has produced an enormous literature essentially either supporting or challenging a statement crystalised fifty years ago by the influential educationalist Basil Bernstein in the title of a classic article for the weekly magazine *New Society*, for many years a must-read for all involved in the caring professions. Bernstein's title (and his conclusion) was stark and continues to provoke vociferous debate: 'Education Cannot Compensate for Society' (Bernstein, 1970). Fifty years on from Bernstein, Rebecca Allen and Sam Sims appear to concur:

> Each year around 17 per cent of pupils leave school functionally illiterate, twelve years of compulsory education having got them almost nowhere. The gap in attainment between pupils who just make it into the top quartile of richest families (the 75th percentile) and those who just make it into the third quarter of richest families (the 25th percentile) has remained high and broadly stable since the 1950s. Standards have proven stubbornly resistant to change and inequalities have not closed.
>
> (Allen and Sims, 2020, p. 2)

Prior to lockdown, and against this challenging background, UK educators and their colleagues in most advanced education systems the world over had gamely continued – consciously or unconsciously – with their career-long efforts to prove Bernstein wrong, demonstrating their concern for the persistence of educational outcomes shot through with the intersectional impact of social class, family circumstance, ethnicity, gender and disability, and a myriad of other, often more nuanced, differentiations. Thus, according to the charity Teach First, which provides a major route into the teaching profession in England and Wales and focuses on placing those who pass through its programme in schools in disadvantaged areas:

- In England and Wales, a child from a disadvantaged background is eighteen months behind when they take their GCSEs.
- A disadvantaged child is three times more likely to be excluded from school.
- The chance of a child from a poorer background going to a higher-performing school is falling.
- Fewer than half of those children who live in poverty reach expected levels for English and maths by the end of primary school.

(Teach First, 2020)

When one drills further into these headlines, the social patterning of this inequality and its impact becomes clearer; for instance, in terms of school exclusion rates, the most recent Department for Education data reveals that exclusion rates for boys are over three times those for girls, and are significantly higher among:

- those eligible for free school meals;
- those with special educational needs;
- children and young people of Caribbean heritage;
- children and young people of white British heritage;
- children and young people from Gypsy Roma and Irish traveller communities.

(Department for Education, 2020a)

And when one looks at the experience of those in care, the picture is even bleaker, a recent report from a leading charity in the field revealing that in 2016:

- 25 per cent of looked after children and 30 per cent of previously looked after children achieved the expected standard at the close of primary school (by comparison with 54 per cent of all children).
- 14 per cent of looked after children and 26 per cent of previously looked after children achieved five good GCSE grades, including English and mathematics (by comparison with 53 per cent of all children).
- Adopted children, care-experienced children and those looked after are 20 times more likely to be permanently excluded from school.

(Adoption UK, 2018)

Many argue that formal educational systems contribute to and reproduce these inequalities; Julian Astle, who leads on education at the Royal Society for Arts, Manufactures and Commerce (RSA), a London-based learned society with 27,000 fellows globally, offers one explanation for this in a recent blog post:

Do we distribute the education budget in a way that is likely to help children overcome the many barriers to learning that poverty places in their way? Is the school funding system designed to give children the greatest possible chance of learning, then earning, their way out of poverty? The answer, until recently, was a resounding 'no', and for a simple reason: the government spent more money on the education of rich children than poor children, thus ensuring education was more likely to compound than reduce social and economic inequalities. It did so simply because richer children spend more years in education than poorer children, and as children grow, so does the cost of edu-cating them, with each phase of education, from primary school to university, more expensive to deliver than the previous phase.

(Astle, 2019)

Such a phenomenon is not uncommon across a range of public services, not just education, and will be familiar with any individual who has studied sociology, or any of the social sciences to A level or beyond. The middle classes use more of these services at any one point in time, are aware of changes in the support available, know how to negotiate their use to deliver the best outcomes, are better at 'nudging' their way up the queue and, as noted earlier, live longer than their less-advantaged peers and so make greater use of the services available as elders; the critique is a long-standing one that is often used to criticise all manner of welfare states, but Astle goes on to suggest that the tide may have turned a little, with regard to the English education system in any case:

> Three changes instigated by Tony Blair and Gordon Brown began this shift. First, school funding was increasingly skewed towards poorer pupils. Second, the school leaving age was increased from 16 to 18, requiring those who traditionally left after their GCSEs – many of whom come from low-income families – to stay in education for an additional two years. And third, despite the introduction of tuition fees, and the oft-repeated claim that this would harm access, the gap between the university participation rates of rich and poor students actually fell over the period (with the highly progressive student loan repayment system ensuring that public subsidies were targeted at graduates with low lifetime earnings). In combination, these changes meant that by the 2010 general election, the government was, for the first time, spending as much on the education of the poorest students as on the richest.
>
> (Astle, 2019)

However, expenditure doesn't guarantee outcome, and the needle is slow to shift, even with the introduction, in 2011, of the 'pupil premium', a funding stream specifically aimed at disadvantaged pupils in English schools, by the then new Conservative–Liberal Democrat coalition gov-ernment. Where there is the political will, interventions can be swiftly introduced but culture takes much longer to change. As evidence of the pace of change in education, Astle cites a 2017 report from the Education Policy Institute:

The gap is closing, but at a very slow rate. Indeed, despite significant investment and targeted intervention programmes, the gap between disadvantaged 16-year-old pupils and their peers [a gap of 19.3 months] has only narrowed by three months of learning between 2007 and 2016 … Over the same period (2007–2016), the gap by the end of primary school narrowed by 2.8 months and the gap by age 5 narrowed by 1.2 months.

(Andrews et al. 2017, cited in Astle, 2019)

So, we can be clear about one thing: COVID-19 didn't create the educational inequalities that it has exposed, although it may well have deepened these inequalities, as Amanda Spielman, chief inspector of schools acknowledges:

Although many children have continued to learn well, and will bounce back straight into their studies, it's a sad fact that children will have had very unequal experiences at home. Not every child will have had a quiet place to work, a supportive adult on hand to help, or access to technology; many will have become demotivated, even with all of these. For some, catching up on lost learning won't be easy. Schools will be thinking hard about how to help the children who need it most, while taking into account the health restrictions, finite resources, staff and space.

(Spielman, 2020)

Certainly, the pandemic has placed such inequality, perhaps for the first time, beyond denial, making it a reality acknowledged across the political spectrum. The Left has traditionally been the most vocal on matters of inequality, not least in the education system, but these were the words of a Conservative prime minister in August 2020, not those of a Labour education secretary or a radical agitator:

Most painfully of all, the costs of school closure have fallen disproportionately on the most disadvantaged, the very children who need school the most. Surveys estimate that while the majority of pupils have been learning at home, as many as a quarter of pupils were doing less than two hours of school work a day.

Keeping our schools closed a moment longer than is absolutely necessary is socially intolerable, economically unsustainable and morally indefensible.

(Johnson, 2020)

Warming to his theme, Johnson continues:

> Children in the richest families spent over 75 minutes more per day on home-schooling than those in the poorest, and one study predicted that the attainment gap between children from economically deprived households and their peers could widen by more than a third ... The longer this continues, the more likely it is that some will tumble out of education, employment or training altogether, never to return.

Although there had been examples that bucked the trend, notably New Labour's Sure Start initiative in the late 1990s and across the first decade of this century, years of compensatory programmes, including the current pupil premium initiative in English schools, have struggled to make a profound impact on educational inequality, to 'close the gap' or, in its latest less-ambitious incarnation, to 'diminish the difference'. In that these programmes invariably seek to provide additional access to learning for disadvantaged children already struggling in the schooling system, some critics have questioned whether 'more of the same' is necessarily the route to a solution; experts in the realm of learning recovery and special educational needs would contend that such interventions need to be much more nuanced, and do not amount to a repeat prescription of medicine that has already failed.

Moreover, attempts to lay blame at the door of poor teaching and poor schools in disadvantaged communities can only explain so much, when the patterns of underachievement are *so* closely aligned with socio-economic disadvantage and *so* concentrated among particular communities.

Post-COVID-19, educational disadvantage is unlikely to ever again be swept away as 'fake news'. The implications for how we deliver schooling – and a wealth of related educational and welfare services for children and young people and their families – *could* be profound and long-standing. In this shared realisation, there is surely the potential for a positive legacy, but only if there is action to address it. The new transparency about the existence of poverty ensures only a starting point.

'Super heads' or system change?

There are many examples of heroic teachers and heroic school leaders (and, of course, heroic students and families) triumphing against the odds, but the association between disadvantage and educational achievement is undeniable and, as we have made plain and at some length, exists in just about every society with a developed education system. Moreover, these success stories are often unhelpful because each contains an intensely unique ingredient: a very particular mix of students or parents, the impact of a particular, school-specific initiative, a teaching force with a particular mix of qualities and, almost always, a driven leader, or in the parlance of the tabloid press, a 'super head'.

Super heads featured strongly in the media narratives around schools and COVID-19 and many genuinely 'super' heads have crossed our paths in the writing of this book: the head who delivers meals to the homes of disadvantaged children; the head who opens the school across weekends; the head among a group of heads who provides that additional courage and leadership for other just as committed but less confident or experienced heads across a group of schools (sometimes to the irritation of their colleagues in local authorities or multi-academy trusts); and (most of all) the head who emerges, through the crisis, as not just a *school* leader, but a *community* leader.

Make no mistake these are fantastic, charismatic, caring people and any education system, any system, any society needs as many of them as it can get. But there are several problems with the 'super head' model as a means of driving *system-wide* school transformation: we can't run a nation-wide system on qualities that are both rare and unique to the individuals concerned because, while we can learn from these individuals, we can't necessarily capture these qualities or transfer them through training courses and manuals (in spite of the continual efforts of policymakers and highly skilled practitioners to do so); we can't ask these individuals to repeat their success year-on-year precisely because of the emotional and physical energy expanded and the personal sacrifices made (their burnout is not so much likely as *guaranteed*); and we can't discount that their success in any one school has a fortuitous element, because of the coming together of a particular group of staff, a particular intake and a particular community spirit, at a specific point in time. In short, the 'superness' is neither easily transferable, with succession a particular challenge, nor vested as wholly in the individual as observers might think. Super leaders build and sustain super teams and, occasionally, they get a little bit of luck and inherit them, untapping gold that has, perhaps, been ignored in the past.

Moreover, for those unlucky enough to be running or working in a neighbouring school, the 'super head' obsession can become both a burden and an excuse: 'If only we had a super head, we'd be fine'. Post-COVID-19, we ought to make it our mission to develop models of headship that are sustainable over time, a task for many of the best in a great profession but not one with a label reading 'Reserved for Superhero' on the seat. Even if such an approach didn't have multiple deficiencies, there aren't enough to go around. And there never will be.

This point is made at some length because, while we ought to celebrate the outstanding leaders who came to the fore during COVID-19, we can only build an education *system* on the *systemic* lessons of the virus. The idea that educational outcomes would improve, or that systemic poverty would be addressed, if every head or principal spent every evening delivering food parcels to their most vulnerable families in *ordinary* (or more ordinary) times is absurd; indeed, they would risk shoring up a society that is accepting of such poverty in the first place, while maintaining an insufficient focus on the educational outcomes that *might* help *some* of the children and young people in their midst escape this poverty.

And there is an irony here; so often the heads held up as heroic for such noble (and absolutely necessary) acts during the lockdown are, almost by definition, the heads who lead our most challenging schools – and at least some of these heads are those castigated in normal times because of poor results. As argued earlier, post-COVID-19, we *must* judge the success of such heads and such schools across a much broader scorecard, and the delivery of an education that is genuinely holistic. Academic metrics will remain vital, but they are insufficient in isolation.

The loneliness of modern poverty

There is something striking about poverty in modern Britain, and in many industrialised and post-industrial societies – it may be experienced by fewer people, but it is experienced more starkly and more acutely by those who do experience it and, ironically, the educational success of greater numbers may have contributed to this poverty. This is to do with the interplay between achievement and inclusion that we return to in the chapters that follow. Perversely, it might be a consequence of social mobility, rather than its absence. Addressing the loneliness of modern poverty ought to be a priority for policymakers and for all of us post-lockdown, and some of the attitudinal shifts that the pandemic may have caused – and the evidence on this is largely anecdotal at this stage – might help us to do so; shifts such as a recasting of the definition and value of key workers, one beautifully summed up by the comment of a parent of a Year 11 child to a head teacher on the day that schools closed for lockdown and as panic buying (especially, mysteriously, of toilet rolls) gripped the nation, and shared with us in the course of our research for this book:

> Mr [redacted], thanks so much for looking after my son from Monday. I am amazed to discover that I am a key worker. I stack shelves in a [redacted] supermarket. If you need any toilet rolls, let me know and I will look after the school.

Let's take a look at this new, lonely, isolating, excluding poverty.

Over the past century, the UK, and most comparable economies born in the industrial revolution and generating, as we have outlined, industrial-style schooling systems, have undergone a radical reshaping. Very broadly, in a process that has accelerated significantly since the 1980s, they have changed in shape from being broadly triangular (with an elite at the top and the greatest number at the bottom) to being broadly diamond shaped (with an elite at the top, the greatest number in the middle and a minority at the bottom). The change is represented in Figure 3.1.

The change is profound. In the old model, to be at the bottom of the triangle brought all of the life-limiting impacts of deprivation, except one: it was not socially isolating, anything but. Trade unions flourished and working-class communities thrived in spite of (and partly *because* of) the toughness of daily life.

However, post-war growth created opportunities and prospects in an expanding white-collar world and 'smoke stack' manufacturing industries gave way to a growing service sector, trends that accelerated during the Thatcher governments of the 1980s and that, politically, were smartly tapped into by the sale of council housing and the extension of share ownership that came with the sell-off of publicly owned utilities. Herein lie the seeds of the change that we have witnessed in recent decades.

In the new model, those in the middle have often been the beneficiaries of the expanding welfare states and education systems, especially over the past forty years. The new middle-class commuter suburbs of 'Metroland' may not offer quite the solidarity of the older working-class communities, as represented – perhaps to the point of caricature, in the paintings of L.S. Lowry and the music of Ewan MacColl – but they are where the bulk of the population now live. Poverty in a diamond-shaped society doesn't just leave you poor, it leaves you alone, isolated, cut adrift. And critically, this group at the base of the diamond lacks one other thing that the old working class had in some abundance – political agency.

In short, in a society, where the poor are an isolated minority, without the prospect of social mobility or the numbers to exercise political influence, the task of educators seeking to give children from these communities a way up and out is even more challenging than in more balanced societies. And ironically, the success of these educators with the children

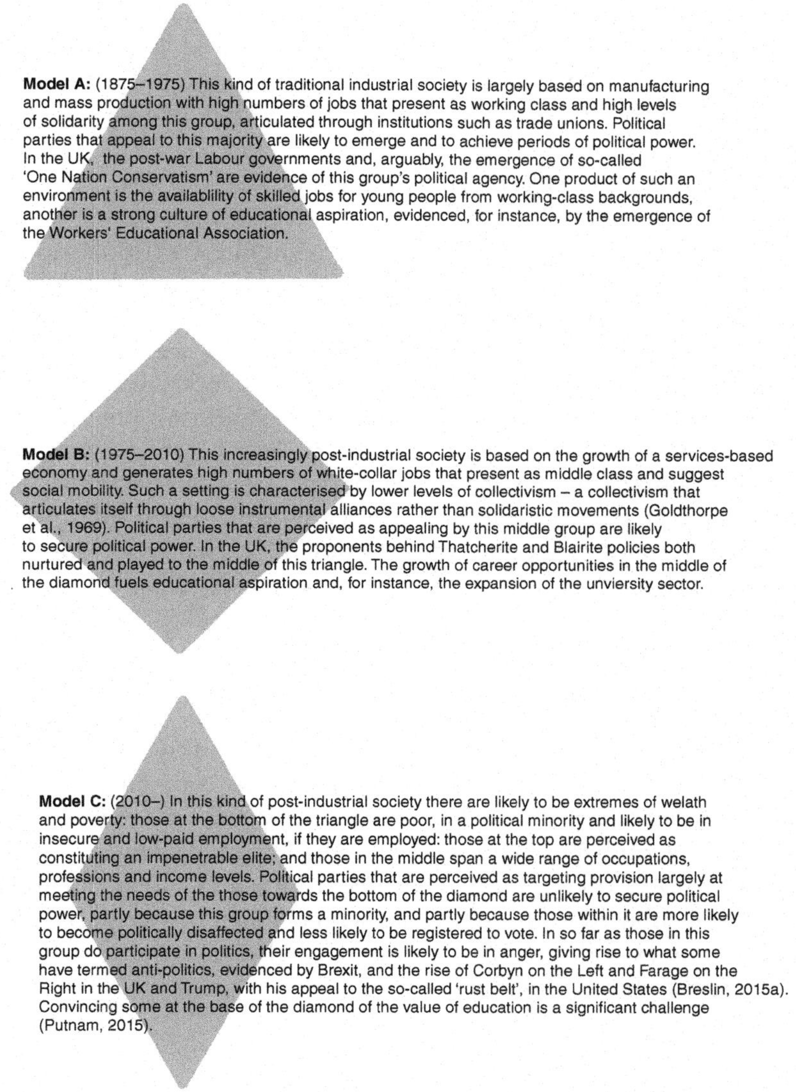

Model A: (1875–1975) This kind of traditional industrial society is largely based on manufacturing and mass production with high numbers of jobs that present as working class and high levels of solidarity among this group, articulated through institutions such as trade unions. Political parties that appeal to this majority are likely to emerge and to achieve periods of political power. In the UK, the post-war Labour governments and, arguably, the emergence of so-called 'One Nation Conservatism' are evidence of this group's political agency. One product of such an environment is the availability of skilled jobs for young people from working-class backgrounds, another is a strong culture of educational aspiration, evidenced, for instance, by the emergence of the Workers' Educational Association.

Model B: (1975–2010) This increasingly post-industrial society is based on the growth of a services-based economy and generates high numbers of white-collar jobs that present as middle class and suggest social mobility. Such a setting is characterised by lower levels of collectivism – a collectivism that articulates itself through loose instrumental alliances rather than solidaristic movements (Goldthorpe et al., 1969). Political parties that are perceived as appealing by this middle group are likely to secure political power. In the UK, the proponents behind Thatcherite and Blairite policies both nurtured and played to the middle of this triangle. The growth of career opportunities in the middle of the diamond fuels educational aspiration and, for instance, the expansion of the univeristy sector.

Model C: (2010–) In this kind of post-industrial society there are likely to be extremes of welath and poverty: those at the bottom of the triangle are poor, in a political minority and likely to be in insecure and low-paid employment, if they are employed: those at the top are perceived as constituting an impenetrable elite; and those in the middle span a wide range of occupations, professions and income levels. Political parties that are perceived as targeting provision largely at meeting the needs of the those towards the bottom of the diamond are unlikely to secure political power, partly because this group forms a minority, and partly because those within it are more likely to become politically disaffected and less likely to be registered to vote. In so far as those in this group do participate in politics, their engagement is likely to be in anger, giving rise to what some have termed anti-politics, evidenced by Brexit, and the rise of Corbyn on the Left and Farage on the Right in the UK and Trump, with his appeal to the so-called 'rust belt', in the United States (Breslin, 2015a). Convincing some at the base of the diamond of the value of education is a significant challenge (Putnam, 2015).

Figure 3.1 The changing shape of industrialised and post-industrial societies.

'of the middle' serves only to consolidate the exclusion of those in acutely disadvantaged circumstances.

Add parental choice and the marketisation of the education system into the mix and, over time, advantaged pupils gather in certain schools and disadvantaged pupils end up in those that remain; the result is a form of gridlock and market failure in what the English school inspectorate tellingly and accurately describe as the emergence of a group of 'stuck schools' (Ofsted, 2020), or what a school leader in one recent research project (Local Government Association, 2019) described as 'career damagingly difficult schools'.

The point is that, system-wide, the more successful the 60, 70, 80 per cent of pupils, the more excluded the 40, 30, 20 per cent become. Likewise, the more that young people move out of disadvantaged communities (for instance, where a university education has enabled them to), the more disadvantaged those communities become. The argument is not that such mobility should be reined in; it is that, post-lockdown, and as a society, we need to manage its consequences. As we argue in later chapters, this is about recasting the balance between attainment-first and inclusion-first strategies, not least in how we school our young people; it is about recognising that the unintended consequence of raising achievement for the majority (those in the middle of the diamond) may be that those at the bottom are further excluded. If that exclusion overly pertains to specific communities, the consequences for the well-being of *all* of us are dire, not just for those that we have left behind.

Moreover, the promotion of austerity from foreboding *condition* to policy *preference* in the decade since the election of the UK's Conservative-led coalition government in 2010 has stretched this diamond, with the elite more secure (and less accessible) and those at the base further marginalised and excluded from the mainstream. None of this makes the challenge of closing the gap easier for policymaker or practitioner, nor does it ease the poverty experienced by those 'left behind'. It was these families that Manchester United footballer Marcus Rashford had in mind when he wrote an open letter to MPs calling for a government initiative that saw school meal vouchers distributed to those families with children in receipt of free school meals to be extended across the summer holidays, an issue that he subsequently spoke about on *BBC Breakfast*:

> It's written from the heart and it's about how my life was … the letter is to open up and let people understand the impact on families, and to know I've done the right thing. What families are going through now, I've once had to go through that – and it's very difficult to find a way out. It's very important for me to help people who are struggling. Whether the outcome changes or doesn't change – that's why I wrote it.
>
> (BBC News, 2020b)

Within twenty-four hours of the broadcast, the 22-year-old footballer had forced one of the first government U-turns of the pandemic, with the prime minister pledging to extend the voucher scheme across the summer break. As such, the government had acknowledged a long held view among both anti-poverty campaigners and school staff of all ranks – poorer children have it particularly tough over the annual summer holiday.

Those 'super heads' who have won plaudits during lockdown for their work attending to the welfare of children from these isolated families at the bottom of the diamond know that when 'business as usual' returns, they are likely to be judged by the same metrics as beforehand. This is not to say that the schools these heads lead should not be judged in terms of the examination performance of the children and young people that they are responsible for – grades can offer exactly the ladder out and the leg up that these children and their families need – but it is to argue, again, for a broader scorecard that recognises the scale of the challenge these school leaders and their colleagues face, and for a plethora of supportive and affirmative funding and resourcing channels to support this work.

In our discussion of learning loss in Chapter 6, we note that there is no affirmative dimension to the funding framework for the provision of tutors and mentors proposed by the government, post-lockdown. If the learning loss is greatest for – and (not quite the same thing) it has the greatest impact on – those from the poorest communities, as the prime minister has acknowledged earlier in this chapter, all manner of educational interventions need to reflect this, as do the resourcing and funding channels through which they are facilitated.

In all of this the experience of lockdown may offer a grain of hope. Many of those in the lower part of the diamond are in employment, but in low-wage, physically exhausting and socially demanding work. The pandemic has rightly identified these individuals – not just the doctors but the hospital orderlies, not just the logistics managers but the truck drivers, not just the senior council officials but the refuse workers – as key workers; maybe a post-lockdown commitment ought to be to enshrine these definitions as *permanent*, and to better look after those who perform these roles for the long term, both in schools and beyond.

Summary and key messages

COVID-19 has laid stark the childcare function performed by our schools, and how vital this is to parental and economic well-being. Policymakers and professionals should acknowledge this as a function of schooling, not a by-product.

This wider role needs to be recognised in funding formulas, staffing arrangements and universal access to wraparound care prior to the start of, and after the close of, the formal school day. The 'extended' and 'full-service' schooling models, proposed but rarely fully delivered during the early 'New Labour' years, might be worth revisiting.

COVID-19 hasn't created either the societal inequalities or the inequalities in educational outcomes that it has revealed, but it may have widened both. With poverty and its educational consequences now clear and politically undeniable, there needs to be a concerted effort to build inclusion, widen participation and raise attainment that bridges the political landscape.

A Standing Commission on Education, driven by school and system leaders and infused with the experience of schooling and childcare professionals and shot through with, and grounded by, the voices of students and parents, might have much to offer, especially in the closing of this perennial gap.

Recommendations

3.1 Closing the gap must remain a driving principle of educational provision.

3.2 Funding streams and mechanisms should reflect this priority.

3.3 The practicality of remodelling school campuses as multi-service community hubs should be explored, with the community hub model informing new build projects wherever practical.

3.4 The scorecard on which schools are judged needs to be much broader, taking into account contextual factors and issues such as well-being, learner experience and inclusion.

3.5 The Department for Education ought to establish a Standing Commission on Education to map out what a post-lockdown education system could and should look like.

Breadth, balance, the curriculum and its assessment

4

In Chapter 5, we turn to the event that will for many long define schooling during lockdown, the UK-wide examination grading crisis of summer 2020, a crisis that emerged partly because no such examinations had taken place. Before we enter that discussion, though, it is important to explore the curriculum through which children and young people progress on their route to a range of assessments and some of the principles that underpin this assessment. Thus, in this chapter, we consider the concept of curriculum and the ways in which it might be assessed. What do we mean by curriculum, what is the purpose of any curriculum we offer and what do we mean by a broad and balanced curriculum?

The English national curriculum

In England, the national curriculum, along with inspections by the Office for Standards in Education, Children's Services and Skills (Ofsted), local management of schools, performance tables and grant-maintained schools and city technology colleges, essentially the forerunner to the current academies programme, arrived courtesy of the 1988 Education Reform Act, the brainchild of the Conservative secretary of state for education, Kenneth Baker. The Act was so ambitious and expansive in its range that '[it] came with the introduction of a set of five training days, taken from teachers' holiday entitlement at the time. These are still known amongst older members of the profession, somewhat begrudgingly, as "Baker Days"' (Breslin and Moores, 2014, p. 45). Remarkably, the 1988 Act is still a significant influence on the shape and form of schools in England today, and its influence as one of the foundation stones of the 'performativity' culture that continues to pervade schooling across the UK and beyond.

Educational progressives had long argued for an entitlement curriculum as a means of ensuring that children and young people – in all schools and from all backgrounds – had access to a shared high-quality diet of educational provision. This was a move that they saw as a natural extension of the shift to comprehensive secondary schooling initiated in the mid-1960s and analogous with other education innovations at the time, notably the extension of further education, the establishment of the Open University and the creation of a new generation of universities and polytechnics and much later (perhaps surprisingly), under Baker's Conservative predecessor, Sir Keith Joseph, the replacement of separate Ordinary (O) level and Certificate of Secondary Education (CSE) examinations with a single, initially un-tiered and at least partly coursework-based examination at the time of its introduction, the General Certificate of Secondary Education (GCSE).

But Kenneth Baker's national curriculum was not what the progressives had in mind. Their criticism was not, as such, its breadth but the level of prescription it initially laid down, across four age-based 'Key Stages' and a multiplicity of subjects, each possessing its own detailed content for the Key Stage concerned in a series of bulky colour-coded ring binders. In short, the national curriculum was, at birth, pretty much the curriculum in its entirety. In effect, the progressives' fear was that it would kill off what they saw as a rich and diverse culture of curriculum creativity and innovation. In as far as one existed, it pretty much did.

Subsequent innovations – and there have been several – have produced a slimmer, more agile and more focused curriculum, but the basic Key Stage architecture remains in place, and at a cost: the loss of a range of subjects. And here is the irony: a 'full' national curriculum crowds out innovation because little else can be fitted in. A narrower curriculum, where the national curriculum occupies only a *proportion* of the school curriculum, deliberately or inadvertently, enshrines in its content a hierarchy of knowledge that accords value to those subjects – or those *elements* of subjects – that are included and denies value to those excluded. In pre-digital times it was common for media editors to talk about quality being defined by what was left on the cutting-room floor. The comparison with curriculum is irresistible but the comparator is not quality, it is the status of the subjects concerned. The modern national curriculum gives greater status to some subjects (those it includes) by denying this status to other subjects (those it excludes). Further, as we shall see later in this chapter, this hierarchy is strengthened by the status given to certain subjects in the assessment apparatus through which the progress and attainment of young people is measured as they progress through these subjects.

Thus, in primary schools, those subjects assessed through End of Key Stage Assessments (commonly still referred to as Standard Attainment Tests or SATs) are sometimes accorded higher status (by teachers, parents and children) than those that are not. In secondary schools, those subjects that are not (often for very good reasons) examined at GCSE (and those that do not count in school performance measures such as the English Baccalaureate) are sometimes thought of in lesser terms (again by teachers, parents and young people), while those examined at A level are sifted into clusters obliquely deemed 'facilitating' and 'enabling' (by a relatively small and self-selected group of elite universities), such that this hierarchy of knowledge, given credence through the national curriculum, extends far beyond it. As such, it gives rise to an educational landscape divided variously into 'hard' and 'soft' subjects, 'academic' and 'vocational' courses, 'old' and 'new' universities and all of the snobberies that pertain to these divisions.

Of course, the focus on a smaller group of key subjects is well intended and has brought some benefits. For example, the National Literacy and National Numeracy Strategies of the early New Labour years were informed by a genuine desire to build inclusion and these were successful not just in raising standards of literacy and numeracy in the primary phase but in areas such as the structuring of lessons, notably through the literacy and numeracy hours that became a feature of the primary day at the time. The concern, two decades on, though, is that this kind of prioritisation may have, in some schools, impoverished the wider curriculum and driven performativity to a point where it is corrosive to the well-being of both children and those who work with them.

Whether or not this is the case, the pause in regular day-to-day schooling opened up by the pandemic may create the opportunity to reflect on the curricular experience that we offer the children and young people in our midst. The case for an entitlement (or 'national') curriculum for all remains persuasive, especially given the persistence of socially patterned gaps in educational attainment and subsequent life chances discussed in Chapter 3, and the reality that key competencies in areas like English and mathematics are vital to accessing the wider curriculum is undeniable.

But maybe our core curriculum, our focus on what are sometimes framed as the 'basics', has become too narrow, too austere, too all-conquering, such that there is, in some settings, an insufficient wider curriculum *to* access. Has not lockdown persuaded us that our sense of the 'basics' needs revisiting and reviewing? What of the development of digital literacies, of the capacity for creativity, of the development of the skills, knowledge and dispositions that future generations will need if they are to flourish as effective citizens in thriving societies, of the ability to learn independently and of the reciprocal altruism that makes us social beings?

Many of these qualities, and many others, would not sit easily as subjects on a timetable, less so as examinations at 11, 16, 18 or whenever, thankfully so. But that does not mean that we ought not take steps to ensure that we create curricula – and maybe a national curriculum – that nurtures these qualities and skills. It is to this wider notion of curriculum that we now turn.

The myth of curriculum breadth

For many, the curriculum is reflected in the school timetable: in secondary settings this amounts to a list of subjects with, further up the school, a degree of choice as students edge towards GCSE and A level, or the equivalent elsewhere. In primary settings, based around integrated day teaching with a single teacher and, for the most part, in a single room, the subject boundaries, other than those chunks of time marked out for English and mathematics (the literacy and numeracy hours as they were initially framed a couple of decades ago that we mentioned earlier), the curriculum is more holistic but arguably less visible.

Perhaps for this reason practitioners in English primary schools have reacted with some trepidation to the return of 'curriculum' and 'subject knowledge' to the inspection framework (Ofsted, 2019) for the first time in almost two decades, an issue that we pick up in Chapter 8, which is concerned with inspection, research and system performance. However justified, though, this trepidation, the holistic spirit can get lost both in the all-too-common presumption, especially in the secondary phase, that the curriculum is just a list of subjects. Rather, the curriculum might be more holistically considered as:

> Much more than just a set of subjects on a timetable or wall chart; instead, [it is] the total learned experience of children and young people. What values and attitudes are we encouraging those in our care to adopt as a result of how we operate as a learning community – expressed for instance through the diversity of our staffing, the value we place on student and parental voice, the style of our behaviour policies and the priority we appear to give some curriculum subjects over others? Educational sociologists use the term 'hidden curriculum' to describe these sometimes unintended lessons that are as powerful as anything that a young person might pick up in geography, English,

science, PSHE [personal, social, health and economic education], or the assembly programme.

(Breslin, 2018)

With this conception of curriculum as a backdrop, let's reflect on the curriculum normality that schools faced pre-lockdown, especially in the secondary phase.

Currently, our secondary school curriculum is a bit like a Billy bookcase from Ikea, or a big box of Lego. You can generate multiple variations. The Department for Education and its agencies periodically steer (and sometimes force) us towards a particular configuration, whether that be based on the Technical and Vocational Education Initiative in the 1980s, the national curriculum launched towards the close of that decade or, more recently, the ill-named EBacc that we discuss in more detail later in this chapter. But fundamentally the nature of schooling at scale is that all the building blocks have to fit together. This drives us towards specific types of learning (academic rather than professional or vocational) and specific types of assessment framework (in England, Wales and Northern Ireland, GCSE at 16 and A level at 18).

Most secondary schools would claim to offer a broad and balanced curriculum and, at first glance, that would appear to be true: English, maths, geography or history, some mix of physics, chemistry and biology (or perhaps some form of combined science course), French, German or Spanish, religious studies, design technology in some form, possibly computer science, maybe citizenship studies, maybe an arts course of some form.

But a closer inspection reveals significant challenges. First, this list, certainly the first two-thirds of it, consists primarily of traditional academic subjects, as does its heavily promoted subset, the EBacc. Second, in most secondary schools, every subject is examined through the same assessment tool, the GCSE, many of these subjects in much the same way. This works reasonably well for those earlier in the list (including maths, English, the humanities, the sciences and languages) but it is questionable whether the model works as well for practical, creative and artistic subjects or a programme like citizenship education (where the consequences of failure do not bear thinking about). Third, the arts and creative subjects and the social sciences are pushed to the margins, with the latter barely featuring at all. Finally, other than a nod from the design technology curriculum, professional, technical and vocational subjects are absent from the mix.

Moreover, recent reforms to GCSE and A level have driven (in the name not so much of standards but of standardisation) this cross-subject homogeneity to new levels with the virtual end of teacher assessment, coursework and modularisation. These all came rapidly back into vogue – or were forlornly missed – in the context of the cancellation of the 2020 written papers. So much for learning through doing, as coursework enables students to do, and for offering those bite-sized chunks that are more manageable for the reluctant and tentative learner, for whom a linear two-year course with a single terminal examination is both fear-inducing and impractical. This is especially important to those sitting GCSE and A level exams in non-school settings, in further education, as returning adult learners (often failed by the system first time around) and to home learners (of which we have already argued there will surely be more post-COVID-19).

In short, an upper secondary curriculum composed of eight, nine, ten, or more GCSEs does not so much offer breadth and balance but variations on a theme, or maybe a couple of themes. It forces a significant range of subjects to compromise their very essence in the name of a one-size-fits-all assessment tool, lest they lose status alongside their more conventionally academic peers. Since GCSE is the only trick in town, those skills and abilities, and the knowledge that resides in these subjects, are recast to fit the template; the examination defining the subject, rather than meeting the subject's, or student's, needs.

And this is before we consider the learning that might accrue from undertaking courses in professional, technical and vocational education, by participating in work-related and workplace-based learning or by engaging in community projects and enterprise initiatives. Too often, the vocational curriculum becomes one that learners *fall* on to because of a lack of success in the academic mainstream, rather than being a positive choice. No wonder that, as a nation, we so often mourn our inability to attract young people into engineering or to build the productive capacity we need, as COVID-19 has once again exposed.

Meanwhile, in spite of the rhetoric, activities designed to develop the much-trumpeted qualities of character, empathy and resilience are marginalised and pushed into extra-curricular spaces as add-ons. The messages conveyed by the system? Give the naughty boys (in this still highly gendered landscape) a car engine (such that vocational education becomes a behaviour management strategy rather than the foundation for a high-skills economy), and build your character after your homework is done.

The politics of curriculum reform

In this context, emerging concerns about the exam cohorts of 2021 are telling. Given the amount of schooling that those entering Year 11 and Year

13 in September 2020 have missed, the response of the English exam regulator, the Office of Qualifications and Examinations Regulation (Ofqual), to propose reducing the content load of the 2021 papers is pragmatic and entirely justified, the proposed cuts are more questionable. Why? Because many of these amount to the removal of the experiential element in the GCSE and A level specifications – the very element that is least like the wider essentially generic qualification but is, arguably, quintessential to the subject disciplines concerned. Thus, as this book goes to press, the proposals suggest the loss of assessments relating to field trips in geography, experiments across the sciences and the removal of oral examinations from language qualifications. As this author, donning the cap of what the website www. conservativewoman.co.uk described at the time as a 'distinctly off-message chief examiner', observed in one front-page report: 'Removing orals from language exams is a bit like removing numbers from maths' (Tony Breslin, cited in Turner, 2020d). This tale essentially highlights the double-edged sword presented by the virus to those intent on educational reform.

For curriculum progressives, the legacy of COVID-19 might offer an opportunity for the sort of critical examination of curriculum breadth proposed above, with a desired outcome being a lesser dependence on GCSE and the possibility of introducing new kinds of learning and new kinds of qualification for those aged 14–16, including a stronger place (and higher status) for creativity and the arts, the social curriculum and professional and vocational education, and to the kind of experiences that are currently scarcer in the secondary curriculum than many educators would like: high-quality work experience and work-related learning to develop employability skills; engagement in business and social enterprise programmes to develop entrepreneurialism and social responsibility; and community engagement schemes to nurture the skills and dispositions necessary to build a culture of active, effective citizenship.

In contrast, for curriculum traditionalists, a similar reduction in the dependence on GCSE is an opportunity to narrow the curriculum, to enhance the place of 'core' subjects and to remove those subjects defined, in their eyes, variously as 'fluffy', 'soft' and of insufficient practical application in the so-called 'real' world. Many of these subjects are vital in developing the creativity of all young people, as well as creating the kind of therapeutic spaces (de Botton and Armstrong, 2013) that many young people will need access to post-lockdown. Stephanie Cubbin, a leading figure in arts education in the UK and an accredited national leader of learning, believes that the pressure to narrow the curriculum, to squeeze the arts and place a premium on a specific and narrow set of subjects is at odds with the direction of parental opinion. She puts it this way:

We were starting to see shifts of parents wanting more [in terms of the arts and creativity agenda] ... in terms of pushing a creativity agenda, having had a lot of creative subjects dismantled and some giant local authorities ... abandoning arts, dance, drama music in their schools altogether ... and, you know, students wanting those things and parents driving for those things, that is important.

(Stephanie Cubin, head of art,
St Marylebone Church of England School, focus
group – secondary education, 15 July 2020)

Given the cancellation of written papers across the UK in 2020 and the proposed narrowing of their focus in 2021 (although a second spike in the virus may yet mean a cancellation of the 2021 written papers and looks already to have secured their postponement to later in the academic year), such a debate about what is on the curriculum and what is not – and what is assessed and what is not – is inevitable and correct, but its outcome is extremely difficult to call.

Should such a review produce the kind of outcome favoured by traditionalists, this will not be the first time that an innovation initially favoured by progressives produces, for them, an unintended outcome. As we have noted, throughout the 1970s and the early 1980s, calls for an entitlement curriculum were led by progressives such as Denis Lawton (Lawton and Dufour, 1973), largely on the basis of equality of opportunity and the need to 'close the gap' in educational outcomes; it is not unreasonable to describe the national curriculum introduced in the late 1980s as constituting their worst nightmare, in terms of its focus on traditional academic subjects, its level of prescription and its marginalisation of the social curriculum and vocational education.

Calls to reduce the number of GCSEs typically sat by students at age 16 in favour of a broader curriculum that draws on several forms of assessment and offers a far wider range of learning experiences remain a legitimate progressive aspiration, but such a reduction in GCSEs also runs the risk of marginalising subjects beyond the classic *conservative* core, while strengthening existing vehicles such as the EBacc. The traditionalists' call to 'focus on the basics' may resonate with some form of 'common sense' but it is likely to result in an austere, impoverished curriculum that favours nobody while removing opportunities for success for those who are already disadvantaged. Mastering the 'basics' of literacy and numeracy is vital if the broader curriculum is to be accessed, but it is equally important that there remains a broader curriculum *to* access.

In any case, the *presentation* of any proposed reduction in the number of subjects accessed by 14-year-olds is also critical, whatever the rationale for it, as the following extract from an article in one of the Sunday broadsheets in July 2020 illustrates, in its title, subtitle and opening words. Thus, under the subheading 'Arts subjects are being ditched so English and maths can be "crammed" while private pupils are to get the full complement', it begins: 'Thousands of children at state schools are to be limited to as few as five or six GCSEs while their peers in the private sector are taught nine or ten' (Griffiths, 2020a). In this context, curriculum progressives will be disappointed by the response, in the same article, of the chief executive of one of England's most prominent multi-academy trusts, Dan Moynihan of the Harris Federation:

> I don't want to be accused of cutting the arts, but we want kids to be successful. I do not think they will be pleased to look back when they are 40 and see that, because of a bit of art or French or design and technology, they did not get the qualification in English or maths they needed to get a job.

Those of us who are monolingual, still feel nervous and out of place in galleries and museums and struggle to put a flat-pack bookcase together, never mind hang a picture, sew a badge on to a child's school uniform or change a bicycle wheel (with any confidence that it will stay on), might look back at the academic 'success' (and narrow austerity) of our (state) school years in a different way.

Perhaps surprisingly for progressives (and maybe depressingly), the champions of curriculum breadth, and of the arts, in Sian Griffiths's afore-mentioned piece are the chief inspector of schools, Amanda Spielman, and the chair of the Independent Schools Council, Barnaby Lennon, both of whom are fervent in their support for a broader curriculum and especially the retention of those kinds of subjects that Moynihan proposes to ditch. Indeed, it has long been an irony that it is the UK's elite and world-renowned private (or 'public') schools that have often offered the most progressive of curriculums, with space for the arts, sport and all manner of endeavour and personal development programmes.

In recent years, for example, the political biographer, historian and edu-cationalist Sir Anthony Seldon has been a notable advocate for the promo-tion of well-being, happiness, emotional literacy and citizenship education programmes, especially during his time as master at Wellington College (2005–2015), the elite English public school, and subsequently his tenure as vice chancellor at the University of Buckingham (2015–2020). Founder of the now well-established Festival of Education, Seldom brought many of these ideas together over a decade ago in a paper for the Centre for Policy Studies think tank entitled *An End to Factory Schools: An Education Manifesto 2010–2020* (Seldon, 2010). Although many might question some of his proposals, its core critique and the title on its spine would not have looked out of place in the library of any self-respecting educational radical.

The curriculum and its assessment: a message about what matters?

Nothing is more instructive of the impact of our 'grades are all that matters' culture than the reaction of young people to the announcement that *their* examinations were to be cancelled, and their incredulity at the idea that they may gain grades without having to complete exam papers. As one parent, preferring to comment anonymously, puts it:

> They were furious and upset that they were losing the opportunity to demonstrate that they could gain their grades … they were also upset at the lost rite of passage that the exam experience (such as it is) has become, and, all along, they'd been told that it was the GCSE grades that mattered.
>
> (Parent, written submission, 31 August 2020)

For these young people, *grades* are the focus, not the knowledge and skills that they have already mastered through attending classes, reading, research and, *of course*, inspirational teaching. We turn to the ensuing – and inevitable – grading crisis in Chapter 5; for now, let us focus on the interplay between curriculum and assessment, and how this reveals all sorts of beliefs about what matters in education and beyond.

A generation or two ago, the cancellation of exams for 16- and 18-year-olds might have brought celebrations in the streets, but not today. Against this background, COVID-19 provides a classic 'what matters' moment. Beyond COVID-19, the ground is likely to be fertile for a much wider discussion about whether a culture of tests, targets and tables should be such a dominant driver of what we do in our schools and, in fairness, the new inspection framework for English schools discussed elsewhere may help to kick start the debate. At the very least, we ought to focus hard on what educational targets should focus on, what tests should assess and what tables should record.

Moreover, this furore over the 'cancellation' of SATs, GCSEs and A levels has also shone a light on the oddity of fixed assessment points in our 'just-in-time' era. Imagine a world in which we all did our driving test on the same day, or a model where only a certain percentage could pass the test or one where the tabloids throw their hands up in horror if the numbers passing moved consistently upward – unthinkable and yet that's pretty much the case with public examining in our schooling system.

Alongside this, observe the irony of a government that removes course-work, gets rid of modular courses (note the recently departed AS-A2 model at A level), marginalises teacher assessment and derides predicted grades, only to fall back on what remains of this infrastructure to provide grades for the lockdown cohorts. Perhaps one legacy of COVID-19 might be a national rethink focused on how we assess children and young people: could the kind of online assessment now used routinely in high-end recruitment (by Ofsted among others) be a model that might work in our schools and be used to assess GCSE and A level on a just-in-time basis, not on a certain day in May or June, but when the learner is ready?

And could we find that continuous, teacher-led assessment is not the enemy of standards that it has too often been portrayed (and betrayed) as? It will be fascinating to track the classes of 2020 and 2021 through to graduation and employment and compare them with their predecessors.

It could be that these horribly messed around year groups might just come up trumps, but, in the meantime, let's resist the urge, in the immediate aftermath of COVID-19, to just go back to 'assessment as normal'.

Toughening up examinations

Those who have worked in full-time education, especially in secondary and further education, for the past two decades will be familiar with an annual moral panic around examination grades. The panic goes something like this: if examination grades improve, allegations of 'grade inflation' come to the fore, with a particular focus on the style of examination papers, the role of coursework and the part played by teacher assessment; if conversely, the quality of grades achieved falls, questions are raised about teaching standards and the integrity of the examining system is questioned, especially where it appears that middle-class children have been denied rightful succession to the university of their choice. In short, there is a reluctance to celebrate either the work of students or those who teach them.

Broadly, with an increasingly system-wide focus on examination grades, some grade inflation over time is inevitable, to be expected and healthy

(Breslin, 2008). Why? Because teachers focus on developing grade-gaining behaviours on the part of their students, because students – recognising the importance put on grades and encouraged by a culture that their parents and peers increasingly buy into – work harder and because, as examination specifications become established, teachers and students build up their knowledge of the kind of questions asked and the types of responses rewarded. The periodic revision of examination specifications produces some blips in this upward progression, but even these blips tend to be flattened out by the tendency of examiners to give students the benefit of the doubt when they are navigating new-style papers.

However, with a system-wide aspiration that characterised the New Labour years towards widening participation, building inclusion and increasing the numbers progressing to higher education, and examination redesign (through the Curriculum 2000 reforms) that supported these objectives, some critics raised concerns about falling standards and what they saw as the emergence of a culture that ensured 'prizes for all'. The specific New Labour objective that at least 50 per cent of young people should proceed to university incurred the particular wrath of these critics, with the often voiced assertion that 'too many people are going to university nowadays', even if these claims more often seemed to come from those who had benefited from a university education, whose parents had done so and whose children would do so, or were doing so. In short, these critics were talking about *other* people's children and, emphatically, not their own.

This climate of grade scepticism and an increasingly hostile view of both the value of university education *in general* (accentuated with the introduction of progressively rising fees and loans in place of grants across this period) and the particular value of *specific* courses (notably those in 'soft' subjects at the so-called 'new' universities) culminated in a range of reforms announced by Education Secretary Michael Gove, following the election of the Conservative-led coalition government in 2010. These were designed to 'toughen up' examinations while reinstalling a claimed loss of confidence in the examining system.

This meant new-style GCSE and A level examinations in schools in England and Northern Ireland and an even stronger emphasis on particular 'core' subjects, at both GCSE and A level.

At GCSE, this core package was embodied in something called the English Baccalaureate or EBacc, a school performance measure rather than a stand-alone qualification, which pulled together a group of subjects that all schools were encouraged to give their pupils access to. Elsewhere, it has been described thus: 'Commonly referred to as the EBacc, it may be

"English" but it isn't a qualification in its own right or a "baccalaureate" in the understood sense of the term, as made popular through the International Baccalaureate (IB)' (Breslin and Moores, 2015, p. 10). Intriguingly, there is no place for the expressive or creative arts, the technical or vocational courses or the social sciences in the EBacc list of anointed subjects. Instead, the EBacc acknowledges the percentage of students in a school who achieve a GCSE pass in English, mathematics, a science, history or geography and a foreign language, while ignoring all else, in spite of calls for it to be broadened to encompass some element of the arts curriculum (Breslin, 2015b).

At A level the self-selected Russell Group of high-status universities mirrored the EBacc by dividing subjects into two groups of subjects, deeming a favoured group to be 'facilitating' subjects and a secondary group as 'enabling'. The facilitating group mirrors the EBacc in its conservatism:

- biology
- chemistry
- English
- geography
- history
- mathematics
- modern and classical languages
- physics

Again, the creative subjects (other than English, which is retained for utilitarian rather than creative purposes) are missing, as are technical and vocational courses, and the social sciences. As such, a traditional hierarchy of knowledge is reasserted, one that bolsters the common mythologies about 'hard' and 'soft' courses and dissuades students from studying the latter at A level. Ken Robinson, author of the landmark report, *All Our Futures: Creativity, Culture and Education* (Robinson, 2001), and long-standing champion of the creativity agenda in schools, who sadly passed away in August 2020 as these pages were being drafted, would surely not approve.

Thus, if Curriculum 2000 had been about widening participation and encouraging innovation that might support this – something that for some amounted to *dumbing down* – Curriculum 2015 amounted to a much more *conservative* assertion of traditional subjects and examining styles, with teacher assessment, bite-sized modules and coursework largely cast aside in favour of externally assessed end-of-course written exams, with a focus on 'real' subjects, 'deep' learning, 'mastery' and, where appropriate, extended writing.

Summary and key messages

The curriculum is a statement of the knowledge, values and skills that we consider sufficiently important to pass on to the next generation; how we value particular subjects and types of learning is reflected in their inclusion or exclusion from the curriculum, as is the depth in which we explore them and the way in which they are assessed.

The pause that the lockdown has forced on schooling may have provided space for the kind of curriculum reflection that is rarely afforded to teachers. School and system leaders need to be assiduous in building on this period of reflection.

The mode of assessment applied to any curriculum, and what is assessed and what is not, conveys a sense of the value placed on different subjects and different areas and types of learning. However, applying near-identical assessment modes across the curriculum is not an appropriate response to this challenging conundrum.

Recommendations

4.1 The return of the curriculum to inspection frameworks is welcome and long overdue but the inspectorate needs to conceptualise the curriculum as more than a list of subjects.

4.2 Future reforms to the curriculum need to critically examine how breadth and balance are achieved, not just across the range of subjects offered but in the variety of types of learning that learners are exposed to.

4.3 Schools should be encouraged to develop practice beyond the specifically academic, such that there is a stronger focus on the development of character, resilience and the whole child.

4.4 Policymakers should urgently address the neglect of the social curriculum, notably in areas like citizenship education, economic and financial literacy and personal, social and health education.

4.5 The Department for Education ought to give serious consideration to reintroducing an expert advisory body with qualifications and the curriculum as its central concern.

Making the grade

5

The class of 2020

In Chapter 4, we began to explore the UK's, or perhaps *England's*, apparently ambivalent attitude to educational success, something illustrated by the annual furore over examination grades, the related and almost annual concern about so-called 'grade inflation' (the process by which the number of students gaining higher grades tends to edge up over the years), the desire to 'toughen up' exams and the tendency towards a system that is *norm* rather than *criterion* referenced – a system in which 'passing' is restricted to a certain number, rather than on the achievement of a certain standard, no matter how many do so. Understanding the place of these preferences and predispositions in British educational culture is vital to understanding the grading crisis experienced by the class of 2020 across the UK, the class of COVID-19 or, at least, the *first* class of COVID-19.

In other walks of public life, increased success might be seen as just that: more people owning their one home, passing their driving test or winning in competitive sports are not seen as a cause for concern, but passing school, college and university exams seems to be. Deep within the different treatment afforded to educational success is a core cultural assumption – that educational success somehow retains its value only if it is preserved for a minority. Of course, in a society where few are educated to a high standard and formally qualified as such, an education does retain a high monetary value and mass education has the potential to both dilute the cash worth of the qualifications of those in the elite and to widen access to that elite.

Nonetheless, it is now widely accepted that societies that are less hierarchical, have higher levels of social mobility and are better educated are both more cohesive and more economically successful. Advanced modern economies need highly educated workers, and lots of them. To build an education system designed to select (and, many would argue, perpetuate and sustain) an elite is to build a system fit for the first industrial revolution, not the fourth (Seldon and Abidoye, 2018), a 'no-brainer' if it is fair to be ironic about such a challenge.

And yet, which way to pivot education systems in the UK remains a bone of contention, as a recurrent debate littered with, on the one hand, reference to gold standards and the integrity of examinations, and, on the other hand, widening participation and building inclusion, periodically demonstrates. The exam results season of 2020 provides ample evidence of this but, first, let us explore how the direction of qualifications reform in recent years made the chaos of grading the exams that never were inevitable.

A brief history of recent qualifications reform

Crises almost always expose the ironies and unintended consequences of earlier policy interventions. What have become known as the Gove reforms (after former Education Secretary Michael Gove) are a case in point. The decision to separate advanced level (A level) and advanced subsidiary level (AS level) – a signature change at the heart of the reforms – is likely to be one that policymakers now reflect on with some concern. To put it bluntly, those AS grades might have been handy this year.

A brief historical tour is called for here: under the earlier Curriculum 2000 framework – the qualifications reform package at the heart of the Blair government's attempts to widen participation – a new qualification, advanced *subsidiary* level, replaced the former advanced *supplementary* level, and the change of wording is vital to both an understanding of the reform, subsequent grade inflation and, ultimately, the rationale for the subsequent Gove reforms.

Advanced *supplementary* level had been introduced just over a decade earlier, in 1989, to encourage students to take a broader range of A level subjects. Advanced supplementary level was of the same standard as A level but had half the content; in short, at least technically, instead of three subjects (the common number of subjects taken for A level and the basis on which UK university offers had been traditionally made), students could take up to six subjects. It seemed a simple solution to what has long been recognised as an overly narrow post-16 curriculum, and one that contrasts, for instance, with that on offer in Scotland, the Republic of Ireland and among many of Britain's European partners: breadth added to depth, with no more than the need for a pair of scissors. It never really took on; schools struggled to timetable it, universities were sceptical of it and few departed from making offers on the basis of three 'full' A level courses and students saw little incentive for studying six subjects, instead of three. A number of students undertook two A level courses alongside two AS level courses, but as a quick fix for curriculum narrowness, advanced supplementary level failed the examination it had set itself. Indeed, such was its unpopularity that, by 1996, only one AS level was taken for every fifteen A levels entered and there were less than 50,000 candidates across England, Wales and Northern Ireland (SCAA, 1996; Breslin, 2008).

The advanced subsidiary level that succeeded its unpopular and unloved cousin, the advanced supplementary level, was a different animal, and the clue is in the term *subsidiary*.

The introduction of the new AS level, one of the more tentative suggestions in the review of post-16 qualifications led by Sir Ron Dearing (SCAA, 1996), which had followed his earlier review of the national curriculum (SCAA, 1994), was to prove the cornerstone of the Curriculum 2000 returns. Fifteen years later, the detachment of the AS level from A level was to be the defining change in the package of reforms introduced by Michael Gove.

Critically, the then new AS level formed the first half of an A level course but was designed to be taken at the end of the lower sixth, by candidates one year into their studies, typically aged 17 not 18. However, the new courses were designed on a modular or unitised basis, with each A level consisting of six units, three AS units and three 'A2' units. The new model offered candidates the opportunity to retake those modules examined earlier in the course that had yielded grades with which they were unhappy. Unsurprisingly, an examination designed for a 17-year-old is likely to produce a higher grade when retaken by an 18-year-old, and this produced surges in grade inflation not previously witnessed.

> Nobody quite foresaw how learners were going to use this, they cottoned on far faster than anybody else about 'cashing in' (AS grades) and that led, of course, to re-sit explosions, and that inevitably led to great timetabling and teaching problems and to the threat of grade inflation with the new A level. In retrospect, you see the seeds of the problem.
>
> (Adviser F, cited in Breslin, 2008)

AS grades gained by students at the end of one year of study proved to be an excellent indicator of performance at A level (and much more reliable than the predicted grade system that preceded Curriculum 2000 and that is, again, in place now), and for this reason some in the university admissions community regretted their detachment from A level but the system architects had not predicted that students, sometimes encouraged by schools judged on the grades achieved by their students, would game the system by *strategically* resitting the AS units in either January or the following June.

Detaching AS level from A level (such that only a minority of schools now enter students for AS level examinations), removing coursework and the teacher assessment often associated with this, reverting to a non-unitised specification structure and the associated modular assessment that comes with this (such that all papers are now usually sat at the same point at the close of the two year course), 'toughening up' content and favouring 'facilitating' subjects (all of which have been introduced in the past five years) has meant that the classes of 2020, 2021 and 2022 (all of which have or will have their studies at least disrupted by COVID-19) faced a very different examination landscape than their recent peers, before the pandemic even emerged on the horizon. Further, the kind of things that might have produced harder evidence for those unable to sit examinations because of the virus (as has been the case in 2020 and may yet be the case in future years) such as grades from examined units, coursework and AS level performance, are no longer a part of the mix.

The seeds of a grading crisis

None of those awarded examination grades in the UK or the Republic of Ireland in August 2020 had sat the examinations that, until lockdown, they had expected to. For students in England and Northern Ireland, these grades will, as the foregoing discussion demonstrates, have been awarded without the help that might have been provided by the former Curriculum 2000 model, which Wales has, effectively, retained. Instead, examination boards and their regulators had to work with teachers to hurriedly assemble a process designed to deliver fair and dependable outcomes for the class of 2020. In doing so, as has already been remarked, they have had to fall back on some of those processes that the Gove reforms had very deliberately stepped away from, notably teacher (or 'centre-based') assessment. And, in the process, the old debates about teacher assessment, objectivity and teacher and school performance have resurfaced, as they do every August, but with additional gusto this year.

Scottish students, where the GCSE and A level model does not operate, gain their examination grades, either a week or a fortnight ahead of their English, Welsh and Northern Irish counterparts, with outcomes for all students announced on a single day. Rarely has the London-based UK press shown such an interest in Scottish education, this headline and byline in the *Daily Telegraph* conceding their non-Scottish interest in the matter: 'GCSE fears as Scottish exam system results are downgraded: moderation slated north of the border amid fears English pupils will face similar disappointment' (Turner, 2020c).

In each of the UK jurisdictions, given the absence of written papers, teachers had been required to go through a rigorous process, which we outline in further detail later in this chapter, that involved, essentially, three steps:

- The identification of specific items of work or internal assessment completed during the course, and the marking of this work and the weighting of its contribution to the grading process.
- The allocation of students to categories based on levels of likely examination success.
- The ranking of students within these categories, both within their teaching groups and across year groups.

The outcomes from this exercise were subsequently submitted to examination boards who then undertook a range of comparative analyses, delivered through a system based on computer algorithms overseen by the regulator Ofqual, or the Scottish Qualifications Authority, with grades achieved by students at the school in recent years, and grades achieved by students at statistically similar schools in 2020, analysed alongside those proposed by teachers.

Job done, or so it might seem; the response to the Scottish results had indicated what might be coming down the line. The weekend before the publication of results for the rest of the UK, the *Guardian* led with the following front-page 'exclusive' badged splash: '40% of teacher predictions for A levels to be lowered' (Adams, 2020a). Adams continued:

> Analysis of the algorithm and data used by the exam regulator Ofqual to distribute grades after the cancellation of exams owing to the pandemic found that a net 39% of assessments by teachers are likely to be adjusted down before students receive their results (on Thursday 13th August). That would mean nearly 300,000 A levels are lower than the teacher assessment of the more than 730,000 A level entries in England this summer. Including GCSEs, which are expected to have a similar downgrade-rate, close to a net 2m teacher assessments will be adjusted downwards and, in many cases, ignored completely.

Of course, this would appear to represent a solid victory for the critics of teacher assessment and a justification for the shift away from teacher assessment and those elements of examinations that may open up the space for greater teacher support, including coursework, but the backdrop to a grading crisis that was to engulf governments, education ministers and regulators across the UK in the ensuing weeks was to prove far more complex.

Teacher 'predications' or centre-assessed grades?

At the heart of the media coverage of this grading crisis sat a debate about the validity of teacher *predictions*. The routine use of this particular 'P word', across print, broadcast and social media, was a disservice to all who had been involved in generating the grades and reinforced the suspicions of both government ministers – already sceptical about teacher assessment – and those members of the public without children in the system about teacher objectivity. The grades generated through teacher assessment were not estimates (or guesstimates) of the type sometimes entered on university application forms to indicate what a young person might get, on the best of days, in the examinations of a summer still months away, estimates sometimes adroitly nudged upwards by middle-class students and their parents. These were *assessments* based on work already *completed* during the course of the foregoing twenty-one months, by teachers who had set this work, and moderated by colleagues in their subject departments, where more than one teacher was involved in the assessment process. Critically, the process for generating these 'centre-assessed grades' (CAGs) had been set out by the respective national exam regulators across the UK, of which that produced by Ofqual for English schools is illustrative (Ofqual, 2020a; 2020b). *Prediction*, as such, played no part.

Thus, although the bulk of media coverage missed this, the grades generated in schools for the class of 2020 were emphatically not 'estimated' or 'predicted'. Instead, a series of pieces of work were assessed by teachers, and students were allocated to grades on this basis, with every student ranked within these grade bands. Each grade band was itself broken into three subgrades, depending on the strength of students' performance.

The process did not, though, stop at this point. Where there was more than one teaching group in a subject (as there ordinarily is in compulsory areas of the curriculum and in popular optional courses at GCSE), teachers had to agree the ranking and grade allocation across the year group, and, critically, heads of department or faculty had to agree their colleagues' final decisions both with their subject colleagues and with senior leaders who had sight of the broader picture across the school or college and alongside comparative historical performance in the subject area. In such a process there is the potential for differential practice between departments within schools and between different schools, but this is not about a lack of commitment or rigour. It may, though, be a product of internal factors, notably the relationship between the senior leadership teams (SLTs) and heads of department, and the degree to which one or other holds sway in this relationship in a particular setting, The potential impact of the SLT–head of department relationship on the CAGs generated is set out in Figures 5.1, 5.2 and 5.3, where the relationship is portrayed as 'collaborative', 'top-down' and 'bottom-up'.

One experienced teacher (a former GCSE examiner, advanced skills teacher and head of department) who participated in the process, speaking on the day the A level results were issued and talking about the approaches used at A level and GCSE, articulated his frustration with the misrepresentation of the process as 'soft' or 'subjective' thus:

> This has been the most demanding assessment process I can remember being part of in thirty years of teaching; at the end of it, as individuals and as a department, we had a very tricky balancing act but the load on heads of department has been especially onerous. They had to take all of this data from colleagues and generate not just a rank order across every teaching group but across the cohort, the year group, while deciding the weighting given to the assignments and pieces of work contributing to the process, in terms of the level of challenge involved and when they were carried out during the course, for instance during Year 10 or Year 11. In a subject like English, that's massive, especially at GCSE, because it's every pupil in the year.
>
> (Teacher of English, in conversation with the author, 13 August 2020)

The following extracts from an exchange of emails between the SLT member responsible for leading on the grading process and the head of English at one school in the East of England illustrates just how diligently the process was undertaken, and underlines how seriously teachers and schools took this responsibility. In an email to her colleagues, the head of English writes:

> Thank you to everyone who has submitted data to the tracker so far with regards to teacher assessment grades for English Language and

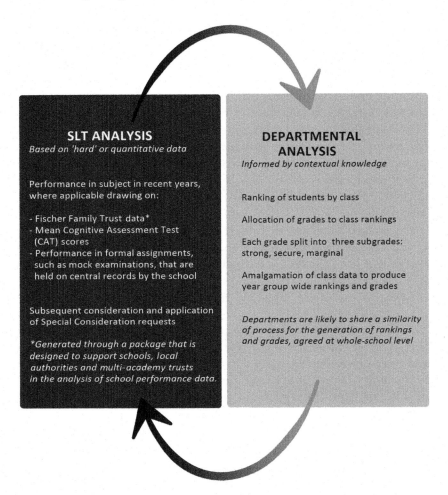

Figure 5.1 Collaborative CAG generation: centre-assessed grading in which the SLT and the department bring an equality of strength to the agreement of outcomes.

English Literature. I really appreciate that people have been working on this so promptly and I am aware that this is a time-consuming and difficult task.

I wanted to make people aware of how this process will work from here on. Concurrently with you inputting teacher awarded grades, I have been examining data measures from the tracker to create a [head of department] ranking of the cohort that sorts all of the students numerically. I will then be applying entirely notional grade

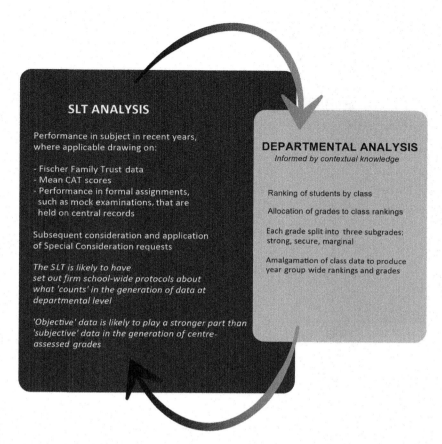

SLT ANALYSIS

Performance in subject in recent years, where applicable drawing on:

- Fischer Family Trust data
- Mean CAT scores
- Performance in formal assignments, such as mock examinations, that are held on central records

Subsequent consideration and application of Special Consideration requests

The SLT is likely to have set out firm school-wide protocols about what 'counts' in the generation of data at departmental level

'Objective' data is likely to play a stronger part than 'subjective' data in the generation of centre-assessed grades

DEPARTMENTAL ANALYSIS
Informed by contextual knowledge

Ranking of students by class

Allocation of grades to class rankings

Each grade split into three subgrades; strong, secure, marginal

Amalgamation of class data to produce year group wide rankings and grades

Figure 5.2 Top-down CAG generation: centre-assessed grading in which the SLT is stronger in the negotiation of outcomes.

boundaries at various points throughout this ranking, as a means of initially allocating calculated grades, before then comparing back with the data that you have supplied. I have currently identified the data measures to be used, but have not run any calculations in Excel, as I have [been] finalising input in to my own classes and didn't want to bias my judgements. I will now be starting to analyse the data for A level over the weekend and will then move on to GCSE immediately afterwards.

It is important that all staff appreciate that we will not be able to report to AQA [the Examination Board] a substantial lift in the grades that our students have attained this year [for A level or GCSE]. I fully understand that many of you will have absolute confidence about the

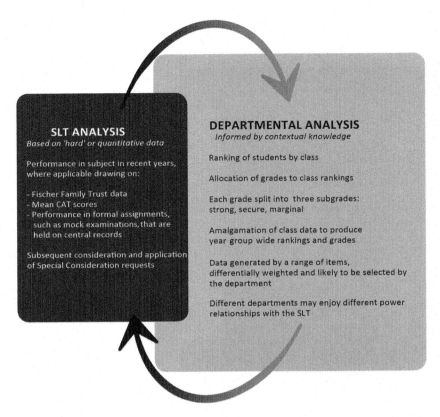

Figure 5.3 Bottom-up CAG generation: centre-assessed grading in which the department is stronger in the negotiation of outcomes.

very high performance of a number of students in your class and will feel that you know them and their work well enough to make this judgement and that you have the data in the tracker and your mark book to back up your view.

The reality of the situation is that we will only be able to award a small number of 9s, in line with last year's cohort. To provide some context, last year we achieved 16 9s for English Literature and 28 8s. For Language, we achieved 12 9s and 28 8s. FFT [Fisher Family Trust data] only predicted that 7 of our cohort would gain a 9 in Language and 6 would in Literature.

I am not asking anyone to move their grades down, as it is important that what you have input into the tracker reflects what you honestly believe your students would have achieved in the real exam. However, I wanted to manage people's expectations and make you aware in advance of the fact that the grades that you have entered will, in the vast majority of cases, have to move down for a number of your students, in order to match the profile of performance across last year/FFT data for the whole cohort.

Therefore – the most important measure for you *is that the rank order of your class is correct, in your opinion.*

I am well versed in all of the arguments that it is unfair that we cannot award more 9s this year to students, simply on the basis that students didn't achieve them last year/it's a different cohort who would have performed differently, etc. and I am in agreement that this process is unfair to students. Arguably, it is as fair as it can be, under the circumstances that we find ourselves in. However, if we do not submit a similar profile of grades to what historical data suggests, *all of our grades will be externally moderated,* and all students will be moved down to match this profile.

I am, of course, happy to field questions and receive comments from people on this, if needed.

Thanks.

[Name redacted]

(Reproduced with permission, 07.35, 24 April 2020, original emphasis)

Later that day, the senior leader leading on the grading process across the school responds:

Hello Team English,

Thank you very much for this [name redacted].

The amount of work that HODs are having to do over the next fortnight should not be underestimated and (I am not just saying this because it's my subject) English is the most complex.

As [Name redacted] points out, all subject grades will be moderated at whole school level by SLT – me and [name redacted]. Special Consideration will be taken into account, where genuinely applicable, at that stage. This should not be factored into your awarding of grades although any information you provide is welcome.

I need to emphasise [name redacted]'s point that results that are hugely different to past years' performances will not be submitted. It is simply not credible that this year's cohort will outperform the

previous two with any significance. For your information, attached are distribution grids for the past two years so you can see the trends.
[Name redacted]

(Reproduced with permission, attachments not included, 13.45, 24 April 2020)

The senior leader concerned subsequently confirmed, after the submission of the draft copy of this text to the publishers, how the process played out. The rigour and thoughtfulness applied to the process and the centrality of the SLT–head of department relationship to the wider exercise, as represented in Figures 5.1, 5.2 and 5.3, is tangible:

> I was in the fortunate position, as a Head of Department, that I was allowed by SLT to select the data from our tracker that I felt was most representative/meaningful to use in terms of producing a mathematical ranking of the cohort, which could then be compared back to the ranking and the grades of individual teachers. I was also allowed to weight it as I wished in the final calculation (which was particularly useful at A level, to ensure that individual class questions did not simply get averaged out with trial examination data, for example). [Name redacted] and [name redacted] then checked the data in the document that I wrote up, to ensure that what was being done was rigorous. [Name redacted] came back to me once I had submitted grades – she moved a couple of students down at A level and a couple up at GCSE to match what she felt was a better grade distribution but there were very few changes at SLT level.
>
> The substantial 'changes' were at [head of department] level from what teachers had originally submitted. Inevitably, across the board, and myself included, the department were more generous in the grading that they allocated (although generally we concurred on the relative ranking positions of their class members). Once I had ranked the cohort numerically from top to bottom on the data and awarded grades in a pattern that matched a three-year average of our performance, I was then able to share these with the department to be reviewed. Some grades were subsequently uplifted to match teacher judgement, as [name redacted] has outlined below although many couldn't be, which did lead to some difficult conversations.
> [Name redacted]

(Reproduced with permission, 16.56, 15 September 2020)

The senior leader overseeing the process concurred, adding:

Where there were really in-depth negotiations, we looked at previous years' trial exam results and how those translated (or not) the
following August.

Teachers were allowed to use their professional judgement if, for
example, they knew of specific reasons why the calculated order did
not entirely reflect what they believed would be the most likely outcome – more applicable to practical subjects and smaller numbers to
be fair.

Special Consideration was applied by SLT at the final, final stage
before submission to exam boards – to replicate what would have
happened had the exams gone ahead.

[Name redacted]

(Reproduced with permission, 16.56, 15 September 2020)

The work that teachers assessed to generate the grades included work
designed to help young people get ready for an examination that never was,
and usually included mock examinations undertaken earlier in the course
and responses to exam questions posed in previous years.

However, in many schools, these activities undertaken in some version
of 'exam conditions' were augmented by assessments of other pieces of
work also designed to *prepare* candidates for an examination, but emphatically not to take the place of it, and some of these may have been carried out
in non-examination conditions and in open-book settings, as work during a
course usually is. Herein lies one explanation for the grades leap: because
one would expect students to do better in 'uncontrolled' non-examination
settings, especially where these assignments are carried out relatively late in
the course. Thus, the issue was, for the most part, *not* one of 'soft' marking
by 'subjective' teachers, but rigorous marking of work undertaken outside
of the exam hall in which one might have expected students to do better.
Ironically, in spite of the higher risk of subjectivity, these so-called *predicted*
grades might have been harsher than those actually achieved.

Of course, *some* teachers, *some* departments and possibly *some* schools
may have felt, given the backdrop of COVID-19, inclined to give students
the benefit of the doubt, but here they were only behaving as conventional
examiners would. In an examination culture in which exams are designed
not to 'catch students out' but to demonstrate 'what students, know,
understand and can do' (Breslin and Moores, 2015), examiners (who are
usually teachers) are encouraged to do exactly the same, and this advice
is accentuated when, as we have discussed in Chapter 4, examination
specifications change or when an examination question is viewed, during
the standardisation phase of the marking process, as having 'missed the

mark'; if this happens several times across a paper causing, say, a shift in four or five marks, this is likely to lead to a higher grade. What do we draw from this? That, even in the most ordinary of years, examining, either by a supposedly 'subjective' teacher or by a distant, unknown and 'objective' examiner is never an exact science. The human factor is always at play in any marking process and different schools with different cultures and different internal dynamics may have, in good faith, interpreted guidance in different ways; this injection of humanity should not be taken as indicating a wide-scale lack of rigour or professional integrity, or an excess of untamed subjectivity, whoever the examiner might be and whatever the process.

Thus, the disparities that the similar Ofqual and Scottish Qualifications Authority interventions (in the form of their now infamous algorithms) appeared to be 'correcting' arose not because of unreliable marking but because the material being assessed was *never* designed for this purpose, because guidance was differently interpreted and applied and because of the internal dynamics of different school communities. Other than mock examinations, at the time of setting, the activities that teachers assessed in 2020 to generate an 'examination' grade were never intended to serve as a potential proxy for the examination paper. It is quite right that exam regulators should seek to design a system that removes unexplained and unusual year-to-year and school-to-school disparities – and in the course of the regular pre-virus examination process there are a range of comparable activities undertaken annually for this purpose – but the outcomes in 2020 should not be used as a stick to beat teacher or centre-based assessment with, or as a reason to refrain from its use in future. Doubtless, it will be.

Making a drama out of a crisis: the algorithm that struck the wrong note

Some decades ago in 1988, the insurance company Commercial Union ran a successful television advertising campaign, with the reassuring strapline: 'We won't make a drama out of a crisis'. Post-lockdown, it might make a worthy title for an induction programme for newly appointed ministers or a professional development programme for their special advisers or senior civil servants. Ministers (or at least those who work with them) will have known the examination grades about to be issued in each of the UK jurisdictions several weeks before they were published, as will their regulators.

In their desire to ensure comparability with previous and future years, regulators, doubtless conscious of ministers' obsession with grade inflation, had decided to explore a means of drawing the 2020 grades into line with those that might be awarded in an 'ordinary' year and settled on that statistician's friend, the algorithm. The ensuing triumph of mathematics was a failure of both politics and educational purpose, but the resultant autumnal feast kept headline writers and education editors gorging for weeks.

Critically, all parties – we must say that because the unsightly blame game endures as this book goes to print – had decided to persist with the application of the algorithm as the mechanism for 'normalising' the 2020 grades after it had already become clear that it would accentuate the differences in achievement between different student cohorts. In particular, this specific desire 'to be led by the science' would contradict a range of attempts by governments of all persuasions since the announcement of comprehensivisation plans in the mid-1960s. Thus, the algorithm would:

- widen the gap between disadvantaged and advantaged students;
- specifically benefit those in low-uptake subjects, typically more popular in independent schools; and
- penalise those schools who had improved significantly over the past three years.

Interestingly, parental wrath and student concern during the period leading up to the issuing of results was not (at least initially) directed at teachers. Their rage was towards the machine, the algorithm and its political masters: the machine had lowered the grades, not the teachers with whom the young people had studied with prior to lockdown, and Ofqual's position had initially been that appeals could not be launched against the majority of decisions: computer says 'No'.

The politics of U-turning

Reactions of parents to the Scottish results had given a foretaste of a saga that would be repeated when the results for the other UK jurisdictions were issued a week later.

Ofqual, the English regulator, blinked first; it had decreed that schools would not be able to appeal against the 'algorithmised' grades, except in very particular circumstances but, with the ensuing storm already causing peripheral damage, it conceded, almost a week before the issue of A level results across the rest of the UK, that schools would, after all, be able to appeal on behalf of students or groups of students that they felt were of exceptional quality or where the school had shown a rapid improvement in grades, overall or in a particular subject, in recent years. *The Times* saw the news as of sufficient importance to merit front-page coverage, leading with the headline: 'Watchdog allows thousands more appeals against A level grades' (Woolcock, 2020b). As did the *Daily Telegraph*, leading with: 'Exams U-turn as pupils win reprieve on A level and GCSE grade appeals' (Turner, 2020a). These 'outliers', the exceptional students and those in the fast-improving schools or subject departments noted above, were always likely to be among those punished by any machine-led levelling or moderation process, a point conceded by the education secretary in the *Daily Telegraph* piece cited:

> It is vital that students with exceptional circumstances are not held back by the way grades have been calculated – including those who are highly talented in schools that have not in the past had strong results, or where schools have undergone significant changes such as a new leadership team.
>
> (Gavin Williamson, cited in Turner, 2020a)

This, though, failed to quell parental concerns in Scotland or across the UK, and just as she had over school closures in March, and the softening of lockdown messaging in April, Nicola Sturgeon did not miss the opportunity to respond to the prevailing mood. Just after 4.00 p.m. on Tuesday 11 August, less than forty-eight hours before A level results across the rest of the UK would be announced, smartphones across the country pinged with the message:

> **Scottish school pupils have results upgraded**
> Tens of thousands of school pupils are to have their exam results upgraded after the Scottish government agreed to accept teacher estimates of scores … All results that were downgraded will now be withdrawn and replaced by the original estimates. The move affects about 75,000 students across Scotland.
>
> (BBC News, 2020c)

It appeared that the Westminster government might have to respond accordingly, and swiftly. It did so, and within hours, but few regarded the education secretary, Gavin Williamson, as going anywhere near far enough.

> Every young person waiting for their results wants to know they have been treated fairly. By ensuring students have the safety net of their mock results, as well as the chance of sitting autumn exams, we are

creating a triple lock process to ensure confidence and fairness in the system. No one wanted to cancel exams – they are the best form of assessment, but the disruption caused by COVID-19 meant they were not possible. This triple lock system will help provide reassurance to students and ensure they are able to progress with the next stage of their lives.

(Department for Education and Williamson, 2020)

He may have offered a triple lock but, by now, nobody was listening to the locksmith. Where his Scottish counterpart had decided to bin the dreaded algorithm created by the Scottish regulator, the Scottish Qualifications Authority, Williamson opted to retain the strategy and add an additional layer: English students who were disappointed by their grades could make their mock grades (achieved in what was mysteriously described as a 'valid mock') the basis for an appeal, which had to be supported (and submitted) by the school.

The mock proposal was immediately, well, mocked. For critics, it revealed a complete lack of knowledge about how schools operate. Unlike public examinations, mocks are internally generated by the school. No two schools in the country necessarily use identical processes or hold the exams at the same point in the course, and different departments within a school may use very different approaches. Moreover, teachers may deliberately mark mocks more or less harshly as a means of motivating individual students or classes to either encourage a particular learner or group of learners, or, in the refreshingly blunt phrase of the Association of School and College Leaders (ASCL) general secretary, Geoff Barton, at the time, 'to give a student a kick up the backside'. The idea that mocks might offer a means of national standardisation told an increasingly sceptical teaching force that those setting the rules had never played the game. In other times, a stadium full of school leaders and heads of department might have offered the ironically polite chant beloved of disgruntled football fans and reserved for unpopular managers and referees: 'You don't know what you're doing!'

Ironically, again, the Gove reforms had contributed to the crisis. Recall that prior to the reforms and following the last significant reform of A level (the Curriculum 2000 reforms), the AS level qualification was an integral part of the A level and examined after the end of the first year of the course. A set of AS grades would have proved very useful to the class of 2020, not least because some schools and colleges effectively used AS as a mock examination, safe in the knowledge that students could resit the AS papers if they were unhappy with their grade. As with coursework, another potential, if not perfect, proxy for the 'written papers that never were' had been cast aside.

In calling for CAGs to be used for this year's examinations in England, as the Scottish regulator had reverted to north of the border, the weary exasperation of one college principal is illustrative, and his analysis astute:

> When is a 'mock' a 'mock'? The injustice is happening today, and appeals take a very long-time. Appeals are not the answer ... the concern should not be year-on-year comparability ... everybody needs to be sensible and pragmatic ... we're in a pandemic!
>
> (Tim Fisher, principal, Queen Elizabeth Sixth Form College, Darlington, speaking to Eddie Mair on LBC (a commercial, news-focused national radio station in the UK) on results day, 13 August 2020)

In the event, with the Scottish decision to revert to CAGs, with the offer of free appeals largely ridiculed (not least because the appeals system would surely collapse under the subsequent demand) as the proposed use of mock results had been and with the GCSE train hurtling down the tracks towards both minister and regulator, Ofqual issued the following statement, which we reproduce in full:

> The arrangements in place this summer are the fairest possible in the absence of exams, however any process for calculating grades will inevitably produce some results which need to be queried. We and the exam boards share the government's desire to do all we can to give schools and colleges every opportunity to appeal.
>
> On Tuesday (11 August) the Secretary of State asked us to consider how a valid mock exam result could be considered as part of an appeal. As many across education have confirmed, the approach taken towards mock assessments varies considerably between schools and colleges. Therefore, any appeal based on mock assessment evidence must include further safeguards to ensure the process is fair.
>
> We are setting out today, Saturday 15 August, the criteria determining what is a valid mock assessment. Exam boards have confirmed they will be ready to process these appeals from Monday – they will provide further information to their centres and contact details are below. Students seeking advice should first speak to their school or college.
>
> This route of appeal is open to any student whose mock grade is higher than their calculated grade. We want to make sure this

opportunity is available to a wide range of students, including those who had not taken a written mock exam before schools and colleges closed. We will therefore allow a non-exam assessment mark to be used too. Successful appeals on this ground will allow the student to receive the mock grade. Mock exams and non-exam assessments do not normally cover the full range of content. Centre assessment grades took into account the student's performance across the whole course. In circumstances where the centre assessment grade was lower than the mock grade, the student will receive the centre assessment grade.

Because of the grade protection in place for students this summer no grades will go down as a result of an appeal.

This applies to GCSE, AS, A level, Extended Project Qualification and Advanced Extension Award in maths.

(Ofqual, 2020c)

Effectively, Ofqual had conceded that their minister had made the wrong call, even if it might be an exaggeration to say it had 'thrown him under a bus': given the choice between differing mock and CAGs, Ofqual would favour the CAG every time. A Nicola Sturgeon-style U-turn, albeit by the back door, had been extracted (rather than offered) from the regulator (if not the minister), but the political damage had been done.

But the story did not end there. Five hours later, late that evening, the Ofqual statement reproduced above was withdrawn, with Sunday's second editions capturing the news and Monday's feasting on a tale of splits between Whitehall and the regulator. A strategy that had been justified on the basis of 'maintaining the integrity of the exam system' had left this integrity in tatters, and the reputation of the government, and of Ofqual, had not fared any better.

In any case, given that university offers in the UK are accepted or rescinded on the day that A level grades are published, the educational impact had already been felt by, and at that stage it was assumed that this impact would prove to be irreversible for, some young people. The weekend closed with widely reported student protests and the threat of legal action from some of those who had missed out. One student's memorable home-made banner, widely circulated on social media, captured the injustice of the moment, an injustice that would prove to be the own goal that would sink the whole intervention, reminding all present that: 'No old Etonians have been harmed in the making of this algorithm!'

By the Monday afternoon prior to the issuing of GCSE results, the game was up, and the inevitable announcement emerged: the English secretary of state, Gavin Williamson, followed Nicola Sturgeon's lead, and announced:

This has been an extraordinarily difficult year for young people who were unable to take their exams ... We worked with Ofqual to construct the fairest possible model, but it is clear that the process of allocating grades has resulted in more significant inconsistencies than can be resolved through an appeals process ... We now believe it is better to offer young people and parents certainty by moving to teacher assessed grades for both A and AS level and GCSE results ... I am sorry for the distress this has caused young people and their parents but hope this announcement will now provide the certainty and reassurance they deserve.

(Williamson, cited in Heren, 2020)

Sturgeon had waited a week or so before offering a single, fulsome apology and the adoption of the CAGs. Williamson had done so after watching the Scottish scenario unfold, enduring five days of negative front-page newspaper headlines in the interim, before offering his own U-turn, arrived at apparently begrudgingly and bit by bit, days ahead of the issuing of the GCSE results.

The headlines failed to abate but Williamson remained in post as this book went to press at the beginning of September. Not so, Sally Collier, the chief regulator at Ofqual, who announced her resignation, with immediate effect, on 25 August, less than a week after the algorithm-free GCSE results were published (but before the delayed and amended results for BTEC vocational qualifications had even been issued). In her resignation statement, Collier offered the view that 'the next stage of the awarding process would be better overseen by new leadership'. Maybe, she was referring to educational leadership more broadly, and not just that which she offered.

Collier's departure was followed, twenty-four hours later, by that of the permanent secretary at the Department for Education, Jonathan Slater. This time there was no 'Did he jump or was he pushed?' question to answer, the announcement from his department conceding that: 'The Prime Minister concluded that there is a need for fresh official leadership' (Department for Education announcement, 26 August 2020).

Attempts to maintain the integrity of the examination system had, as we have already observed, had the reverse effect, with schools who did not see their grades improved by the ditching of the algorithm complaining that they had lost out and legal threats and press briefings flying in all directions. The class of 2020 are unlikely to have their grades frowned upon in years to come and the unique experience that they will have developed throughout lockdown and, in particular, across an exam results season that was agonising for students, parents and teachers, and excruciating for all onlookers, may have enabled many of them to have developed levels of resilience that may make them employment and university ready in a way that no set of grades can hope to. The lockdown lessons from the episode are many and varied but, as an object lesson in how not to make a U-turn, this will surely feature in politics examinations, and political folklore, for years to come.

An avoidable mess?

All of this could easily have been avoided: deep in the desire to introduce algorithms to 'standardise' teacher marking and 'normalise' this year's examination grades against other years is the set of attitudes that underpin a decade of qualifications reform in England. These make clear assumptions about such marking, which we have outlined elsewhere in these pages; it is worth restating these assumptions briefly here.

In the Gove reforms to GCSE and A level, teacher assessment is viewed as inherently subjective (because teachers are familiar with the students), overly negotiable (because middle-class parents and students are thought of as being adept at pressurising teachers into making favourable judgements) and unreliable (because teachers are differentially experienced in marking work that contributes to public examination grades). There is some evidence for the first two of these risks when the discussion is about *predicted* grades, and the third may have been accentuated by the removal of teacher-assessed coursework from the assessment mix by the Gove reforms, as this diminishes the opportunity for teachers to be involved in the assessment of public examinations.

But, critically and as we have underlined throughout, the class of 2020 were not subjected to 'predicted' grades or teacher 'estimates', but to a regulator-designed process of centre-assessed grading. This was never going to produce comparability with past and future years because the form of activity being assessed was not, itself, comparable, because no written papers were taken. And the application of algorithms to the teacher-assessment process produced its own unintended consequences, but consequences that regulators were aware of well in advance of the publication of results. The decision to 'carry on regardless' in all four jurisdictions was an act of political folly that combined intransigence and arrogance by all of the decision makers in this drama, matched only by the indignity of the denial of responsibility that followed.

To teachers, who had shared many of the worries of their exam groups throughout lockdown, all of this was especially galling. The adjustments made to their marks were taken as a slight by many, and not just by those one might cast as serial rebels. The day after the A level results were issued, Dame Alison Peacock addressed members of the Chartered College of Teaching thus:

> You were not listened to. Back at the start of July, we told the Department for Education that our teachers must be heard and supported when it comes to exam results ... As we prepare for a new school term amidst ongoing uncertainty, we need to see that our government respects education and listens to our teachers. The past 24 hours will just further demoralise a profession already under huge strain. This is not right.
>
> (Dame Alison Peacock, chief executive, Chartered College of Teaching, email to members, 14 August 2020)

It may have suited the government's long-standing narrative on teacher assessment (subjective, soft and unreliable) to see the marks downgraded, but would it not have been more honest to concede that grades would rise because students were being assessed (retrospectively) on a range of activities not (pre-pandemic) designed for this purpose and often delivered in non-examination settings, and prepare the public for this?

Instead, guided by the regulator, the boards used the kind of year-to-year standardisation techniques used every year to draw the grades of 2020 (a very different kind of year) into line with those of the recent past. That, as we have seen, in both England and Scotland, the application of the algorithmic analysis widened the gap between advantaged and disadvantaged students doubled the irony. It was always going to, because it tied schools to previous performance patterns, smoothing away, as we have noted, the efforts of outliers and fast-improving schools in the process. The algorithm methodology may have 'standardised' the grades against those earned in more ordinary years, but it also baked in the inequalities repeated in those results, year on year.

Graeme Tiffany, a detached youth worker and academic, who had participated in one of our *Lessons from Lockdown* focus groups, unpicked the problem with such methodology adroitly in a blog published after the issuing of the Scottish results but just prior to that of the English A level results a week later. It is worth quoting Tiffany at length:

> What is happening this year appears to have done more than reproduce existing inequalities. It has patently exacerbated them. A key driver is the governments' obsession with 'moderation', the desire to

ensure that no one year is more or less advantaged compared with that before or, indeed, the year after. One set of commentators argues this is essential to ensuring the 'integrity of the system', while others argue that this constitutes little more than the maintenance of the status quo. Whichever it is, such statistical moderation is premised on an assumption that the ability of students in one year is broadly in line with that of the year before, and likewise, will be in relation to the next.

Put another way, the concept of 'ability' takes on a fixity without philosophical foundation. What is revealed is the discriminatory reality of a system that labels children 'low', 'average', or 'high' ability even as infants, on the basis of broader, historical, sociological population data. This data also has a discrete geography. Low, average, or high performing schools tend to be defined as much by postcode as by league tables. While we know postcode is a reasonable proxy for poverty, especially in countries with high levels of inequality (like the UK), to use this also as a proxy for ability is something altogether different.

The Scottish Qualifications Authority ... has pointed out that had adjustments not been made, teachers' recommended grades would have resulted in an uplift of between 10% and 14% (depending on the level of qualification) compared with the previous year. As stated, this is inevitably viewed as a threat to the legitimacy of 'the system'. Albeit fanciful to many, the idea that this uplift might have been some compensation for months of disrupted formal education was never entertained. Nor was the idea that we might throw some significant research capacity at studying these unique circumstances, thereby testing long-held views that a 'less bright' student will inevitably struggle in higher education.

(Tiffany, 2020)

And this astute recognition of the practical impact of the application of algorithms by UK regulators intent on protecting the integrity of the system needs to be viewed alongside the personal impact on individual students, not least those seeking to satisfy university offers, even if they were ultimately successful:

My image of university was intrinsically linked with that of a close friend, and, upon logging onto the UCAS tracker on the morning of August 13th, we found that I had been one of the lucky ones and that she had not. The algorithm – which was not only classist, but discriminated against anybody with extenuating circumstances that had impacted their prior academic performance – had decided that I would be going to university without her. This friend had intended to retake her A levels this summer, having taken them last year shortly after her mother was diagnosed with cancer. The algorithm was unsympathetic to her circumstances. In the week that followed, she endured days of U-turns and emails back and forth between herself, her school and the university, until her place was confirmed based on her centre-assessed grades. Her experience is one of thousands.

(Amy, Year 13 student (Hertfordshire), written submission)

Algorithm or not, there remained one group of outliers in this cohort who were not going to be saved by any kind of intervention, by any minister or regulator: bright but none-too-hard working students who put in a late shift in the run-up to the written papers will probably underachieve the grades they might have gained in normal times. Data from the initial sittings of the new-style papers first examined in 2017 suggested that these students were net beneficiaries of the Gove reforms, with their performance bolstered by the shift away from near-continuous, modularised assessment and course-work and the shift towards a single set of end-of-course papers.

Proportionality and perspective

These pages have been written as the grading controversy unfolds and amid headlines that might cause readers, including this one, to press the panic button. The application of the now infamous algorithms to results in England and Scotland was the wrong solution to a problem that one could argue didn't exist, but let's put that aside for now and consider the benefits that may have emerged from the crisis. In short, let's offer a slightly more dispassionate reading. Michael Callanan, an experienced teacher of English, another member of one of our *Lessons from Lockdown* focus groups and a long-term supporter of the project that this book arises from, reminds us that:

The news that just short of 40 per cent of A level grades were lowered may not make great headlines, but only 3 per cent were dropped by more than one grade and it seems that Ofqual have held to the rank order offered by centres and, if that is the case, in determining the rank order, teachers have had the strongest hand in the assessment of their students since the removal of coursework. The fact is that boards go through an internal adjustment process every year, and it is very rare for every one of our students to get the grades that we expect for them. Our expectations have been raised this year because of our engagement in the process.

(Michael Callanan, teacher of English, Parmiters School, Hertfordshire, in conversation with the author, 14 August 2020)

Moreover, headlines equating the loss of a grade to ruined lives feed a disproportionality about the importance of examination grades as the sole marker of achievement in our educational culture. As we have seen in Chapter 3, to have an education or not makes or ruins life chances; to end up at one university rather than another is less likely to do either, although the Westminster government's subsequent announcement that all students must be offered (and that it would fund) the first-choice place secured by their amended (centre-assessed) grades, if necessary on a deferred basis, means that relatively few will suffer this fate. And, in any case, in a year in which universities are expected to have multiple vacancies because of the expected dearth of overseas students, and with the lifting of the 'cap' on course numbers in many areas, universities may have some flexibility to raise numbers.

Examinations and education: a time for reflection?

Through all of this, a common theme emerging from various official sources is that the priority has been about protecting the integrity of the examination system and that the class of 2020 might somehow be disadvantaged in some employment application years from now if their year is seen as a 'soft' one. Frankly, the idea that employers will, many years from now, either recall or use such knowledge seems fanciful. True, some will continue to look at GCSE and A level grades alongside the class of degree an individual gains; however, the broader trend, especially among larger 'blue-chips', is towards publicly declaring their commitment to judging potential employees or candidates for promotion across a much broader scorecard, with exam grades a part of this mix, but not its totality. To quote Callanan again:

It is sad that another generation of teenagers have woken on results day to news of what's gone wrong with A levels or GCSEs, when, this year of all years, we should be celebrating their participation, their hard work, their resilience and their achievements.

(Michael Callanan, teacher of English, Parmiters
School, Hertfordshire, in conversation with the
author, 14 August 2020)

For most, A level and GCSE grades, like professional qualifications, are an access currency and a means to an end, superseded by all sorts of subsequent achievements, and barely discussed by the spring of the following year, but that news was quietly ignored this year, as it is every August.

Moreover, the typical response of politicians – and many students, parents and educational professionals – has been to rue the absence of examinations this year, or as Gavin Williamson put it, the day after announcing both the closure of schools and the cancelation of the 2020 written examination papers:

Any route that we go down is not as good as having a proper set of exams – that's why we do it as we do it every single year. This isn't something that any education secretary would want to be making the decision on.

(Williamson, speaking on *Good Morning Britain*, 19 March 2020)

The view that the cancellation of this year's written papers exposes the need for an education system so firmly based on such modes of assessment is not, though, universal, as this 15-year-old student demonstrates in a cogently written letter to the *Times Educational Supplement* (*TES*), published just after the cancellation of written papers was announced at the outset of lockdown and reproduced in full here:

Two weeks ago, COVID-19 caused something no school child could ever have expected: the cancellation of exams. Unsurprisingly, this unprecedented situation prompted a wave of articles, with columnists starkly divided between those who religiously endorsed exams and those who saw an opportunity to progress beyond the archaic system of GCSEs.

And I, a 15-year-old boy with perhaps nerdy tendencies, find myself agreeing with the latter group. But why?

I have sat countless exams throughout my years at school, having a formula drilled into me. A formula incompatible with creativity. A formula hardly seen outside an exam hall. A formula called 'GCSE'. Selfishly, these exams devour two, or even three, of our peak years of education, before spewing out floundering teenagers, who quickly realise that this formula can't write a compelling job application, is incompatible with the demands of A levels and is really an initiative-stunting burden. Tragically, initiative is the precise quality required for the innovation that our future so desperately needs.

Ultimately, GCSEs have one sole purpose: to get pupils into their desired colleges or sixth forms. So, it's ironic that, come September, GCSEs are not only forgotten but also often their rigid principles must be meticulously erased from your memory before you continue your education and enter the 'real' world. These exams are like a Dairy Milk in the height of summer. The thought of the rich, creamy chocolate is delightfully exciting. But when we finally peel the wrapper off, we only find a sludgy mess of oozing liquid, its worth quickly disappears. The futile saga of GCSEs interrupts your prime years of education, like the dreary minutes we must spend wiping the sticky chocolate off our hands.

Perhaps the scrap of paper we are handed in late August would be worth the sacrifice if it was a valid reflection of aptitude. But it's not. It's merely a measure of your capacity to cram your head with dates and the colour that sodium hydroxide turns copper sulphate.

The UK is the only European country to enforce national exams at 16, exams that are more a memory test than anything else. And, unfortunately, we need a pandemic to jolt us into the 21st century. Having defiantly waved goodbye to the EU, I hope we haven't become too proud to have a 'European-style' education overhaul. Maybe, just maybe, my cohort of Year 11s will survive without exams at 16.

(Alexander, 2020)

And, while the education secretary may not be a fan of Alexander's standpoint, he did find support from a perhaps unexpected quarter, two head teachers, both leading high-achieving schools, who spoke to us during the research exercise that informs this text. Responding to the closing question in our one-to-one research interviews that sought to illicit one step they would be inclined to take in the wake of the lockdown, and in the wake of the grading crisis, they were candid and unequivocal:

On the exam fiasco, you know, that what I hope comes out of this? That we actually get rid of exams, they are an anachronism- they are a Victorian model, [not fit for] the twenty first century ... How do you measure the worth of your school? Is it exam results? Or is it how you communicate with parents? ... How do you measure the worth of young people and the progress that they've made, the qualities that they have? Not, through an exam ... You will never close an attainment gap if the prime judge is an exam at the end ... [Those] from a more disadvantaged background, they don't have the role models, they don't have the consistency of a place to study, they don't have access to, you know, data because (of poor access to) Wi-Fi, they cannot afford tutors. Eh, so why are we putting them through it?

> (Head teacher (speaking on condition of anonymity),
> research interview, 22 August 2020)

[We need to consider] whether or not we have exams in the future. The exam system that we have doesn't help – closing the gap isn't easy anyway, but the exam system makes it harder. We need a complete rethinking of our exam systems.

> (Head teacher (speaking on condition of anonymity),
> research interview, 24 August 2020)

These views may not be universal (or even widely held) by school leaders; they are given expression here, not so as to endorse a call for the abolition of exams (although there is a case for this at 16 given that this age no longer equates with the end of full-time education and training) but to underline a broader point, emphasised throughout these pages: in light of lockdown, we ought to move creatively forward, not dash hurriedly back to what was in place before. Such reflection will require professional and political courage, but we will need this if we are to build a schooling and education apparatus fit for the future, rather than the past.

Summary and key messages

The grading crisis of 2020 lays bare a range of assumptions that lie deep in English educational culture. These need to be critically explored and acknowledged in ongoing debates about educational standards and in any moves to recast educational provision post-lockdown. These impact not just on practice in the upper-secondary phase, but in primary, further and higher education and on our attitudes to different types of learning and approaches to learning, especially in the so-called vocational domain.

Given the persistence of local lockdowns and the uneven, intrinsically unpredictable path from lockdown nationally, the Department for Education and Ofqual should come to an early decision about whether there will be a return to written papers in public examinations in 2021. Rescheduling the 2021 examinations so that they take place in late June and July rather than May and early June (as proposed by the Labour party on the day this book goes to press) is one option (and cautiously welcomed by the schools minister, Nick Gibb), but this ought to be aligned with a late start to 2021 undergraduate programmes so as to let the marking process take its course and to separate the awarding of grades from the awarding of degree places. Such a separation this year would have significantly reduced the stress on students intending to progress to higher education and, three years on, who will recall that degree programmes started in November, or even January, rather than October?

If written papers are not to be used, multiple lessons from this year's experience need to be learned, especially around the impact of algorithms and their apparently disproportionately negative impact on already disadvantaged students and on those in improving schools. Moderation and standardisation, whether carried out by humans or machines, should improve the accuracy of grading judgements but they must not do so at the cost of further enshrining long-standing and socially patterned inequalities.

Further, question marks about aspects of the methodology used in 2020 should not be used either as a(nother) stick to beat teacher assessment with or to dash back to traditional examinations as soon as possible, as it appears Conservative proponents would like to. Teachers have gained invaluable professional development from their engagement in the marking process for public examinations during 2020, and this should be seen as a resource to be drawn on in future years.

Recommendations

5.1 Future reforms to the qualifications structure across the UK ought to seek to reintroduce elements of teacher assessment and coursework alongside external assessment and marking.

5.2 The Department for Education and its agencies, awarding organisations and the profession need to work together to produce an agreed model to be implemented in the event of the cancellation of timetabled exams.

5.3 Decisions about whether and when to stage written examinations in 2021 should be made and announced without delay.

5.4 The government ought to commission a major longitudinal study tracking those who would have sat SATs and written GCSE and A level papers in 2020, tracking well-being, academic success and early career progress.

5.5 It is vital that there is a full and transparent enquiry into the 2020 examination grading crisis in each of the UK jurisdictions.

Catching up on 'lost' learning   **6**

In recent years policymakers and educational commentators have become increasingly focused on school attendance. To some degree, this emerges from the debates about well-being and welfare that we discuss at length elsewhere in these pages, with school seen as a 'safe place' for children and young people and one in which many gain respite from difficult and disadvantageous home circumstances, as well as constituting a public but controlled space in which vulnerable children are visible by virtue of their attendance.

Attendance is also, though, seen as vital to progress and attainment. Not unreasonably, goes the mantra, 'If you're not in school, you can't learn!' The weekly school newsletter detailing the attendance of classes and year groups, the awarding of certificates and prizes for those who attain maximum attendance for a term or a year and the observations on attendance in school inspection reports are all evidence of the prominence of attendance in current discourse. And, while overly presuming that those who attend *will* learn might be to confuse aspiration with reality, the notion that 'turning up' is at least a prerequisite *for* learning is not without merit. From such an analysis, it is clear that if not turning up equates with 'missing out', then lockdown takes missing out to new levels and applies it to a near universal demographic. Hence, the language of curriculum catch-up, long the preserve of special educational needs and disabilities (SEND) coordinators and inclusion leaders, enters the educational mainstream. 'Catch-up' is now presented as a challenge for all. Post-lockdown, it is likely to remain so.

Narratives of lockdown

But there is a danger here in jumping to the conclusion that *all* children have struggled during lockdown, both in terms of curriculum coverage and well-being, which we turn to in Chapter 7. As we have emphasised throughout, the reality is that lockdown has produced very different experiences, and sometimes for learners in the same circumstances. Of course, there have been challenges and failures, and these have had their greatest impact on those children and young people least equipped to carry this burden. However, the following freelance SEND consultant's account of what she describes as an 'unexpected success' in using a technological platform for the first time with a student who struggles with day-to-day, regular schooling, is instructive:

> [I work with] this Year 5 student, aged 10 – he has ADHD [attention deficit hyperactivity disorder] – and I thought, 'This is going to be interesting!' But he and I have flourished on an online platform in a way that I would never have thought could've happened before this. I would have thought it had to be in the room, eye contact, face to face. He loves it. He does two hours a day. I spend [time] with him every day and he's always there before me; ready to start, ready to learn.
> (Georgia Holleran, independent SEND consultant, focus group – special education and alternative provision, 8 July 2020)

Moreover, while those in school – those deemed vulnerable or the children of key workers – have had experiences that are necessarily very different to the pre-lockdown normality, most schools have worked hard to ensure that their experience has been, at least, enjoyable. Thus, the curriculum and its organisation have often been very different and sometimes very innovative, such that while some 'learning' may have been lost, other learning has been gained. The following extract from the lockdown diary maintained by a Year 6 pupil, the son of a key worker and the oldest attendee in his school, is instructive, and his experience clearly educative. His day ends with 'staff-room time' in recognition of his senior status, an innovation that takes the kind of 'vertical tutoring' (Barnard, 2010) proposed by one of our research participants, the experienced head teacher Peter Barnard, to a new level:

> 21 April 2020
> Today was an alright day at school. We made bracelets from wool and they were platted to perfection, but I got help from the teacher which made it a bit easier. We had four different types of string and we

had to choose [what to make] and mine was a rainbow. Also, I made another one that was a bit longer that I used to decorate my bike. I neatly wrapped it around the stem and it actually looked really good … we then did about two hours of work, and I had a big chunk of work, and I managed to do it all … when I had finished the teacher put maths games on the laptop. I did that until it was lunch … lunch was really nice … afterwards, me and my friend went outside and played on the *tiny* red tricycle. After that, we went to the staffroom and had 'staffroom time'. Basically, we go to the staffroom [and] then get sweets and chocolate and also talk [with the teachers].

(David, Year 6 pupil, Hertfordshire, written submission, 29 August 2020, original emphasis)

And, elsewhere, the emphasis on creativity was also evident, with this drama teacher and former actor staging a production of *Henry V* for broadcast, mid-lockdown, on YouTube, a couple of days after we spoke:

We started as a company of seventy, but we've now gone down to about fifty, [and it has been] a deeply meaningful and prolific representation of … students engaging … and that has been sustained. You know, students are attending two or three zoom rehearsals per week and the production on Thursday is being attended by Tom Stoppard. It's being attended by him because at the very start of lockdown when I left the school … we had just been to see *Leopoldstadt*, Tom Stoppard's recent show in the West End about two Jewish families going through the period [from] the turn of the century up until post-Holocaust times and the [Year 11] students that I took to see that … which included disadvantaged students from different backgrounds, students with English as an additional language … they'd all been very, very moved by [the play] and they'd written reviews. So, I sent Patrick Marber [the director] three of the reviews that the students had written and he passed them on to Tom Stoppard … that was the last thing I did … email the reviews … before I left school [at the start of lockdown]. And I was delighted, just like beyond happy … when Tom Stoppard sent me an email personally saying how brilliant the reviews were and how he had been moved by the email that I'd sent to Patrick. And so I've maintained that connection … and, yesterday, his assistant got in touch with me and said he's going to be there when we're, we're gonna, we're going to [perform] it.

(Suzy Marston, head of drama, Chesterton Community College, Cambridge, research interview, 14 July 2020)

Nonetheless, at least among ministers and their advisers and in media headlines, lockdown has been presented as a near *universal* deficit, one that has impacted most on the most vulnerable and socio-economically disadvantaged students and one that needs to be *recovered* from.

A paucity of curriculum thinking?

For one former colleague, Chris Waller, the recently retired and highly respected former professional officer at the Association for Citizenship Teaching (the subject association for those involved in teaching citizenship and related areas of the social curriculum), reflecting on the language of catch-up and recovery and the absence of a *pedagogic* grasp of the challenge, fired off an uncharacteristically angry Facebook post, as the catch-up narrative gathered pace in mid-lockdown:

> I cannot believe the lack of philosophical discussion in the media about how learning can continue in lockdown. If QCDA [the Qualification and Curriculum Development Agency that had been abolished shortly after the election of the UK's Conservative-led coalition government in 2010] had been around, I am sure the debate would have been more public and thoughtful and nuanced. The cry of 'send the kids to school' never broaches the purpose of them being there or how the curriculum might adapt to a new normal. In the past, thinkers like Ted Wragg or Tim Brighouse might have taken to the air. We could have had thoughtful discussions about process-based learning and students as researchers in their home setting, whilst also having limited teacher time at school. If ever there was a single illustration of the emptiness of Gove and Williamson and Cummings and their vision of learning and schooling and the damage they have done to teachers as leaders in learning, then this has revealed it. We continue to prepare students for a life that may not be there.
>
> (Chris Waller, independent education consultant,
> Facebook, 19 June 2020)

In a subsequent post in the same discussion, citing influential figures in the curriculum debates that bodies such as QCDA, and its forerunner, the Qualifications and Curriculum Authority (QCA), hosted, Waller poses a key question, not just in light of lockdown but in light of the new concern for curriculum at the heart of England's recently revised inspection framework (Ofsted, 2019): 'Where has the language of curriculum design, innovation and evolution gone? Jerome Bruner must be spitting blood!' (Chris Waller, Facebook, 20 June 2020).

Undoubtedly, in the so-called 'bonfire of the quangos' proposed by Conservative Party leader David Cameron in the wake of the 2008 financial crisis and during the long build-up to the 2010 general election, and subsequently delivered by the UK's Cameron-led coalition government in 2010, education was a specific target and the Qualifications and Curriculum Development Agency one of the first on the list; moreover, others to disappear or merge (including the National College for School Leadership and the Teacher Development Agency) in the years that followed primarily held an advisory or development focus. Those spared from the bonfire, and in some cases strengthened, were focused on regulation, compliance and oversight: Ofsted (the school inspectorate), Ofqual (the examination regulator) and the Education and Skills Funding Agency. This is not to say the latter functions are not important, but it is to emphasise a focus on compliance and monitoring, rather than development and advice, an imbalance that Waller's terse response draws our attention to and that may help to explain the paucity of educational thinking that critics of the catch-up agenda point to.

Certainly, when the disappearance of the institutional knowledge of curriculum development and related matters that transpired with the abolition of QCDA and similar agencies is combined with what a teacher in one of our focus groups described as a 'hollowed-out civil service, reduced in the name of the "Big Society" and, pre-lockdown, focused on rewriting regulations for a post-Brexit Britain', the paucity of curriculum thinking claimed by Waller is at least plausible. Maybe, there is value in revisiting the idea of arms-length educational agencies tasked with the purpose of providing support and advice, both upwards to ministers and outwards to the profession, in areas such as the curriculum and qualifications. With local authority support services playing a much reduced and essentially non-curricular role (and likely to struggle for funds in the tight public funding climate that will surely follow the virus) and curriculum 'intent, implementation and impact' again the focus of Ofsted (2019), and given the need to address the uneven and highly nuanced learning needs of individual pupils and particular cohorts in light of the pandemic, such expertise would surely be most welcome at this stage, and may have an enduring role.

Plugging the gap: the National Tutoring Service

Nonetheless, universal problems require universal solutions and politicians often seek 'oven-ready' and 'off-the-shelf' ones. Thus, on 18 June 2020, the government proposed its response: a £650 million funding package for schools to address 'catch-up' coupled with a £350 million National Tutoring Programme, which according to one of its architects, the Education Endowment Foundation, is 'a government-funded, sector-led initiative to support schools to address the impact of COVID-19 school closures on pupils' learning' and consists of two pillars:

> *Tuition partners*: schools will be able to access heavily subsidised tuition from an approved list of tuition partners. These organisations – which will all be subject to quality, safeguarding and evaluation standards – will be given support and funding to reach as many disadvantaged pupils as possible.
> *Academic mentors*: schools in the most disadvantaged areas will be supported to employ in-house academic mentors to provide intensive catch-up support to their pupils.
> (Education Endowment Foundation, 2020b)

The Education Endowment Foundation, with its particular focus on 'closing the gap' between 'advantaged' and 'disadvantaged' young people and its origins in another of the National Tutoring Programme's delivery partners, the social mobility-focused Sutton Trust, is surely right in its assertion that:

> There is a substantial attainment gap between pupils from disadvantaged backgrounds and their classmates – and this is likely to have grown significantly since school closures. There is extensive evidence showing the impact of tutoring to support pupils who have fallen behind. However, access to tutoring is often limited to the schools and parents that can most afford it.
> (National Endowment Foundation, 2020a)

The second, mentoring-focused strand of the proposed programme, designed to be live by the time this book is published in early 2021, builds on a range of successful widening participation practice and a number of specific projects that have already enabled a significant number of young people from disadvantaged backgrounds to access higher education and set off on the track to elite careers, but the substantive, catch-up focused tutoring strand is more problematic.

Translating a practice, tutoring, engaged by better-heeled parents to give their children a marginal advantage into a national programme targeted at those who are from *disadvantaged* homes is fraught with difficulties. Why?

Because the use of tutors by middle-class parents is an intensely personalised activity, one that is entirely unregulated or quality assured and that takes place, usually with scant regard for safeguarding, in either the child's or the tutor's home. In any case, it is often less about 'catch-up' and more about insurance policy, for instance in terms of passing an '11-plus' style exam or securing a particular GCSE or A level grade in a specific subject, possibly to secure a place in the sixth form or at university.

The Education Endowment Foundation is right to identify the impact of such tutoring in the securing of middle-class advantage, and thereby its role in *widening* the gap with which it is concerned, but it is a significant jump to assuming that this kind of intensely bespoke, one-to-one activity carried out in home surroundings can be simply transferred into the circumstances of the disadvantaged, howsoever defined, or that it can be easily recast into group activity in schools or through mechanisms like lunchtime or after-school clubs, or in specialist classes with 'catch-up' or 'recovery' pasted above the door or on the whiteboard. Indeed, we have already seen how attempts to keep schools open for 'vulnerable' children during lockdown often failed to reach their target market, because to send one's children to school was to publicly declare their 'vulnerability' to the world. This kind of public badging of particular children and young people as needing 'catch-up' flies in the face of labelling theory and may simply confirm their status at the bottom of the class.

In short, the National Tutoring Programme raises as many questions as it seeks to answer: How will children be identified as needing tutoring? Who will staff the programme and will those involved need specific training? Will the tutoring be 'in-class', through classroom withdrawal or in extra-curricular spaces, or will it be delivered largely online? How will it dovetail with teacher-led main class teaching? Is tutor content likely to be bespoke to individual pupils or specific cohorts in particular schools, or drawn from generic schemes of learning or particular online platforms? Is the proposed funding sufficient to meet post-lockdown needs? And, critically, how will the impact of specific interventions and the programme as a whole be isolated and evaluated? As this experienced teacher and working tutor, who, at the time of writing, is pondering leading a pitch to become one of the programme's delivery partners, puts it:

> How do you measure any kind of impact? We're in danger of spending a significant sum of money doing something that is essentially pointless. Those who are to be effective as tutors will need to grasp the difference between 'tutoring' and 'teaching', as will the

schools where they are engaged. They will also need to understand the behaviour and motivations of young people who will often have very particular needs.

> (Michael Callanan, delivery director, Orwell Youth Prize, research interview – tutoring and curriculum recovery, 29 July 2020)

Another personal tutor, writing in the *TES*, also emphasises the distinctiveness of tutoring, as distinct from teaching, and that the time given to relationship building, which those pushed to deliver catch-up might be encouraged to ignore, is critical:

> Personal tuition needs to be exactly that: personal. Tutors need to get to know the children if they are going to be confident in understanding what motivates and engages them. This may well require a 'trial and error' approach in initial sessions but, with clear lines of communication already established, the opportunity to build a programme which suits the child should be more straightforward.
>
> (Gamble, 2020)

The welcome granted to the proposed programme from school leaders was, clearly for some of the reasons advanced by Callanan and Gamble, cautious, welcoming the investment but curious about the detail of the programme's application and the wider funding package, as Geoff Barton, general secretary of the ASCL notes:

> We welcome this vital and significant investment in helping children to catch up with lost learning as a result of the coronavirus emergency. It will help to support the work that schools are already undertaking in drawing up catch-up plans … [but] there are clearly going to be questions about the planned model for the National Tutoring Programme. Could the £350 million of funding be better used by simply providing it to schools to fund catch-up programmes, rather than subsidising tutoring organisations? And, if schools are expected to pay towards the cost of the tutors, how does this square with the fact that school funding has been very uneven for many years and some institutions will have far less capacity to afford these costs?
>
> (Barton, 2020)

On the broader funding package, Barton continues:

On the £650 million funding to be shared across state primary and secondary schools, we are confused by the assertion that head teachers will decide how the money is spent, when this is immediately followed by an expectation that it should be used on small-group tuition.

Before concluding:

It remains frustrating that we haven't had the opportunity to discuss any of this with the government ahead of this announcement and that we once again find ourselves having to piece together the detail. We really do need a much more collaborative approach so that the government and profession can together work on developing a really effective, joined-up national plan.

Barton's colleague Paul Whiteman, general secretary at NAHT, was similarly welcoming but circumspect:

While we now await further details, on the surface, this announcement does appear to be a positive development, and it clearly represents a considerable investment. NAHT will now seek clarity from the government about exactly how the money will be allocated. We also want to find out more about how their proposed tutoring scheme (also announced today) will work in practice.

(Whiteman, 2020a)

Perhaps there was relief on the part of both Barton and Whiteman. A week or so earlier, the government had trailed the idea of summer tuition and the possibility of keeping schools open during the 2020 summer holidays. As we noted in Chapter 1, teachers – and heads in particular – had worked through the Easter and May half-term breaks and often various bank holidays to keep schools open for the children of key workers and those deemed vulnerable; the sighs were audible when this proposal emerged. It was quietly dropped. It may have proved to be the straw that would have broken this camel's back, for parents and teachers: 'Parents did not want this either. No way did I want to do either the school run or continue with virtual learning across the summer. We all needed a break!' (Parent, written submission, 31 August 2020).

How well the support package, and the National Tutoring Programme in particular, plays out will begin to become clear around the time that this text lands in bookstores and on library shelves, but heads and teachers are clearly nervous about attempts to direct school practice from the centre and through the prism of external, private or third-sector suppliers with unclear lines of accountability and, in some cases, unproven expertise, delivering something more akin to booster classes than personal tutoring. Just as established and dedicated home-schoolers had complained about the appropriation of their terminology (but not, necessarily, their methodology) during lockdown, the tutoring community was now making similar noises. Perhaps 'booster classes' is a more appropriate description, given the intended purpose and their likely role as extra-small group lessons in specific subjects, rather than extended tutorials, delivered on a one-to-one basis.

Certainly, whatever the 'catch-up' strategies employed, these will need to align with what particular pupils are doing in particular schools. As the influential system leader Leora Cruddas, chief executive of the Confederation of School Trusts, puts it: 'Where tuition can have value is where it's done alongside the curriculum. If the government is going to be spending money, I would suggest that those programmes … are strongly aligned with the work a school is doing' (Cruddas, cited in Weale and Adams, 2020). Perhaps there was (or is) another solution, at least in terms of the portion of the funding going directly to schools: might the idea of a pandemic premium (preferably with a different, more imaginative and less foreboding name), modelled on the principles of the pupil premium and pupil premium plus funding framework in English schools, deliver the fourfold aspiration of discrete funding, targeted intervention, school autonomy and impact accountability? English schools are increasingly effective at delivering against hypothecated funding streams such as pupil premium and sports premium and demonstrating the impact of the autonomously designed and bespoke interventions that this funding enables, internally to their school and trust governing boards and externally to agencies such as Ofsted, and the Education and Skills Funding Agency.

Such a model might address another issue raised by critics of the government's 'catch-up' plans as they currently stand, namely that they fail to address the differential impact of COVID-19 and pre-existing disparities in pupil outcomes. According to research by the Education Policy Institute (Hutchinson et al., 2020), prior to the pandemic, disadvantaged pupils' learning lagged eighteen months behind their more affluent peers by the time that they sat their GCSEs, while various surveys since lockdown have suggested that the learning loss suffered by those from poorer backgrounds has been greater during lockdown.

However, there appears to be no distinction between the additional funds to be allocated to schools in affluent and deprived areas, such that the risk is that this 'catch-up' funding will not enable catch-up *between* different cohorts; in short, the Education Policy Institute argues that the *wider* post-lockdown gap between these groups will remain, much to the bemusement of its executive chair, David Laws:

> It is difficult to see the rationale for such a decision … it means that schools where as many as half or more of children are in poverty won't have the extra resources they need to pay for interventions that we know can make a difference.
>
> (Laws, cited in Weale 2020b)

As the former coalition government schools minister widely credited with the introduction of the pupil premium funding framework in English schools, Laws's observation carries particular weight.

Summary and key messages

Children and young people have missed a significant amount of formal learning during the lockdown, and there will be gaps to address, but the language of 'catch-up' ignores the alternative learning that some have bene-fited from. The focus on 'recovery' risks an over focus on the deficit side of the balance sheet and portrays schooling as merely the 'filling of empty vessels' with 'knowledge'; policymakers and system leaders need to address this austerity of curricular and pedagogic thinking.

Moreover, it reveals an expertise gap that has widened as local author-ities and national agencies have moved from a developmental focus to one concerned more narrowly with 'school improvement' and with compliance and monitoring. This austerity of pedagogical thinking has been accentuated as curricular provision has become concentrated around narrower subject hierarchies, as outlined in Chapter 5.

The language of 'catch-up' risks the development of a mindset that presumes *all* children and young people return to school with a learning deficit rather than a body of new knowledge that their particular experi-ence or mindset may have facilitated. Schools and teachers need to capture this. If a deficit mindset is allowed to flourish, not just in classrooms but staffrooms, there is a risk that this will translate into reduced aspirations and low aspirations are *always* the enemy of high achievement, especially among those already disadvantaged.

Recommendations

6.1 Schools ought to be encouraged to take a diagnostic approach to ensure that both the learning losses and the learning gains of lockdown are captured.

6.2 Catch-up programmes need to be tailored to the needs of specific cohorts and individual students.

6.3 Funding streams need to be affirmatively structured so that provision is targeted at those with the greatest need.

6.4 External interventions, such as mentoring programmes, should complement the work of schools in addressing identified gaps in learning.

6.5 School-level practitioners need to be enabled to work with those providing tutoring services, to deliver bespoke solutions in a cohesive manner.

Pupil well-being and emotional recovery　　**7**

Whatever the difficulties of 'lost learning' or 'catching up', and whatever the merits of focusing on this, as a profession and as policymakers, we have a toolbox of potential strategies and tactics (albeit sometimes costly and needing smart and targeted implementation) to address these challenges. Thus, summer programmes, after-school clubs, crammer classes, booster sessions, programmes that enable special access to the most disadvantaged, volunteer-based tutoring schemes, dedicated funding streams such as pupil premium and so on can all be called upon to 'replace' the hours, days, weeks and months of lost 'curriculum' time, addressing in the process what has been described as the 'obsession with coverage' (Dufour, 1990). But children in the UK, and in very many other countries affected by the pandemic, have missed out on more than curriculum content. The leader of the UK's second largest teaching union puts it this way:

> [Children and young people] have missed out educationally. They have lost out socially and physically. And, emotionally, too, our children have endured anxiety, pain and yet more loss … a plan that recognises that the emotional well-being of children is key to enabling all children to reconnect with education … a plan that recognises that our children are living through a triple crisis of the coronavirus pandemic, a deep economic crisis and institutional and systemic racism as attested by disproportionate impact of the pandemic and the Black Lives Matter protests in the wake of the continued impact of institutional racism and racial injustice.
>
> (Dr Patrick Roach, general secretary, National Association of Schoolmasters and Union of Women Teachers (NASUWT), online debate at the Tolpuddle Martyrs Festival, 22 July 2020)

Looking forward to the possibility of schools reopening in September, one of the parents who spoke to us (a parent who also works for a national charity at the heart of the well-being landscape), identifying what she considered to be priorities for teachers to address, concurred and was unequivocal:

> The first thing is a massive plea that schools focus on well-being and positivity above all else. Even if the kids learned nothing in September and that, you know, they could make this into a celebration of every-thing that every child has achieved during lockdown, whether that's learning to find a recipe, whether it's doing circuits with their dad, or whether it's reading *Lord of the Flies*, or anything in between, you know? And that would just be a wonderful, wonderful start to the, to the new year.
>
> (Alison Woodhead, director of public affairs, Adoption UK,
> focus group – parents, guardians and carers, 22 July 2020)

Emotional recovery is a little more complex, and a lot more challenging than curriculum 'catch-up' although this is not to belittle the task facing teachers and those who support them in achieving the latter.

The 6-year-old who has 'missed' the best part of a term and a half of schooling has also missed hours of socialising, not just in the classroom but in the lunch queue and the playground and in the myriad of 'play dates' generated in the school yard and at the school gate that lockdown, or rather 'social distancing', has ruled 'out of bounds'. To miss out on a term and a half of schooling is to miss half a school year; to our 6-year-old, that's a fair proportion of their fledgling educational career and a lot of socialisation.

The sociability of teaching and the fear of parents

And, of course, it is not only children who may have been traumatised by lockdown, social distancing, the normalising of mask wearing in public spaces and so on. Teaching younger children to 'distance' from their friends goes against the grain for most teachers, especially when it is accompanied by resultant changes in pedagogy – the sudden shift away from collaborative learning and group work, and the re-emergence of single-desk rows, usu-ally reserved for the annual examination season at the top-end of secondary schools.

Teaching is a fundamentally social profession built on relationships in both classroom and staffroom. Those teachers and teaching assistants who spoke with us in the range of focus groups that we convened during the summer of 2020 mourned both these shifts in classroom practice and spoke of how they missed the children and their colleagues during lockdown. As we detail elsewhere in these pages some, on the grounds of personal fear or because of the need to 'shield', were reluctant to join the planned return to school in June 2020 and, as we have seen, this reluctance was sometimes clunkily communicated by the teaching unions during the preceding month or so, but it should not be inferred that they didn't *want* to return to school. The following blog post is illustrative of this:

> I want to go back to school. Because when school is on I know I'm really good at my job. I'm organised at work; I can get stuff done and I can do what I love doing – teach students – and can do it well … Every teacher I know and have spoken to wants exactly the same thing. The emotions I feel are the same as any teacher's. We are a madly driven profession, one wildly and chaotically in love with its work, one which feels the strongest pulls of vocation – of being called to labour. Whether things should be like that is a different question.
>
> (Boxer, 2020)

The other driver against any kind of return to school during the second half of the summer term came from the concerns of some parents but, as illustrated in Figures 7.1 and 7.2, by the close of the second week after their planned return, this fear appeared to be in decline, a pattern that was to continue for the remainder of the term, especially in primary schools and especially among those who were not deemed 'vulnerable'. In the secondary phase, schools tended to use a wider variety of attendance strategies, some calling students in on particular days for a form of academic tutoring, others adopting more conventional teaching strategies, involving full or half classes.

Nonetheless, the interplay – throughout the crisis – between parental fear and child fear, is a factor that should not be ignored, as this local newspaper columnist and working schoolteacher observes:

> Maybe, it's a bit early for hindsight … This could be a temporary blip, like previous financial crashes or bank runs. Yet, no matter what happens, we must seek to instil calm for the sake of the kids. We cannot (as adults) put the fear we are all feeling onto them … The truth is we are transferring our tangible angst onto offspring who should be worried about the next episode of *In the Night Garden* and not on the importance of wearing face masks and standing on gaffer-taped lines.
>
> (Ellis, 2020)

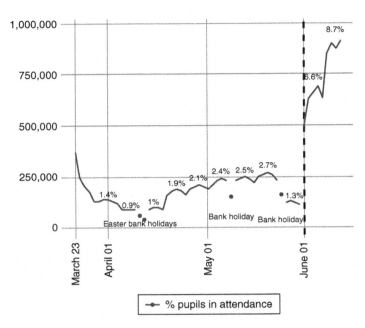

Figure 7.1 Growth in attendance of pupils in education settings between 1 June and 11 June 2020, by comparison with attendance patterns earlier in lockdown. Source: Department for Education (2020b).

While the dismissal of the 2008 financial crash as a 'blip' is rather cavalier, this kind of adult angst was a factor in the lukewarm response of some parents to the news that schools were to reopen at the start of June, and it remained so as September loomed. This parent, talking to the *Guardian*, articulates the kind of concerns that, at different points during lockdown, exercised many, especially those in larger families or with older relatives living at home:

> I have mixed feelings. On the one hand, I desperately want my children to have a proper and full education and not the poor substitute that I provided for them during the school closures, despite my best efforts, but on the other hand, I don't trust the government to have my children's best interests at the forefront of their decision-making around re-opening schools ... I am very worried about the risk of allowing them to return. With five children at the same school, our family completely destroys the bubble concept that so many schools are adopting and relying on to reassure parents ... My mother lives with

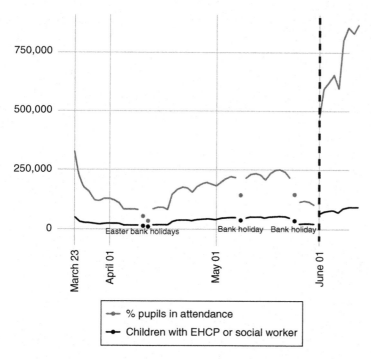

Figure 7.2 Growth in attendance of all pupils and of children with an education and health care plan (EHCP) or social worker in education settings between
1 June and 11 June 2020, by comparison with attendance patterns earlier in
lockdown.
Source: Department for Education (2020b).

> us, this also means additional, unnecessary risk for her … I believe the
> decision to hurriedly return children to school is driven by economic
> reasons and not educational or health ones.
>
> (Kay Tart, cited in Lightfoot, 2020)

In short, the ambivalence about returning to school came (and still comes)
from multiple constituencies, with school leaders seeking to accommodate
and reassure fractured classrooms and staffrooms; no constituency offered
a single, consistent response, perhaps unsurprisingly as no two schools or
communities are the same, with each school necessarily applying its own
bespoke risk assessment and responding to its own circumstances. Thus,
among parents and children, there were attendees and absentees and,
among school staff, the picture was the same.

Perhaps this shouldn't surprise us; certainly, it wasn't (and isn't) unique to our schools, causing some commentators to ponder on whether the lockdown had been *too* successful, at least in getting the vast majority of individuals to shun social spaces or, to a significant degree, a return to the workplace.

There may be elements of truth in this, as there may be in the claims that some, forcibly freed from the rat race, had begun to 'enjoy' lockdown and find a new karma in their existence. However, there may be another driver at play here – a culture of risk aversion, thirty years in the making. Moreover, as noted in Chapter 1, the inevitably bumpy exit from lockdown, with the reimposition of local lockdowns (or at least local *slow*downs) in a number of areas across England, but notably concentrated on areas high in socio-economic disadvantage and with large BAME communities in June, July and August 2020, was in marked contrast to calls for a full return to school, in all areas, in September 2020 in England, Wales and Northern Ireland, and a month earlier in Scotland.

Here, threats by the Westminster government, in contrast with those in the UK's devolved administrations, to fine parents who did not return their children to school at the start of the autumn term were met with incredulity by both teachers' and parents' leaders:

> We don't think that it is the right approach to fine parents for the non-attendance of children as soon as schools fully reopen in September, and the government should not expect schools to take this action. There will be many frightened and anxious parents out there, and this is very much a case of building confidence that it is safe to return, rather than forcing the issue through the use of fines. The government must show a greater understanding of the realities of the situation, and we would recommend that there is a period of grace while normal patterns resume.
>
> (Geoff Barton, general secretary of the
> ASCL, cited in Weale, 2020a)

Cited in the same article, Kevin Courtney, joint general secretary at the National Education Union, the UK's largest education union, added:

> Working with families in a constructive and supportive way, using scientific information to address concerns, is a far better route than fining parents. This can often alienate the very individuals schools most need to reach out to and would always be a last resort.
>
> (Courtney, cited in Weale, 2020a)

This echoed the response of Parentkind, the national body representing parent–teacher associations:

> More work needs to be done by government and schools to reassure parents and carers that it is safe for children to return to school. A significant number remain undecided about returning their children to school next term, and the majority of parents and carers are wanting the right to make the decision themselves. The government needs to be understanding of parents' legitimate concerns and talking about fining them is not helpful.
>
> (Jolly, 2020)

And these national voices appeared to find resonance at the chalkface with the website of one broadsheet running a story about the response of head teachers under the headline and byline: 'Head teachers may refuse to fine parents who keep children at home in September: unions predict school leaders will use loophole in the law to avoid fining parents who fail to send children to classes' (Gardner, 2020). As well as in the letters pages of the national press:

> Sir … it is a sobering thought that the education secretary (Gavin Williamson MP) appears to be so devoid of persuasive or constructive ideas that he considers one of the best ways of ensuring a full return to school life in September is to fine those parents who may choose to keep their children at home for perfectly understandable reasons.
>
> Although there is little disagreement that it is preferable to have every school open and operating as normal, with the strict proviso that it is safe to do so, freedom of choice must continue to remain paramount. The threat of fines and possible court action should be removed immediately.
>
> (Claughton, 2020)

In any case, the threat of fines did not seem to shift the needle on parental attitudes on the issue of a September return with the same paper subsequently reporting on a survey of 13,500 parents by Childcare.co.uk, an online community for parents and childcare providers, that:

> 26 per cent did not intend to send their children back to school. Of these, 80 per cent believed that the government was reopening schools for economic reasons, 67 per cent felt it was unsafe [to do so] and 63 per cent said they did not care if they were fined.
>
> (Woolcock, 2020a)

This discussion is pertinent here because it paints a broader picture about concerns around the pandemic, and the inability to insulate, or inoculate, schools, teachers, children and their parents from these concerns. In the early days, the messaging about COVID-19 was clear, and centred around 'stay home'. Libertarian pundits of the Left and the Right, such as Claire Fox at the Academy of Ideas (who was elevated to the House of Lords late in lockdown) and Peter Hitchens, a *Mail on Sunday* columnist, railed against this failure to 'trust the public' and called on policymakers to 'treat people as grown-ups', but the softening of messaging that they and others had called for did not produce a concurrent reduction in concern. Rather, it contributed to anxiety, with the government facing calls for clarity and finding itself in the invidious position of opening up some areas of the economy, partly for the economic survival of those parts of the economy, while closing down others.

Thus, as the words of this paragraph were first drafted on the last day of July 2020, they landed on-screen during a week that had seen the reopening of gyms, the introduction of compulsory face coverings in shops (a couple of weeks after their reopening), the announcement that those returning from Iberian holidays or trips to Luxembourg would need to quarantine for two weeks and the hosting of 'small-crowd' test events in domains as diverse as cricket and comedy, and, subsequently, their postponement. As portrayed in the opening chapters, whether or not the shutdown of schools came too late or not, their partial 'reopening' in June 2020 had been a much more patchy affair, with parental and pupil take-up, at least initially, notable for how tentative and partial it was; two months later, in August 2020, confusion about arrangements for the upcoming autumn term in England, Wales and Northern Ireland, and the proposed full opening of all schools, remained rife, in spite of near full attendance in Scottish schools that had returned three weeks earlier.

The varied experiences of childhood trauma

In all of this the trauma of children takes on multiple forms and facets and becomes more complex as they process the mixed messages from peers, parents and the media. It is worth exploring this a little further because it reveals a much more nuanced picture than the one sector leaders, caught up in a political metanarrative, paint. The reality is that, while there have been some broad commonalities, particularly around being distanced from friends, the psychological demands of lockdown have impacted differently on the well-being of *different* children, and differently on the *same* children at different points in the lockdown. As this senior leader in a special school puts it:

> I know it's very early days, but it does seem [that] actually some of the children absolutely thrived and [have] grown [during lockdown] and they haven't regressed and they've come back into school able to engage again. And that gives me great hope for September when we're opening fully, that actually our children will embrace school and we can, we can, we can carry on carrying on.
>
> (Jane Lovis, deputy head teacher, Pebble Brook School, focus group – special education and alternative provision, 8 July 2020)

Another teacher, formerly UK-based and now teaching overseas, also pointed to the benefits for at least some children, and some families, during lockdown. Reflecting on his own experience of lockdown in Dubai (where schools were also closed), he commented:

> I've enjoyed it, for the most part. It's new to me and as such, I've had the chance to experiment and assess what works well with the classes I teach (in terms of online teaching strategies). For some students, it has been great. Some have adapted well. I do get the feeling that some have not gotten the best out of it and real specific intervention will be needed for them in the future. As a parent, the time with my daughter has been incredible. Yes, she's bouncing off the walls and going 100 mph from morning 'til night, but I can't imagine a time when we'll ever spend this much time together.
>
> (Glenn Amoah, teacher of secondary English, Ministry of Education Dubai, United Arab Emirates, written submission, 27 June 2020)

A University of Bristol study, published later in lockdown and based on the survey responses of a thousand young people in the South-West paints a similarly nuanced picture, concluding that anxiety levels among young teenagers dropped during the pandemic, with the BBC News website reporting that: 'Those who felt least connected to school before lockdown saw a larger decrease in anxiety, raising questions about how the school environment affects some younger teenagers' mental well-being' (BBC News, 2020a). One of the study's authors, Dr Judi Kidger, added: 'As schools reopen, we need to consider ways in which schools can be more supportive of mental health for all students' (BBC News, 2020a). And this broadly positive (or at least non-traumatising) experience of lockdown was reflected in the comments of some of the young people who joined our focus groups:

> Well, me and my friends ... none of us have really been stressing about it. From my end, the people I speak to, none of them were really bothered about having teacher-assessed grades or not having to do their exams ... I think the news and stuff has made it out to be a lot worse than it actually was.
>
> (Ben, Year 11 student (Merseyside), focus group –
> students (11–16), 25 August 2020)

Another member of the group, ironically the son of a broadcast journalist, agreed:

> I'd say the same. I think it's actually been much better than it's made out to be by the news. Me and most of my friends weren't stressed and have fairly enjoyed lockdown and not having to do grades. I know a couple of people who were stressed to begin with, but I think they're [in] the minority.
>
> (Jack, Year 11 student (London), focus group –
> students (11–16), 25 August 2020)

For others, lockdown has provided a chance for quality time with siblings:

> I'm quite lucky because I have two brothers who are living at home at the moment with the family [during lockdown] ... I think we've had fun together as a family. One of (my brothers) is also quite into exercising [and] gym work ... he's managed to [stop] me getting bored and [has been] getting [me] out of the house ... doing exercise, doing runs. So, I think, in a way, [it's] brought us together a little bit more than usual because they're usually at university, and I hardly ever see them, but we've just had six months of ... seeing each other ... overall I think it's been good for us.
>
> (Ed, Year 11 student (London), focus group –
> students (16–19), 26 August 2020)

Highlighting these cases is not to belittle the very difficult experiences of lockdown had by some young people, especially those living in the midst of abusive relationships or domestic violence, or experiencing the kind of disadvantage that those cited above have not had to contend with. A head teacher who took part in one of our research interviews reveals the following contrast:

> I suspect that many children in the area that we serve, that we're in, have had an experience [that] will have been very advantageous for them, rather than any kind of deficit ... but, also ... we [now] recognise some families [as] vulnerable, who prior to lockdown we would not have identified as having particular vulnerabilities ... particularly around domestic violence, relationships that maybe could be hidden. There are four or five families we now have concerns about who were not on my radar before ... Over the holidays I've been in contact with two of those women and we are [now] building a relationship with [professional] support ... which means that when the children come back ... we can offer something that's more tailored to those children ... We know the damage that domestic violence, and witnessing it, can do to children.
>
> (Head teacher (speaking on condition of anonymity), research interview, summer 2020)

Rebecca Brooks, the author of an early lockdown report on the experiences of adopted children (Brooks, 2020a), also pointed to this more varied picture than popular narratives might have us believe:

> We found that more than half of the parents of secondary school children who responded to our survey said that the children were less stressed when they weren't in school. And this is coupled with a lot of comments of children making remarkable progress or doing much better than parents thought they would.
>
> (Rebecca Brooks, education policy advisor, Adoption UK, focus group – special education and alternative provision, 8 July 2020)

Many of the families and children that Brooks focuses on periodically struggle with school as a result of adoptive trauma and consequent attachment difficulties, something that we discuss further later in this chapter. Other children struggle with school for other reasons, including bullying, and for these children, lockdown may also have provided a relief, rather than a challenge.

Thus, while the simple narrative that the lockdown has been universally damaging suits political protagonists on all sides of this debate and makes for good news copy, the realities that schools will face on the return of children in all year groups will be much more complex. Here, it might be useful to identify some pupil 'types', not to suggest that young people fit easily into these boxes (because some children will have moved *across* these categories at different points *during* the lockdown), but because it gives a sense of the breadth of the schooling challenge ahead. Three types are perhaps prominent:

1. *Lockdown thrivers:* these are the children who feel that they may have discovered something that works more effectively for them than the schooling they had experienced before lockdown. On the one hand, this group includes the kind of child referred to by Georgia Holleran (the independent SEND consultant who took part in one of our focus groups in Chapter 6) who has thrived during lockdown because it has offered the opportunity to do something very different to that which takes place in the schoolroom that they are assumed to be missing. They may have struggled with the structure of schooling, the busyness and noisiness of school corridors and school yards, the (often necessary) nature of school regulation or the demands of the school timetable. Alternatively, this group may include children who are living in comfortable settings with good Wi-Fi access and families newly won over by the potential of home-schooling and with the resources and cultural capital to support and richly resource schooling at home. Either way, the children in this group are likely to have discovered news ways of learning with which they are particularly comfortable. Post-lockdown, winning some of these children (and their families) back will be no easy challenge for schools; the likelihood is that some of these lockdown thrivers are likely to switch to home-schooling permanently.

2. *Lockdown survivors:* these are the children who have, by and large, 'got through' lockdown, who have gained some new experiences and developed some new skills but who have missed the sociability of school and the structure that it gives to the day and the week. This group are likely to welcome the return of school, but may return with new perspectives and some sense of what life could be like without school. Prior to lockdown, many of these children will have survived school in much the same way, without necessarily engaging or flourishing. Post-lockdown, engaging these children will be vital to securing their renewed commitment to schooling. If many in this category are the low-maintenance, broadly compliant children that some schools may have taken for granted in the past, they might prove to be a different proposition afterwards and schools need to be ready for this.

3. *Lockdown strugglers:* these are the children who, for a myriad of reasons, may have found all or part of the lockdown incredibly difficult; they may have experienced abuse, ongoing family discord or domestic violence, they may live in challenging socio-economic or cramped conditions or they may struggle much more profoundly with anxiety, loneliness or with the schoolwork set during lockdown, such that any failure to 'catch up' is likely to impact on their already fragile self-esteem. Some of these children will have been unable to access secure Wi-Fi, or the equipment to make the most of such access, during lockdown. Post-lockdown, identifying and delivering bespoke pastoral and curricular support to these children is vital, especially if they are dependent on a stable school environment, because this is so markedly different to what they face at home.

The point is that each of these very broad categories, of which membership is fluid over time, holds a tremendous diversity of need, circumstance and experience within it. Thus, these are not categories defined by the classic distinction of perceived or (somehow) measured ability. Instead, they are defined by the complexities of motivation, pre-existing conditions (such as ADHD and autism), personal disposition (however formed but likely to be heavily influenced by issues of attachment and adverse childhood experiences) and family attitudes and situation.

Too often in the past, schools have mixed the former with the latter, confusing the former (ability) with all kinds of behaviours that may present as difficult to manage for the school, or at least for the *mainstream* school or practitioner. For this reason, post-lockdown, the skill sets held by those who work in our special schools, in alternative provision and as SEND coordinators, those leading on the social curriculum and overseeing PSHE and pastoral provision, pupil counsellors, family liaison officers and educational psychologists are likely to be at a premium. Late and post-lockdown, the wider schooling system will need to acknowledge – and *invest* in – the expertise of these groups as never before. In the 'new normal' these skill sets will need to be 'in the room' from the start, not in an office, or former storeroom, down the corridor or at the end of a last-ditch and reluctantly made phone call.

And, this will be especially the case in the weeks immediately after schools return to something like full-scale operation. Why? Because during this period, very many pupils and students, whatever their age, circumstance and location on the matrix presented here, are likely to feel levels of anxiety, not unlike those that they first experienced on their first day at primary or secondary school; thriving or surviving during – or for most of – lockdown is an indicator of future need, but it does not preclude the possibility of high anxiety in those first few days and weeks back, especially if strong pressure is being exerted to 'catch up' during this period.

The primacy of well-being and relationships

Let's be clear: for schools and for those who lead and work in them, this is difficult stuff. Whatever the importance of *curriculum* catch-up (with which we might assume that most young people will need some support), curricular need is measurable and progress towards it can be quantified; addressing multiple deficits in well-being less so, especially when the latter often presents itself in much more oblique ways. Although a direct citation is difficult to find, the phrase 'culture eats strategy for breakfast', is widely attributed to business leadership guru Peter Drucker. In terms of current debates about the priorities of schooling post-lockdown, one might draw a similar conclusion about well-being and catch-up: *securing well-being is a prerequisite for curriculum catch-up, not its poor relation.*

Probably for this reason, as we shall see later, many of the education professionals who spoke to us (especially those in the primary phase, working in SEND settings and in socio-economically disadvantaged areas), placed well-being, and the diagnosis of need in this respect, at the top of their priority list upon the return of 'full' schooling. In this regard, Rebecca Brooks makes a useful distinction between 'catch-up' and 'recovery', reserving 'recovery' for discussions about well-being and thinking of 'catch-up' as a much more instrumental activity, essentially focused on curriculum. It is worth quoting her position at length:

> What children need – in fact what society needs – after the pandemic is not 'catch-up'. It is 'recovery'.
>
> 'Catch-up' implies a narrow emphasis on curriculum goals with a focus on getting all children to the same endpoint as quickly as possible. 'Recovery' acknowledges that the impact of this crisis has been far wider than 'missed learning' and that we will need to begin where children are, rather than focus on where we would like them to be, and how to get them all to that same point as quickly as possible.
>
> Some will return to education having made surprising progress, not only in learning of all kinds, but also in terms of their mental health and well-being, which are foundational to learning success. Others may have maintained their learning to a degree but be carrying an emotional burden which will guarantee that they buckle under the

pressure of 'catch-up' programmes. Still others will arrive on shaky ground in all areas, having endured a period of their lives where survival was the only attainable goal.

There is no possibility of a regime of 'catch-up' that will restore all children to their curriculum targets in a few weeks. We cannot rely on extra tuition and summer classes and hope to continue on after that as if COVID-19 never happened. To imagine that we can not only ignores the impact of COVID-19, but also the inequalities that already existed in education and have, if anything, been exacerbated in recent months.

Recovery is not a one-size-fits-all process that can be achieved with a quick burst of energetic activity. It will probably be years before our society, our economy and our children come out from under the shadow of this crisis, if ever, and we must be willing to enter into a long period of recovery that recognises not only where we want to end up, but where we really are right now.

(Brooks, 2020b)

The challenge of reintegration that Brooks vividly outlines might be helpfully viewed through the lens offered by approaches that might be described as 'inclusion first' and 'attachment aware'. It is worth saying a little more about each of these approaches and the contribution that they might make to well-being focused schooling, post-lockdown.

Inclusion first

To education professionals focused on raising attainment, the notion of delivering a package of strategies that might be described as 'inclusion first' (Breslin, 2008) may appear to signal a softening of ambition in terms of outcomes for young people. It is not; rather, it becomes a necessity because, for all of their success, attainment-first strategies ultimately consolidate the exclusion of those who, for whatever reason, find school most challenging. In short, the more successful schools are in raising the achievement of the majority, the more excluded those left behind become:

When there is significant and self-evident under-performance in the system, the increases in student success are reasonably easily won. When this is (no longer) the case, schools and teachers are left to focus their efforts on more 'challenging' students – students who are already conscious of their relative lack of success in an achievement culture

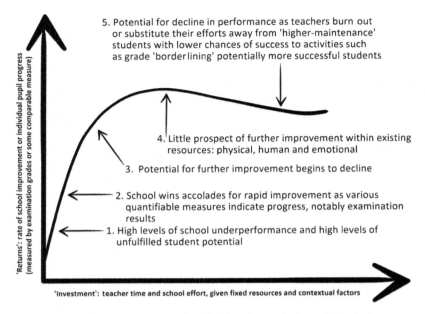

Returns (both in terms of grades achieved and teacher motivation and retention)
diminish as the student cohort becomes both more disadvantaged and more
challenging; economists would dissuade us from investing our energies in such
learners.

Figure 7.3 The diminishing returns to attainment-first strategies.

and who are the most likely to be already dealing with (or succumbing
to) socio-economic disadvantage and social upheaval beyond the
school's gates or control.

(Breslin, 2008, p. 79)

This process is reproduced in Figure 7.3.

Achievement-focused attainment-first strategies are effective (and necessary) in delivering success for those young people who ought to have been
achieving in the first place, but a curve that begins with steep rises reaches
a plateau as this underperformance is removed from the system, and as
teachers and schools reach optimum performance levels within current
resource levels and curricular and pedagogical frameworks. This serves in
part as a summary of the consequence of adhering doggedly to attainment-
first strategies in the English education system for more than a quarter
of a century. To date, policymakers (and, arguably, school leaders) have
failed to acknowledge the need to shift from *attainment-first* to *inclusion-first*

strategies if they are to *widen* participation and reach those learners left behind by a culture frequently described as 'test, tables and targets'. This influential policy shaper suggests that the pendulum, pre-lockdown, was already beginning to shift in this direction:

> I think that we were beginning to see … shifts in the tide in terms of a focus on inclusion and exclusion, and there was considerably more interest in … issues related to special educational needs, in relation to reducing exclusion and so on … I think we were beginning to see a turn of [the] pendulum which may not have made itself manifest every way yet, but I think it was … starting, percolating. I think [we've had] a big focus on improving results, which I think some people have talked about as a negative thing. I personally don't necessarily see it as a negative thing [but] I think that has unintended consequences.
>
> (Loic Menzies, chief executive and founder, Centre for Education and Youth, focus group – secondary education, 15 June 2020)

And this change in direction is not just important for the children concerned. It is vital also for their teachers if they are to avoid the demotivation and burnout that follows from recurrently unsuccessful practice, especially when those students who struggle most are disproportionately present in schools in areas of high deprivation, schools that can be 'career damagingly difficult to work in' (Local Government Association, 2019). These learners need to have their exclusion addressed if they are to flourish as achievers, and that means a degree of system re-engineering, of changing what schools are *like* and how teachers and support staff *work* in schools. It needs the pendulum shift that Menzies is beginning to identify.

The point is that, post-lockdown, if the impact of proposed policy interventions is marginal and the gap between differentially advantaged learners widens significantly, the importance of addressing the exclusion of these pupils, cut further adrift from their peers in terms of achievement, becomes vital – not just for these children and young people, but for the schools and communities that they are part of. Inclusion-first strategies are key to their success not because inclusion is achievement's less favoured cousin, but because inclusion is a prerequisite for the achievement of these learners and achievement's more narrowly focused and easily quantified sibling, test and examination attainment.

Attachment aware

In recent years there has been a growing interest in attachment-aware or trauma-aware schooling and in the impact of 'adverse childhood experiences': traumatic events in childhood that are likely to impact on a child's ability to form secure attachments, both as a child and in adulthood. Such a failure can manifest itself in a range or mental health needs and impact profoundly on an individual's well-being. The Attachment Research Community, which has more than 200 UK schools in its membership, describes attachment theory in the following terms:

> Attachment theory explains how children build an internal working model of themselves and the world through relationships. Trauma, abuse, neglect, separation and bereavement have adverse effects, which means the child and adult's sense of safety and relationships need to be rebuilt in order for them to learn.
>
> (Attachment Research Community, 2020)

Attachment-aware schools, with their focus on 'connection before correction' and their understanding of children with attachment needs as being 'connection seeking, not attention seeking', find the kind of 'one-size-fits-all', 'zero-tolerance' behaviour strategies still favoured in a minority of school settings an anathema. Although this kind of analysis is often most commonly applied to adopted and care-experienced children, the experience of some children during lockdown is likely to be traumatising, while others will have found the initial entry into lockdown incredibly difficult and still others may find the re-entry into school similarly challenging.

For those children who have had the most difficult experiences of lockdown, possibly because of a family bereavement (conceivably a bereavement caused by the virus), or because of family instability or domestic violence, abuse or simply because of isolation, loneliness and anxiety, the outcome is likely to be trauma and the experience adverse. If the results of these experiences are left unaddressed, these 'lockdown strugglers', to use the term coined earlier in this chapter, may find that they struggle with attachment and related issues long beyond lockdown itself. This correspondent offers a stark warning, and a proposed solution:

> Experiences of insecurity, loss and trauma in the school-age population are likely to have proliferated during the pandemic, and opportunities to address such adversity have not been available to most

children. There is no one-size-fits-all solution to supporting all those children but there is one lesson from my work. COVID-19 has caused many grandparents, parents or teachers to die in a short period. We found bereavement support for school children prevented long term ill-health and could be delivered economically in small groups.

(Cann, 2020)

There is now a growing literature on the impact of adverse childhood experiences and their impact on subsequent life chances. And, for a significant number of children, lockdown will have been an adverse childhood experience of just this type. In addition, there are a range of organisations – especially among those who work with adoptive families, those involved in fostering, those who work with victims of both child abuse and domestic violence and those who work with families suffering bereavement – that hold or are developing significant expertise in this field.

Moreover, the rise of the well-being and safeguarding agendas – and, in particular, a concern for young people's mental health – in the day-to-day practice of all UK schools has created a sensitivity to these issues, now profiled strongly in inspection frameworks and other regulatory apparatus, which ought to be a resource that schools should fully utilise, post-lockdown, especially during the period in which some sort of normal schooling resumes.

The fear is, of course, that in the concern to achieve 'safe' schooling – masks, bubbles, spacing, sanitiser, staggered start and finish times, staggered breaks and lunchtimes – insufficient time is given to the diagnosis of what will be highly individualised well-being related needs. For this reason, a number of school leaders and other practitioners who have spoken with us have emphasised that well-being will be their highest priority when children return:

> The first thing we've got to do is look after well-being, because you can't learn unless you're emotionally stable and feel in a good place. So, well-being, well-being, well-being has got to come first before anything else ... If we don't get the well-being right first, we are not going to help those children to be life ready, work ready or world ready in any sense or any way.
>
> (Karine George, former head teacher and co-founder, Leadership Lemonade, focus group – primary education, 14 July 2020)

It's down to relationships – relationships built on trust, and trust in a place where there's [been] fear. What about if we don't get those results? We'll get those results! If we go for deep learning with a real emphasis on well-being and positive relationships, [we'll be] okay – achievement flows from inclusion.

(Daniel Kerbel, head teacher, Grange Primary, Harrow, London, focus group – primary education, 14 July 2020)

It is worth reiterating, though, that to focus on well-being is not to deprioritise matters of curriculum catch-up and academic progression. From an inclusion-first perspective, addressing issues like trauma and attachment is a prerequisite for learning to take place. One possible legacy of all of this, as we have already argued earlier in this text, is that those focused on inclusion-related issues, pastoral care and special educational needs and disabilities will gain a stronger voice in school staffrooms and leadership teams. That would be no bad thing.

Ensuring staff well-being

This focus on reintegrating, or reinducting, children and young people into schooling life, while *diagnosing* where their individual experiences of lockdown leaves them, will be critical to the success of any catch-up strategies and to their ongoing experiences of schooling, and the same is very much true of staff.

Just as pupils have had differential experiences of lockdown, so it is with staff. Indeed, they too will have been, at different times, lockdown 'thrivers', 'survivors' and 'strugglers', and heads and senior leaders will need to use a full range of human resources strategies to ensure that staff are not just in attendance, but mentally *ready* to teach, to lead, to enthuse. And all of this in a public environment where, as we have discussed elsewhere in these pages, the signals are inevitably contradictory as lockdown is, necessarily, both eased *and* reasserted, reflecting a range of competing priorities: reopening schools, rebooting the economy, monitoring the decline (or otherwise) of the virus, re-establishing some sense of normality, or at least some kind of routeway to it. Nothing illustrates this better than a news report that surfaced on the first day of August, citing one of the government's leading advisers and posing a stark question – one that we have already explored in an earlier chapter:

I think we're in a situation whereby most people think that opening schools is a priority for the health and well-being of children and that when we do that we are going to reconnect lots of households. And so actually, closing some of the other networks, some of the other activities [that connect households] may well be required to enable us to open schools. It might come down to a question of which do you trade off against each other and then that's a matter of prioritising, do we think pubs are more important than schools?

(Professor Graham Medley, Scientific Advisory Group for Emergencies (SAGE), speaking on the *Today* programme, BBC Radio 4, 1 August 2020)

Reflecting on the staffing challenge that emerges as schools reopen in this highly fluid environment, one head teacher who spoke to us picked up the well-being focus taken by her colleagues cited earlier, but noted the importance of staff well-being in all of this:

We are going to be compassionate. We're going to be kind, we're going to show [the children] that we want them back – that they're important to us, but it's not going to be linear. It's not going to be straightforward. And so, we also need to get ourselves ready for the marathon, even though we don't know where the marathon is, we don't know the routes and we don't know how long it's going to be. We've got … to look after ourselves as well as our children.

(Diane Rawlins, senior deputy, Arbury Primary School, Cambridge, focus group – primary education, 14 July 2020)

Attending to issues of staff well-being (and to the very different experiences of individual members of staff within the same staff body), of lockdown and their varied dispositions to a return to work is as important to attending to the well-being of children, not because staff are more important than children, but because staff well-being is a prerequisite for pupil well-being, and the latter is a prerequisite for effective, purposeful and enjoyable learning. For school, federation, trust and local authority leaders and governing boards, the fractured team dynamics that are at risk of emerging in such a setting may prove to be the greatest challenge of the crisis. It is to these and the other challenges facing system and school leaders that we turn in the following chapter.

Summary and key messages

Addressing the well-being of children and young people, and staff and volunteers, upon their return to school has been the priority for the vast majority of education professionals, school governors and parents who have spoken to us in the research that we have undertaken in the writing of this book.

System leaders and policymakers need to prioritise well-being in the same way. Inclusion and well-being are prerequisites for learning, not alternatives to it.

Recommendations

7.1 It is vital that the emotional, psychological and attachment needs of children and young people are not ignored in the pursuit of academic catch-up.

7.2 Schools, system leaders and policymakers should pivot their efforts towards inclusion-first and well-being focused strategies, both in the immediate aftermath of the pandemic and in the longer term.

7.3 Schools must be enabled to better develop an understanding of trauma and attachment and how vulnerabilities in these areas might be addressed, an understanding that is likely to be vital in supporting the needs of children returning to school.

7.4 Education professionals must recognise that some students have thrived during lockdown and therefore develop strategies that sustain their flourishing in a school setting.

7.5 System-wide, there needs to be a much stronger focus on matters of staff well-being, including the well-being of heads and senior leaders, if schools are to retain the capacity to enable the children and young people in their care to thrive.

Leadership and governance

8

Whatever the debate about the health consequences, the government's objective to keep schools open as long as possible in the early months of the virus because of the multiple impacts of closure (on vulnerable children, on the NHS workforce and on the many others now newly – and belatedly – acknowledged as *key* workers) has shone a light on the importance of all who work in our schools: school leaders, teachers, teaching and laboratory assistants, those making and serving school meals, those looking after children during break and mealtimes, site managers and after-school club staff, school bursars and business managers, cleaners and maintenance staff, sports coaches and librarians, student counsellors and educational psychologists, specialists from the variety of professions that support those with special educational needs and disabilities and so on. Beyond COVID-19, the status of the school workforce, and hosts of other key workers, will find its proper place in our hearts and in our minds. Not before time.

But status does not sit in a vacuum. While most understood that school leaders, teachers and support staff were (and, as we go to publication at the start of September 2020, remain) in largely uncharted waters, there was tremendous variety in the experience of parents (as we explored in greater depth in Chapter 2), both within the state sector and between the state and the independent sector, a point not lost on one parent with a younger child in the state system and older stepchildren in independent schools:

> I remember [in] that first two weeks feeling that I was sort of coping, but feeling very overwhelmed by it … In terms of the school, I don't actually recall much communication from them in the first two weeks,

I felt that they were sort of responding. They were quite in shock and, as a school, they were quite disarmed and kind of struggling to know what to say ... Whereas like I said, [with] my [privately educated] stepson, there was a seamless transition into home-schooling through Microsoft Teams and, you know, all that, all the other platforms that we've got.

(Participant, focus group – parents, guardians and carers, 22 July 2020)

And this was, to some degree, reflected in the comments of those teachers from the independent sector who participated in our research but, of course, supporting disadvantaged children was not a burden, as one independent sixth-form college leader in the independent sector put it:

We were able, in the school closure [period] to deliver all of our lessons online, you know, and that worked well. We provided a fair bit of extra pastoral support as well online ... So, to be honest with you, we've been in a fairly privileged position, I would say.

(Sean Buckley, principal, LSI Sixth-Form College, focus group – independent sector, 20 July 2020)

Doubtless this ability to offer a more seamless transition into home-schooling may have had something to do with resourcing (something we shall return to later) and, as another colleague from the independent sector conceded, the contractual relationship between parents and providers in fee-paying settings. But, as outlined in Chapter 2, the overwhelming response of parents throughout the crisis has been empathetic and supportive, what-ever the sector:

It struck me how, what a massive challenge it was for the teachers to, all of a sudden, shift to this ... online world and how there was a big skills gap between what they needed [to be effective] in the classroom and what they needed to be [effective] online.

(Manjit Shellis, assistant director of wider learning, Digital Education Partnership, focus group – parents, carers and guardians, 22 July 2020)

But what was the experience like from the other side of the lens, for teachers and, in particular, school leaders? In Chapter 1 we explored the experience of teachers during lockdown; now, we turn to the challenge of reshaping and reorientating teaching and the wider school workforce, post-lockdown.

Teachers' professional development and initial teacher education

As we outlined in Chapter 2, the level of parental interaction during the pandemic has emphasised the need for schools to reconsider how parental engagement is managed post-lockdown. Likewise, the emergent digital technologies have revealed the need to build digital literacy and develop accompanying pedagogies profession-wide, a challenge that we explore further in Chapter 10. Both have an impact on how we train, recruit, develop and retain teachers. Taken together, both emphasise the importance of access to high-quality teacher education and continuing professional development opportunities, and the equivalent for the wider school workforce, especially when a post-lockdown recession might mean a surge of interest in joining the profession and when those joining will bring new skill sets, especially in the digital sphere, a point not lost on those in the teacher education community:

> I think there is a degree to which we need to recognise the expertise that they [newly qualified teachers] are now bringing into schools because they, themselves, have been online learners. And now they are going to be online teachers. That's some incredible resource actually – that schools don't have in the same way [and] that established teachers don't have.
>
> (Vic Crooks, assistant professor in history education, University of Nottingham, focus group – teacher education, 27 July 2020)

Across the UK the long-standing Postgraduate Certificate in Education (PGCE) spans an academic year with, usually, a couple of extended periods of teaching practice of several weeks duration, one earlier in the course and one towards the close of the year. The practical difficulties of delivering such a programme with schools partially closed are obvious but, as with others in the schooling arena, inventiveness and creativity were the order of the day:

> We put in place quite quickly ... an online system of delivery for professional development and for keeping [in] touch with students on a group, as well as a one to one, basis. [First] we had whole groups, cohort sessions, then we had smaller sessions and then we added one-to-one ... and ... very quickly, early on, we said PGCE secondary students will not be in schools. We didn't wait for the government or

the schools to make those decisions, [although] we did consult with the schools.

> (Kim Cowie, lecturer in education, University of Newcastle
> focus group – teacher education, 27 July 2020)

But, this ability to embrace the digital risks underplaying the qualities of 'in-the-room' teaching and teacher development:

> I think there are real dangers in the ways that institutions have shown how quickly it's possible to say it's okay, we've set up alternative [online] tasks, alternative kinds of assessment, alternative ways of communicating. We can develop this expertise very quickly … [but] … I think there's a real danger of downplaying, the expert knowledge and experience of teacher educators in knowing how teachers learn … there's a real danger in sending messages that we can … you know, … put it all online.
>
> (Caroline Daly, professor of teacher education, University
> College London, focus group – teacher education, 27 July 2020)

Building on this theme that we can't 'put it all online', Daly continues:

> We need time to work with teachers who are still learning – whether they're student teachers, employment-route teachers, trainee teachers – we need time for them to spend with experts [from] a range of sources [and] from a range of perspectives, doing those things that are really complicated, that are highly contingent, that are 'in the moment', that enact things around learning that preserve the importance of things like physicality, dramatisation, physical literacy, all kinds of social and verbal interactions that are actually incredibly hard to replicate online.

Arguably, this is not just about teacher training. It's about teaching itself and the nature of schools as social spaces. It's about, as Graeme Tiffany puts it in one of our other focus groups, *presence*:

> I go back to this central point for young people: presence, and what Rhydian Brooke calls, 'the miracle of presence', is so important for them. And if you ask them what they miss they'll tell you clearly: 'I miss my friends. I miss my friends and I miss being able to engage with my teachers in a kind of a conversational, questioning kind of way'.
>
> (Graeme Tiffany, detached youth worker, University of London,
> focus group – secondary education, 22 July 2020)

And teachers and trainee teachers likewise. This is not to say that there are not benefits that the socially distanced, remotely mentored student teachers of 2020 have gained, but that they have had one kind of preparation, and not another:

> Some of [the lockdown-trainees] have gained brilliant experience in, in kind of medium- and long-term planning, which they wouldn't necessarily have had … Some of them were absolutely fantastic and took on whole schemes of learning and have spent vast amounts of time doing planning in a way that they wouldn't necessarily have had the time or the flexibility to do in a standard year. So, I think there have been some real benefits … [but] … I've spoken to several of them and they are, they're worried about standing up in front of the class-room. They know they can do it. They've got reams of paperwork and files and all sorts of wonderful reports telling them that they're doing it, and that they have had enough training and we've got confidence in them, but actually having not stood up in front of the class since March … [it's] a terrifying thought. And I think experienced teachers are kind of having a little bit of a, you know, an extension of, of the kind of 'summer holiday blues' … when you kind of think [come September], can I do this again? I think that's massively extended in these trainees.
>
> (Sophie Igo, assistant head and initial teacher training lead, Chesterton Community College, Cambridge, focus group – teacher education, 27 July 2020)

Whatever the practical difficulties, though, that lockdown has posed to those in initial teacher education, it has been as insightful to this community of educational professionals as it has been to those elsewhere in the educational landscape:

> I think it's made us understand how complex initial teacher education is these days; so many different routes, so many different phases, so many different age profiles on our programmes, so many different [types of] school and setting that we're actually working with. And it makes you reflect, I think, on the nature of your partnerships and how strong they are and the different kinds of trainees that you've got.
>
> (David Kerr, head of initial teacher training, fellowship and engagement, University of Reading, focus group – teacher education, 27 July 2020)

Kerr, in common with many at the chalkface, feels that there might be a 'reset' opportunity in all of this – one that might enable reframed teacher education programmes to capture this complexity – but worries, as early as July 2020, that teacher education providers are, already, being guided to revert to pre-lockdown norms:

> The question is whether [the] DfE [Department for Education], Ofsted and others [will] allow us to be more flexible in the way we plan our programmes, going forward, because there's a danger that [after lockdown], we just go back [to pre-lockdown practice] because we're forced [to do so] by things like the ITT [Initial Teacher Training] Core Content Framework and [the Ofsted] inspection framework. We all have these great ideas now about what we'd like to do – online mentoring, online meetings – but there's a danger that we'll be forced back to the ... usual pattern just because of the way that we're actually inspected and governed [by] the forces in the centre.

And Professor Rachel Lofthouse, who had enabled us to pull the teacher education focus group together, concurs:

> We've been forced, as have schools, to be extraordinarily adept at being flexible, adaptable and agile – you know, on an almost daily basis having to come up and resolve issues. But ... when we've gone back, for example, from UCET [Universities' Council for the Education of Teachers] to the DfE and asked them to be a bit more flexible and agile around the juggernaut of policies that are coming, we've essentially met [with] what I see, from my position, [as] a bit of a brick wall.
>
> (Rachel Lofthouse, professor of teacher education, Carnegie School of Education, Leeds Beckett University, focus group – teacher education, 27 July 2020)

For Kerr, the answer lies in stronger partnerships with both schools *and* those engaged in system leadership and governance, but he remains concerned that this opportunity might be slipping away:

> There's a real need to have a good dialogue with our school partners, so that it's a real partnership, but also with DfE and Ofsted, so that we don't just capture the learning – they also capture the learning ... there's been a kind of window of opportunity here. It's a question of whether we can grasp it and take it forward.
>
> (David Kerr, head of initial teacher training, fellowship and engagement, University of Reading, focus group – teacher education, 27 July 2020)

Fundamentally, these comments raise questions about the kind of places we want schools to be – and the tasks, as a society, we need them to fulfil – and the kind of profession we want teaching to evolve into, not simply in the stressed months of an inevitably unevenly easing lockdown, but in the longer term. In this regard, one key theme shone through in our focus group and one-to-one research discussions, which was raised by Steve Chalke in the late-lockdown tweet cited in our Preface; namely, that of *resetting* our education system, rather than merely *restarting* it.

Headship during lockdown: the logistical challenge

As any teacher, school leader or school governor will testify, there is no downtime in the lives of those who lead our schools and never has been, but the range of players involved in such leadership are routinely united around one theme: lockdown has posed challenges to school leaders that no preparation or training programme, or no body of school experience, can have prepared school leaders for. Indeed, many of the heads who have spoken to us, through focus groups, in specially arranged one-to-one research interviews and in casual conversations (sometimes entered into during attempts to recruit participants for the focus groups and interviews) have described the past few months as their most challenging in headship.

Since lockdown, there has been much discussion about, as we explore in other chapters, the impact of cancelling SATs, postponing inspections and performance tables, about the teacher assessment of GCSEs and A levels and about curriculum catch-up and personal recovery. Rightly so. However, these debates barely scratch the surface of what heads were managing during lockdown on a day-to-day basis and in the period leading up to the planned reopening of schools in August 2020 in Scotland and the following month in England, Wales and Northern Ireland, and the nuanced nature of the some-times hourly judgement calls that they were having to make, a task that they remain passionate about getting right but one which is far from easy. The sheer range of the calls being made on both their expertise and their energy was daunting and differed as lockdown progressed and then eased.

As lockdown approached and in early lockdown, the questions included: Who counts as a keyworker? Who counts as a vulnerable child and how are we going to support these children, especially if they don't come into school? Which of my staff are available to be in, and which, for reasons of vulnerability or shielding, cannot be? What level of support can we realistically sustain for home study? What is the content of our offer? How confident with the technology are we, and how confident are our children and our parents? And, finally, what will all this cost – what about the budget? The context in which these early challenges had to be addressed was one foreign to school leaders – *foreign* because of the sheer unpredictability of the situation. This London secondary head puts it starkly:

> Back in the middle of March, in that final week, my overriding feeling was that people were voting with their feet. We lost control of the situation; we are trying to get ahead of situations constantly, because we're leaders. That's what leaders do. We anticipate. We study, we plan, I've got SIPs [school improvement plans] and SEFs [school evaluation forms] … coming out my ears. And I've been [good] enough to inspect these last couple of years, and I've seen them all over the place. I've got one on the floor here now next to my desk, which I was [working] on for September, but for the first time, really, and I've been teaching for thirty-two years now in London, we weren't ahead of the game.
>
> (Daniel Coyle, head teacher, Newman Catholic College, research interview, 17 August 2020)

Coyle continues:

> Parents were coming to the school door and saying, I'm taking my son away, now; I've just watched the news [and] I'm not happy. Now when you combine that with the understandable anxieties of staff as well … It became a situation where for the first time as leaders, we really didn't have a clear way forward. And by Friday lunch time … there was hardly anybody in school. It was weird, absolutely weird. And normally when you get to the end of term or something like that, that's a real positive, happy feeling around the school. It wasn't like that at all … just this massive swathe of anxiety.

Before going on to describe the first weeks of lockdown thus:

> We lived in a vacuum for the best part of ten days, professionally … at home, with the family, people in the neighbourhood [were] asking me similar questions: what's going to happen to schools? Professionally, [heads were being] bombarded with questions that we simply couldn't answer. And I found that really, really destabilising from a leadership point of view. And … at the same time … you had your own anxieties as well. I look back and I find that was the hardest thing, people voting

with their feet, not being able to provide answers for parents, for staff, for yourself, but at the same time having to [wear] that mask of calm authoritative leadership.

Another head teacher, who leads a large primary school, also in London, concurs, using almost the same words:

> We've all had stressful periods of headship, but it's the first time where I felt that my skills and knowledge were just not enough; I was actually, really, relying on the government and their scientists to tell us the right thing to do.
>
> (Ann Bowen-Breslin, head teacher, Hillingdon Primary
> School, research interview, 18 August 2020)

Bowen-Breslin goes on to explain the challenge of 'closing' and how school leadership teams adapted to the new landscape that they were required to navigate, often without a route map:

> Given the stress you have about closing a school just for a 'snow day', it was kind of 'this isn't really happening' … in the last week we had an increasing number of parents who were not sending their children into school, which we didn't challenge because we felt that the country was just in such upheaval that we didn't want to add to the stress of parents, and we felt we could understand why they were starting to say, 'I don't want my child to come in' … the government were making their announcements about key workers and vulnerable children … I was really concerned about this … everybody else was being told to stay at home and yet school staff were being told to go to school. And that struck a real nerve … I think the only thing that kept us all calm was the fact that we weren't NHS staff – they had the toughest job – and we had a vital role as educational professionals and we had to hold our nerve … So, we made sure very, very quickly [that] we got a system in place for key workers [and] for vulnerable children, so that we had a booking system in place within the week … that meant that we had an efficient system for booking in [vulnerable] children [and those of] key workers. And it meant that we could then plan the staffing that we required each week.

And she grabbed hold of the one piece of the scientists' advice that has endured:

> I think instinctively as well, right from the beginning, I was model-
> ling – telling everyone to socially distance. That was the only thing
> that I grabbed hold of that actually would stop [the virus] … So, when
> I had to speak to staff as a group, staff stood on the playground and
> socially distanced … I think we were very probably ahead of the game
> in terms of knowing that that was a really key, important thing to
> model; it was incredibly stressful, not least because it's the first time
> I've had to put adults first – I had to consider the needs of adults as well
> as children, if they were to be kept safe, and we needed them to be
> well if we were to continue to provide the children with an education.

Thus, as schools moved into what might be termed 'mid-lockdown',
attention turned to an additional set of concerns: What has school felt like
for those who have attended throughout? What has it felt like for those who
have remained at home, and what kind of curriculum have they experienced?
How do we deal with the June returners, alongside those in the same classes
who have chosen not to come back to school? And what about their arrival
times, their lunch breaks and their physical organisation on the school site?
Which classes? Which bubbles? Which friendship groups to keep together
and which to break? Here, the formal and informal networks that heads
maintain were vital and gave clarity to, sometimes trumping, the advice
from the Department for Education, the local authority, the multi-academy
trust, the professional association or trade union:

> It was, kind of, it was just step by step. Have we talked about this? Have
> we looked at this aspect of it, or that? [What about children] moving
> around the fields? How are we going to sanitise and clean? What does
> a deep clean really look like? I was also looking at other schools. So
> there [were] … conversations with other heads … I don't think any
> school has got a piece of work that they can say that's all their own;
> you know, I've taken bits and pieces from other schools.
> (Mary Ann Cooper, federation head teacher, Bushey
> Primary Education Federation, research interview,
> 27 August 2020)

And, as the end of the summer term approached, the focus turned
to yet further concerns: How are we going to be able to say goodbye to
those moving on to junior or secondary school, or to college, university or
employment, or to much-loved staff who are leaving us? And how are we
going to welcome those joining us, as we haven't held the range of induction and transition sessions for parents and children that have usually been

completed by now? In truth, for many, the traditional goodbyes didn't take place and the welcomes were postponed until August and September.

Now, as this book goes to press, and with the August and September restarts underway or looming, head teachers, working with their leadership teams and governing bodies, have spent most of their summer 'break' working through the challenge of planning the reinstatement of full-time schooling for all and, again, the questions change: How do we deliver social spacing in full (or near-to-full) schools? Where are the points of entrance and exit, and will we need one-way systems and multiple changeover times to stagger pupil and teacher movement? Do we move pupils to teachers (as is the norm at changeover in secondary schools) or do teachers move to pupils? How do we deal with visitors, and physical education (PE) and drop-off arrangements? And what of risk assessments (and who signs these off), masks and the wider paraphernalia and protocol of pandemic? Oh, and what about the governing board or parent council, and the local authority or multi-academy trust guidance, and the latest pronouncement from the education secretary, and the parents, and *that* Facebook post and the fact that the school down the road has opted for masks and we have not?

The scale of the reopening challenge is hard to convey in these pages, but the multiple-page letters that many heads felt obliged to compose and send out in late August captured the sheer operational complexity of socially spaced schooling. Thus, Ian Cooksey, head at Watford Grammar School for Boys, begins his letter to parents:

> Dear students and parents/guardians,
>
> I am delighted to be able to write to you about the imminent resumption of school. I know you will be excited too, but there will also perhaps be some anxiety about the uncertainty of what school will be like, whether you are a new Watford Boy or a returning student. School will be different in September in some ways, but it should feel like the same welcoming, safe and productive environment. This letter is long, but it contains a lot of important information about how we will keep you safe in school. I urge all students and parents to read it carefully – perhaps, as teachers often say, more than once!
>
> (Ian Cooksey, head teacher, Watford Grammar School for Boys, letter to parents, guardians and students, 21 August 2020)

After the annual welcome to new students and arrangements for their induction, Cooksey goes on to discuss a myriad of issues including arrangements for arrival and departure, the shape of the recast school day (as presented in Figure 8.1), the organisation of the school into a series

A reminder that we have changed the structure of the school day in order to make school safer ... Basically, you will either have break 1 at 10.30 and form time at 11.00 or vice versa. And you will have break 2 at some time between 12.30 and 2 p.m. This all means you will have your own playground space for your year group in every break time.

Period 1	8.30 a.m.	9.30 a.m.
Period 2	9.30 a.m.	10.30 a.m.
Form time and break 1	10.30 a.m.	11.30 a.m.
Period 3	11.30 a.m.	12.30 p.m.
Break 2 and period 4	12.30 p.m.	2.00 p.m.
Period 5	2.00 p.m./2.05 p.m.	3.00 p.m./3.05 p.m.

Figure 8.1 An example of a newly recast 'COVID-safe' school day.
Source: Reproduced courtesy of Watford Grammar School for Boys (2020).

A big change to our usual practice is that each year group (and the sixth-form) will have a zone in the school where nearly all their lessons take place. This means that in the main your teachers will come to your classroom rather than the other way around. Your zone will have strict access rules and may have a one-way system.

Year	Zone	Access and one-way systems
7	Main block – ground, 101–109	Enter and exit via doors at east end of corridor (2 doors) – *no* one-way system
8	Maths 1–6 + 111, 112, 208	Enter and exit via door at far-west end of main corridor – *no* one-way system
9	English block	Enter and exit via front entrance to English block – *no* one-way system
10	Main block – first floor 200–207	Enter and exit via door near Matron's office – *no* one-way system
11	STEM block	Enter at sixth-form centre end; exit at science block end – one-way system
12–13	Science block Ec1–4, PE 1 and 2	Science – one-way system as usual. Sixth-form centre entrance via the art/DT corridor entrance and exits on to the sixth-form patio and the general science exits

Figure 8.2 An example of the use of 'zones' in an attempt to render schools 'COVID-safe'.
Source: Reproduced courtesy of Watford Grammar School for Boys (2020).

of 'zones' (as presented in Figure 8.2), allocated areas for student recreation at break time, the operation of the school canteen, social distancing, handwashing and sanitising, face masks, the arrival at school in PE kit on particular days, stationery and equipment (which of course can't be shared in the traditional 'lend us your ruler' manner during these COVID times), toilet facilities, illness, classroom conduct, arrangements for the daily cleaning of the school, adaptions to the school's behaviour policy and special arrangements for clubs, societies and trips, assemblies, the use of the school library and the treatment of visitors.

Any reader who has had cause to write a public letter to a wide and diverse audience, in which the message is focused on a break with long-established practice, will understand the amount of intelligence and emotional energy expounded in getting not just the content but the tone right. Across England, Wales and Northern Ireland, heads like Ian Cooksey will remember September 2020 as the month in which children returned to school, and August as a month of preparation, a body of work summarised in letters such as his.

And, after all this essentially *logistically* focused thinking, there is the *learning* – the purpose of it all – to consider: what does our re-entry curriculum look like? Specifically, what is the balance between 'catch-up' and 'recovery' or 'curriculum coverage' and 'well-being', and can we personalise this balance so that it works for each individual child, or at least different categories of child – the lockdown thrivers, survivors and strugglers that we identified in Chapter 7?

And finally (at least for secondary heads in England), where does the latest advice from the Department for Education leave us, and our work over the summer, given that it landed in heads' inboxes days before the restart at the beginning of the August bank holiday weekend? This comment from the head at a Scottish secondary school that reopened on schedule in early August provides a foretaste of what those south of the border would be likely to encounter, and how school life, at least in the short term, would be very different:

> Previously, the young people would have come into the dining hall. They would have met their friends. They may have had some breakfast, if they hadn't had breakfast before they left [home]; it was an opportunity to gather and just start [the day] together, we can't do that [now]. And so, pupils have to come in and go straight to class. So, at the moment we're actually using – and this is with the agreement of health and safety – all the different fire exits. So, [a named pupil] would come straight [in through] the fire exit closest to her maths class and go straight into class ... [a member of the] senior leadership team will be there with a hand sanitiser, making sure that they're sanitising hands on entry into the building ... [At changeover] the teacher will

go around with a spray, spray the desks, the pupils will clean their
desk area and their seat … and they'll sit down and they'll begin the
learning.

(Allyson Dobson, head teacher, Dalkeith High
School, research interview, 24 August 2020)

In Scotland, this earlier August restart, and the decision to not to seek an
earlier return during the shorter summer term, arguably gave head teachers
a longer run in and, for this head, leading Scotland's largest secondary
school, this opened up the potential to engage students in the process and
provided additional space for reflection:

> We asked … about fifty kids at the end of June "What would you
> like, how would you like to come back to school – you know – under
> what kind of conditions?" Because I think we, we were, certainly
> I and my senior team, we were starting to think that we were really
> overcomplicating things. I think when you're working from home
> without kids in a school, you cannot but catastrophise. But you are
> overcomplicating things, we must do this, we must do that. The clear
> message from the kids was "We … want to be back and we want you
> to get on with our learning. And, you know, don't make us do mean-
> ingless, pointless things that the adults think you have to do … involve
> us in … the decision making."

(Campbell Hornell, head teacher, Lasswade High
School, research interview, 22 August 2020)

Hornell continues:

> So, we kept it very simple … and … touch wood it's actually going
> well, the staff have been brilliant. The kids have been super, you know,
> really, really, by and large, responsible in terms of complying with new
> things, and parents, by and large, they have been really understanding
> and reasonable and patient and realising that, you know, it's not going
> to be absolutely bang on 100 per cent, correct from day one; we can't
> do that.

And the need is also to produce something that accords with memories and
expectations of what school is about and how it functions:

> You know, it's, it's a real balance between trying to get a normal school
> experience that students are used to, especially the older students.

There's kind of 'muscle memory' [about how] school operates in a certain way – certain rhythms – but the public health measures and requirements mean that it can't be the way it was ... And that's where the leadership, I think, comes in – good judgment around what is the appropriate balance between the normality school experience, and what's required now. I think it's actually [about] reassuring people and building [in] them the confidence that it's safe to come back. And that's, that's where the judgment comes in, I think. And that's what you get paid the big bucks for.

And then, throughout lockdown, there's food vouchers, and sometimes food banks to be operated, and deliveries of meals, or laptops, or dongles or iPads to be made, and all this while anticipating, digesting and acting on the latest advice from the Department for Education, the local authority, the multi-academy trust. Referring to the necessarily evolving guidance issued by the Department for Education, one senior leader put it this way:

> One of the trickiest things for us, was that ... all of the announcements were so public and that nothing ever came to school leaders before the public knew about it. And that caused quite a lot [of pressure] in terms of a workload ... quite a lot of additional work ... barrages of emails from parents, from teachers just [asking,] 'What's going to happen?
> (Donna Hubbard-Young, senior deputy head, Chesterton Community College, research interview, 3 August 2020)

And, on food banks and vulnerable children and their families, Hubbard-Young continues:

> Especially in the early stages, things like the food for the free school meals children, because the voucher system didn't get up and running for an incredibly long time, [posed a challenge] ... we set up our own food bank at school, and set up all the logistics for that. And then the food bank was going quite well. But as the vouchers just took longer and longer [to materialise], we realised that, really ... this coming in to collect a bag of dried goods, like pasta and sauces and things ... it wasn't really ... touching the sides. So then, the school chef set about making sort of proper meals that could be frozen and then just defrosted and cooked ... sausage casseroles and curries and things like that ... some people could come and collect them, but then we had, like, a big delivery service. So, we had like the senior leadership team out in their cars ... dropping off like boxes of food and things like

that. Because in those early days, we just couldn't tell how long things were going to sort of go on for … like I said, the easiest thing, by far, was the teaching and learning, because that's what everybody knows [how] to do.

For Hubbard-Young, this range of support activity was vital, given the divides outlined in Chapter 3, and how much clearer the pandemic had rendered these:

It confirmed for us things that we already knew … we've always known that the home–school partnership is incredibly important, and there's huge amounts of research, isn't there, that shows that children will do better with the support from home? And we've always known that, but it was becoming sort of very starkly obvious that where children had support at home, they were flourishing and they were flying but …

One site manager, a recently retired police inspector who knows a thing or two about crisis management and logistics planning after thirty years on the streets of London, gave a fascinating and empathetic insight into the responsibility that rested with heads throughout lockdown:

The thing is, all you see as a parent, all I see as a parent, is the home learning, but they've been organising so much more than that: who's in, who's not, how the theatre they are dealing with is changing all the time; all the new guidance from the DfE, and then from the local authority or your union; behind that folder of learning that lands on your doorstep [as it did in the first few days] or desktop, is this enormous long logistical tail, and it's all got to be done … and it falls on the head, it all lands at her door.

(Paddy O' Leary, site manager, Bushey Primary Education
Federation, research interview, 2 August 2020)

In another of the focus groups staged to capture the experience of school leaders and governors, classroom practitioners and parents to enable us to scope out the shape of this book, one contribution captured the uniqueness of the challenge, and also offers a glimpse of the optimism that keeps many school leaders going, even in normal times: 'This is all completely new. We're all making it up as we go along but, because of this, we've lost the fear of getting it wrong. That's liberating' (David Miller, head teacher, Pebble Brook School, focus group – special education and alternative provision, 8 July 2020). The liberation theme is picked up in a blog by a key influencer in the UK's school leadership landscape, Emma Knights, chief executive at the National Governance Association, the membership body for England's 250,000 volunteer school governors. Reflecting on the past term and the challenge of leading schools through the pandemic, and looking to the academic year ahead, she observes:

> Without a doubt the last few months has strengthened the relationships between most senior leaders and their boards: each appreciating the other's role and the effort and care with which it is carried out. But some key components of governance, in particular that annual review of the vision and the setting of the strategic priorities for the year, have understandably been delayed in some schools and trusts. This suspension can't continue ad infinitum. These discussions between boards and senior leaders should be liberating.
>
> (Knights, 2020)

Warming to the liberation theme, Knights continues:

> I say liberating because we are still in the pause from Ofsted inspections … liberating because there are possibilities for teaching and learning that six months ago might have written off as fanciful. Liberating to think about what has been learnt during this COVID period and how the opportunities afforded by technology, by relationships with parents and pupils, and by goodwill and gratitude that has been generated can all be built on … liberating because schools have truly been at the hearts of their communities, offering a service to key workers and vulnerable children while the rest of us stayed at home, and helping to keep poorer children well fed … liberating because we do not need to be dictated to by big data … liberating because we can build on the collaborations, too many to mention, which have strengthened between schools, trusts and other public services during COVID times.

And although Knights's daily focus is on school governors and trustees, her audience here is all involved in the leadership of schools. Indeed, she is right to observe that, in many cases, the pandemic has had the impact of bringing the range of players in the leadership landscape of schools together, blurring traditional lines of demarcation and questioning long-established practices and areas of responsibility.

We shall return to the challenges facing head teachers in due course, but it is worth exploring the role of governing boards in maintained schools, trust boards and their interplay with local school-based boards (where these have been retained) in multi-academy trusts and (in Scotland) parent councils during the lockdown at this stage, not least because of the key responsibilities that these volunteer committees undertake in overseeing and ensuring the effective running of schools and in providing support to heads and principals, and other senior leaders, during lockdown.

Governance during lockdown

It is a shame that Richard Steward, in his adroitly named and often insightful text *The Gradual Art of School Improvement* (Steward, 2020), begins his chapter on governance, caustically entitled, 'The Myth of Governance', with the sweeping aside: 'I have met very few head teachers who do not complain about governors, about the decisions they make, about the time they waste and generally about their lack of effectiveness as school leaders' (Steward, 2020, p. 106). This may, of course, be a consequence of Steward's own experience of governing boards as a head or of the particular network of heads that he maintains, but it also misses the point about governance and the lay governance that so exercises him: the purpose of governing boards is to provide support and challenge, and to do so with the detachment and inquisitiveness that comes with the degree of 'outsiderness' that different board members or multi-academy trust trustees bring to the governance table. Referring to his own experience of being grilled by the Education and Skills Select Committee at Westminster, the former national schools commissioner (and experienced head), Sir David Carter, draws the comparison with the best of school governance:

> The scrutiny was rigorous and detailed, precisely as it should be. The committee's inquisition was challenging but also an example of what good governance is truly about within the education system. Hard questions, intelligently asked, and then thoughtful answers, carefully considered, are a vital pillar of how we ensure public services work for the good of the public (and do not run to make life more comfortable for those in charge).
>
> (Carter with McInerney, 2020, pp. 171–172)

According to the Department for Education (2019), the formally stated purpose of school governing boards is threefold:

1. To ensure, for the school or federation, clarity of vision, ethos and strategic direction.

2. To hold executive leaders to account for the educational performance of the school or federation and its pupils, and for the performance management of the staff.

3. To oversee the financial performance of the school or federation and ensure that expenditure delivers value for money.

In reality, there is an additional vital function that governing boards must perform, which is stressed in the latest inspection framework for English schools (Ofsted, 2019), but remains obstinately absent from the headlines set out in the Department for Education guidance:

• To ensure that the school delivers on a range of statutory and regulatory responsibilities, especially with regard to safeguarding.

Moreover, in schools that maintain *local* governing boards (as the vast majority of English schools do), these boards play a significantly broader role:

> Beyond these formal and legal responsibilities, governing boards, and school governors as individuals, do much more than just govern. Critically, individually and collectively, governors serve as a channel of engagement for a range of stakeholders. Although they are absolutely not representatives of these stakeholders, in emerging from these groups and organisations they give the process of governance legitimacy in the eyes of different stakeholder communities (including parents, staff and the local authority).
>
> (Breslin, 2017, p. 12)

In this context, the impact of the absence of an effective governing board on pupil outcomes is clear:

> Where schools were graded as 'inadequate' during Ofsted inspections, senior leaders were reported to have not been effectively challenged and held to account by governing bodies (DCSF, 2008). James et al. (2010b) found that the 'lack of a capable governing body is not a neutral absence for a school; it is a substantial disadvantage', emphasising the significance of the role of the governing body.
>
> (McCrone et al., 2011, p. 11)

But, as with all aspects of school life, governance can be time-consuming for these volunteer governors – especially those who serve as chairs or who lead subcommittees concerned with areas like curriculum and standards, staffing and human relations, finance and resources – and burdensome for heads or principals because of the need to manage the scrutiny that good governance brings and to facilitate meetings and provide reports to ensure that this scrutiny is effective and purposeful.

Of course, the governance is as much about support as challenge, and in difficult times this support, and with it a concern for the well-being of school leaders, is vital. Entering lockdown, it became paramount. The support–challenge nexus is a crude descriptor for a very nuanced role, typically mediated on a day-to-day basis through the relationship between the head and chair. During lockdown the weight of activity had to fall at the support end of the support–challenge continuum and, by necessity, any burden of governance had to be minimised. In short, governing boards needed to pose themselves a searching question, one articulated in a blog drafted in the build-up to the writing of this text:

> As governors, one of the things we have to do is to find a way to take (any burden of governance) off the table, to go governance-light, without going governance-free; we cannot do the latter because our legal and moral responsibilities as members of governing boards (as recent advice from the Department for Education and the National Governance Association makes clear) do not disappear. However, we must do the former, and go governance-light, because, frankly, much of the really important stuff that we do in ordinary times will, like the economy, just have to wait. By comparison with those challenges facing heads on a daily basis, our predicament is much less pressing. Nonetheless, it remains important.
>
> (Breslin, 2020)

On reflection, the phrase 'governance-light' might not have been the best choice of wording, but our discussions with school governors reveal that this has been broadly the direction of travel taken and it would seem to be in line with Department for Education guidance issued early in lockdown: 'School leaders should stay in touch with the governing board in a proportionate way, including providing information on the welfare of staff and pupils, so that they can retain a strategic overview of the situation and the school' (Department for Education, 2020b). Thus, although practice has varied from school to school and trust to trust, governing boards have taken a number of steps, many of which may endure beyond the return of full-scale schooling:

- reducing the number of scheduled meetings;
- moving these meetings online;
- tightening the focus of meetings, by reducing the number of agenda items;
- removing the expectation of written reports from the head or principal and other senior leaders;
- postponing subcommittees, except where their work has a particular and immediately necessary task, such as budget setting;
- maintaining weekly contact between the chair and the head or principal, in particular to ensure that the head is continuing to get any support needed, especially in respect of their own well-being;
- using the notion of short 'pop-up' meetings where the head wants the board's advice or input on a particular issue, or where the head needs, or would like, some form of authorisation (e.g. on a major piece of 'big ticket' expenditure) that can be triggered at the head's request;
- removing the expectation that those governors who are NHS employees or other key workers, or staff governors other than the head, should *attend* meetings during lockdown, while ensuring the door remains fully open to their participation and that they are kept fully informed of discussions and decisions;
- adjusting meeting timings so that they reflect 'work at home' days and other aspects of members' lockdown schedules;
- underlining a high trust culture in which heads and senior leaders, as those working on the ground, feel that they have board buy-in and, where necessary, formal sign-off for any, as the Department for Education (2020e) puts it, 'urgent, time-bound decisions', such that senior leaders are enabled to take such decisions 'in the moment', free in the knowledge that the governing board is, well, *on board*.

Of course, this kind of governance-light approach will mean some catch-up activity further down the line, but it may also cause us to focus, as never before, on what *really* matters and on the *quality* of our collaboration and partnership as governors and senior leaders. Long term, this may lead to better, more effective governance and a range of practices that weren't even on the horizon a couple of terms ago:

> If we'd have been asked in February, you know, do you think governing boards could go virtual? We'd go like, well, why? What? What are you trying to achieve? Or you, you know, Ooh, that's ... a big deal – we'd have been really cautious about it, but the fact everyone had to has

made [us think] … Now people [are] going, right, we'll keep the good
bits of this.

(Emma Knights, chief executive, National Governance
Association, research interview, 22 July 2020)

This mix of virtual and 'in-the-room' activity could produce a more agile,
more responsive governance, with a mix of short 'pop-up', online meetings
and scheduled longer sessions, making meetings less onerous but more
accessible, a point picked up in our discussions with a number of governors
and trustees:

> It meant that we [had to be] very much more agile. You know, [that
> we] could respond quickly. If I wanted to get an answer out of the
> board, I could just issue a request. I could have a board meeting in two
> days, [on] Zoom, with a single subject on the [agenda] you know: 'Are
> we going to open or aren't we?' … And we were very focused at the
> time on supporting the school in terms of making sure they had the
> resources, whether that was risk assessments, board time, [access to]
> simple, practical advice … And I think that made a huge difference
> for us.
>
> (Colin Platt, chair of governors, Monks Risborough Church
of England Primary School, focus group – school
governors, 21 July 2020)

Another school governor who spoke to us has this kind of agility in mind,
when he looks to governance beyond lockdown: 'We need to keep the rapid-
ness of decision making (developed during lockdown), this fantastic ability
to move at speed. If governing bodies can deliver that in normal times, I think
governance of schools will be far better for it' (Dan Hall, parent governor,
Bushey Primary Education Federation, focus group – school governors, 21
July 2020). Sometimes, perhaps because of this speed of movement, some
governors who spoke with us talked of a blurring of strategic and operational roles, not because board members were interfering in operational
matters but because the need was to bring all hands to the pump, and heads
welcomed this support:

> I've never had so much contact with the school and with the leaders
> as I've had in this last period, because I've found they've been using
> me as a sounding board and I've sometimes found myself helping

them make operational decisions, which I would never normally find myself doing.

> (Rosemary Hoyle, chair of governors, Wrawby St Mary's
> Church of England Primary School, Lincolnshire, focus
> group – school governors, 21 July 2020)

Platt concurs:

> Trying to manage this whole COVID-19 meant that we were taking a much more operational interest than we might otherwise have done. [Heads] simply … have the bandwidth to do so [while] having to struggle with all of the coalface-type firefighting – excuse me, mixing metaphors – that the school is having to put up with … trying to create social distancing in a corridor that's only a metre wide, [dealing with] limited toilet space.
>
> (Colin Platt, chair of governors, Monks Risborough
> Church of England Primary School, focus group –
> school governors, 21 July 2020)

And, in some respects, this may have left aspects of governance neglected; on a day-to-day basis, during lockdown, decisions are likely to have been taken that have not been subject to the process of governance that we have come (rightly) to expect in ordinary times, or as Dan Hall puts it:

> We have a fantastic head who has absolutely been all over it, and they've been making the right decisions, they've been doing phenomenally well, but one of the things that worries me is [that] I'm not sure we've done a great deal of governance … We've been supportive and we've been, you know, we've been there for her … but she [has] had to make rapid and quick decisions, and you can't bring a board together all the time … or do everything through the chair.
>
> (Dan Hall, parent governor, Bushey Primary Education
> Federation, focus group – school governors, 21 July 2020)

Thus, post-lockdown, some of the processes of everyday school governance may need to be re-established. Maybe, though, just maybe, in among all of this and as we edge towards a less socially distanced landscape, school governors might benefit from the 'power of the pause' that we have discussed in earlier chapters, using any time and space freed up by lockdown to think creatively and pre-emptively in a way that the pace of an ordinary school year denies us. To return to Knights's earlier cited comments, this is important because:

> Some key components of governance, in particular that annual review of the vision and the setting of the strategic priorities for the year, have understandably been delayed in some schools and trusts. This suspension can't continue ad infinitum. These discussions between boards and senior leaders should be liberating.
>
> (Knights, 2020)

Right now, in late August 2020, in what most hope is late lockdown, most school governors might yearn for 'the pace of an ordinary school year' (and that may yet be a year or so off) but, in the interim, governors and boards would be wise to consider the longer-term impact of the system shock delivered to our schools, and the wider education system, by the virus; schools and school governance might never be the same again. For governors, with their responsibility for setting the tone, vision, values and strategic direction of their schools, this might just be a rare opportunity to play their part in shaping the new, as yet unknown, post-COVID-19 educational reality.

Leadership beyond lockdown

As we remarked at the start of this chapter, headship during lockdown has been, for most school leaders, one of the defining experiences of their careers to date, and certainly among the most challenging. The foregoing discussion of school governance outlines how SLTs and boards have worked together, even if some of the high principles of the head–board relationship have been necessarily placed on hold, notably the wildly oversimplified distinction between the operational and strategic domains so beloved in the governance and leadership literature. Such distinctions are prominent across the textbooks in these fields – another is the oft-claimed demarcation between leadership and management – but the reality is more complex, with these differing activities coexisting on the same Venn diagram rather than in closed and separate, albeit neighbouring, domains. And, great practice occurs in the shared, negotiated, blurry space where the circles overlap, not in the tidy comfort zones at the outer edges. The blurry bits require collaboration, empathy, trust, the ability to come to shared judgements and, with this, negotiation and compromise. The heads and senior leaders and the school governors who spoke to us throughout the research exercise that underpins and informs this text spoke of these qualities, and of the potential for a better mutual understanding of what each can contribute to the shared process of educational leadership post-COVID-19, a point not lost on Emma Knights:

> I think one of the things we've generally found is that in most cases, relationships have been good between senior leaders and governing boards. If anything, they seem to have got better. If you had to generalise from all the different things, we know, they've strengthened. The NAHT are saying the same; our organisations have had fewer disputes (between boards and heads) reported to us.
>
> (Emma Knights, chief executive, National Governance
> Association, research interview, 22 July 2020)

In any case, the strategic–operational divide is unhelpful in discussing the relationship between boards and heads for two reasons: first, because it ignores the *collaborative* relationship between heads, SLTs and boards in which volunteer governors and professional leaders bring *complementary* but *different* expertise to the table, as portrayed in Figure 8.3; and second, because it deskills both, casting volunteer governors on some distant high ground and heads as operational managers, free of strategic thought. Rather the Venn diagram has three circles, as set out in Figure 8.4, with boards setting (and with heads and staff governors as *members*) strategic *direction*, heads (or, in clusters of schools, executive or federation heads) and their leadership teams developing educationally appropriate *strategies* to take the school or group of schools in this direction and employing a skilled team to *operationalise* this strategy and deliver desired outcomes.

During lockdown, the work of heads and boards has further exposed the limitations of a simple binary divide between the strategic and operational domains. It has also opened the possibility of different ways of working. As was remarked in Chapter 1, organisations can tend to reproduce themselves long after the purposes of the original behaviours have been exhausted. Change becomes the enemy because it challenges long-standing orthodoxies that we have long forgotten the need to question. System jolts, such as that provided by the pandemic to the educational infrastructure, cause us to look afresh at these conventionalities, bringing new attitudes, skills and practices to the table, which, in turn, reveal new potentials and opportunities, as this experienced head and local authority school improvement adviser, who now works with school leaders and governing boards as a coach and mentor, observes in conversation with other colleagues in the primary sector:

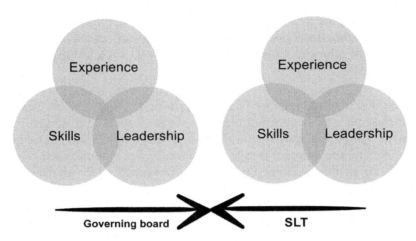

Figure 8.3 Differing but complementary skills and expertise, united by shared values and objectives: the meeting point between voluntary governance and professional leadership.
Source: Breslin (2017, p. 17).

Figure 8.4 Strategic direction, strategic leadership and operational management: a more nuanced tripartite reality.
Source: Breslin (2017, p. 48).

What I've seen … is the resilience that parents have and that young children have … My personal focus is about building on the potential [this offers]. You know, I think [we] saw this potential in the first phase of lockdown and I think, going forward, I think we'll continue to build on this potential [with] the relationships that we've started … I [also] think we've become far better at listening and, because we've become far better at listening, we've identified the strengths of people – we've identified the areas where we can support them and develop them. So, let's not lose those coaching skills – listening to people and building potential, because I think that is going to be fabulous potential, going forward.

> (Annette Szymaniak, consultant head teacher, Monks Risborough Church of England Primary School, focus group – primary education, 14 July 2020)

During lockdown much was made of the relative absence of so-called 'vulnerable' children from schools kept open for these young people and the children of key workers. In fact, it became clear that some parents were keeping 'vulnerable' children at home precisely because of the fact that their attendance would amount to a public declaration of vulnerability, a bit like the way the separate meal queues of 'paying' and 'free' school meals children amounted to a declaration of poverty for some and not others in the 1970s and 1980s. This comment from a parent to one of the heads who participated in our research interviews is illustrative of the point:

One of my mums said that to me, and, uh, she said it in a child protection meeting … social services were putting her under pressure about why the children were not [coming] back to school. And she said, 'Well, 'cause everyone is gonna know I'm vulnerable, innit'. And I just, I think I said to her, 'You're right' … I just thought that crystallised [the problem]; it can't be clearer than that.

> (Head teacher (speaking on condition of anonymity), research interview, summer 2020)

Non-attendance, though, did not necessarily amount to a lack of contact:

I wanted every family contacted on a weekly basis, so we reallocated admin staff [and] support staff and created four separate teams based in each house from about week 3, [and] then made a phone call to every family, every week. And in total, over 20,000 phone calls were made. And how do I know it's 20,000? Because we set up a spreadsheet where … they just had [to] tick that they'd made the contact. And what we found was that the families loved that. And you know, why you ended up with a relationship, [with] relationships being formed … you have the extreme stories where somebody had been on the phone for an hour with [a parent] because they'd hardly talked to anybody else … I've got learning assistants, non-teaching staff who work with additional needs students, now much more confident in terms of their ability to [take] initiative and to be delegated tasks about, you know, making contact with families … I think it's helped to build confidence.

(Campbell Hornell, head teacher, Lasswade High School, research interview, 22 August 2020)

This head of sixth form, newly appointed to role in January 2020, identifies a similar silver lining in the chaos of COVID-19 and feels that he has developed exactly the confidence that Hornell is talking about:

The most insightful part of this situation was phoning [the] home of every student in my year group. In my previous role I knew the backgrounds of those in my form and believed I knew a lot about their home life. I was confident that I would be able to utilise this skill in my new role [across the] year group. I was naive. I called every single [sixth former's] home … numerous times during lockdown. I heard about the numbers of people living in a small space, I got to know their sleeping habits, I learnt about their families' work lives. I had conversations with students and their parents or carers where they [felt] able to be vulnerable. I was told [about] family histories, their fears, their aspirations. I heard about the hobbies that they picked up, their views on the news. I was asked questions, I was told jokes, I was cried at. I thought that I knew my students well before this process, I now know that I had no idea … We have seen the human side of each other, and (I feel they will feel) more willing to come to me in future.

(Zak Jalil, head of sixth form, Newman Catholic College, written submission, 29 August 2020)

Jalil continues:

It is easy to remember this time as a period where there was no clarity, where people were making comments and integral decisions about schools [even] though they have not stepped into a school since their last exam. I will, however, remember it as the time where I knew that I was in the right job. I feel as though I am now more competent in my

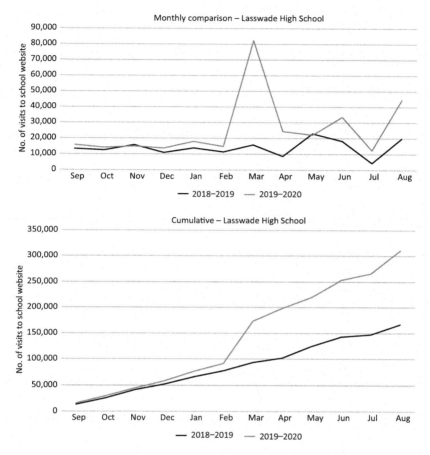

Figure 8.5 Website visits to Lasswade High School during lockdown compared with March–June 2018–2019.
Source: Google Analytics via Pigeon Penguin Web and App Development.

role than I ever could have been. I know my students and they know me. We have mutual respect and I am able to give them the best advice for them. Is that not what we all want as educators?

During lockdown, Cornell also witnessed a surge in visits to the school's website. Figure 8.5 uses Google analytics to show the increase in this kind of online traffic during lockdown, comparing website visits with the comparable period for 2018–2019.

Building on these relationships and sustaining them during the delivery of near-full capacity schooling during late and post-lockdown will be a considerable challenge, but one that, as Jalil's optimism underlines, it is worth seeking to meet.

Summary and key messages

In the main, school leaders, teachers and the wider school workforce, and those involved in initial and continuing teacher education, are emerging from lockdown with their professional status enhanced and a much richer public understanding of the complexity and range of the work that they do; this knowledge and goodwill needs to be nurtured and sustained in both the practice of schools and the behaviour of policymakers.

But during this period new expectations about the performance of schools have taken root, and these expectations might just prove to be a double-edged sword. On the one hand, schools have been revealed as being far more than the 'exam factories' that some had come to see them as, and the prospect that, in future, schools might be judged on a wider score-card that considers well-being, personal confidence, resilience, community commitment, employment readiness and other so-called 'soft' measures and qualities *alongside* academic and technical qualifications is a positive. On the other hand, this arguably extends the scale of the burden that lands on the shoulders of school leaders, governors, teachers and the wider school work-force. Delivering on both sides of this equation simultaneously is a consid-erable challenge and may be harder when lockdown has passed. Certainly, the second academic year of lockdown – a necessarily more varied, more partial, messier lockdown – is likely to bring its own challenges, as this head acknowledges:

> There has been terrific goodwill from parents and staff, but the challenge is to build on it. At the start of lockdown, we were going into summertime, and the sun was shining. That's gone now – we're heading into winter. What worked before [in the spring and summer terms] won't necessarily work now.
>
> (Mary Ann Cooper, federation head teacher, Bushey Primary Education Federation, research interview, 27 August 2020)

And, similarly, the goodwill of heads and other senior leaders needs to be maintained and nurtured – the conclusion of those who have joined our focus groups, taken part in our research interviews or offered written evi-dence is clear: school leaders have performed like heroes throughout the lockdown, with the majority working without halt between the end of the February half-term break and the start of the summer break, often in areas that they have had no previous experience.

And, almost all will have spent the ensuing summer 'break' engaged in the logistics of 'restart', the logistics of bubbles, one-way systems, deep cleans and, of course, socially distancing in schools brimming full with children and young people, and all who support their learning. And just as Cooper is concerned about lockdown in the colder climes of winter, another head, three weeks into the restart in Scotland, confides that some of the young people who have behaved so admirably thus far may develop what can only be described as a lockdown fatigue of their own:

> In four weeks' time, will the kids be fed up with it? The one-way systems, the hand sanitiser and the wiping down of desks and chairs, the split lunches, the time spent outside; You know, will they be fed up with it and will some of them kind of metaphorically rebel against it?
>
> (Campbell Hornell, head teacher, Lasswade High School, research interview, 22 August 2020)

Policymakers and system leaders need to work with the professional associations that represent heads and principals to ensure that their well-being is sustained during the current academic year, so that burnout, system-wide, is avoided. And they need to do much more to underline and affirm the importance and relentlessness of the efforts of heads and senior leaders – and the creativity of their thinking – and that of school governors and all in the school's workforce.

Recommendations

8.1 The positive profile of the teaching profession as it emerges from lockdown ought to be used as the foundation for future recruitment and retention campaigns.

8.2 Initial and continuing teacher education providers need to be enabled to capture the lessons from lockdown for teachers' initial training and professional development and enabled to innovate in so doing.

8.3 Access routes to the teaching profession should reflect the needs of potential teachers, teachers and schools in a digitally enabled, post-lockdown age.

8.4 System-wide, the well-being of school leaders ought to be an absolute priority, guiding the approaches of school governors, system leaders and policymakers alike.

8.5 System leaders ought to commission a study of the role and effectiveness of different school governance frameworks and strategies in independent, maintained and non-maintained schools during lockdown.

Inspection, research and system performance

9

The decision, within days of the lockdown being announced, to postpone Ofsted inspections in English schools was met with audible sighs of relief by teachers, school leaders and governing bodies. In England, schools were only months into a new inspection framework, launched in September 2019 (Ofsted, 2019) and trialled extensively over the previous twelve months. In as far as any new inspection framework is welcomed, the reaction to the change in direction by the inspectorate heralded by the new framework was warmly received in staffrooms, and by SLTs and governing boards.

The inspection framework in English schools

The new framework had promised a return to a concentration on curriculum (something that had not featured strongly in inspectors' concerns since the turn of the century) and to focus less on outcomes and performance data and more on what it termed 'the quality of teaching'. In particular, the new framework invited schools to set out their curricular *intent* and placed a stronger focus on children's personal development, coupling this with a new concern for staff and pupil well-being, while asking an underpinning question: 'What's it like to be a child in this school?' In the words of the relatively recently appointed chief inspector of schools, Amanda Spielman, in her keynote address to the National Governance Association's summer conference in June 2019, the intention underpinning the new framework was to put:

the real substance of education, the curriculum, back at the centre of inspection and support leaders and teachers who act with integrity. To put it another way, we want to help people put as much time as possible into the things that make the most difference for children.

(Spielman, 2019)

Nonetheless, given that inspection reports are public documents – ones that come with either career-enhancing or career-ending potential – any new framework is met with some trepidation by the profession, and especially by school leaders.

For primary school practitioners, the new framework with its focus on curriculum and, therefore, on distinct *subjects* – even though subjects are far from the totality of the curriculum either taught or experienced by learners (Breslin, 2018) – this trepidation was accentuated, given that teachers in primary schools are typically not defined by their teaching of a specific discipline. Rather, across the UK, primary schools are organised on an integrated-day basis whereby, other than for a handful of areas such as PE, a single teacher delivers the breadth of the curriculum, works across subjects and does not, necessarily, organise the teaching day on the basis of discrete subject areas, other than a typical focus on literacy and / or mathematics at some point during each day. In England, the inspection reports produced by Ofsted are strongly formatted and, under the new framework, it is not uncommon to find comments such as these in the 'What does the school need to do to improve?' section with which reports close, whatever the overall judgement about the school (in this case, the school was judged to be 'Good' overall):

> For many subjects, the curriculum is not coherently planned. Leaders' plans do not identify the key things pupils need to know and the order in which this knowledge should be taught. Teachers' expertise in the curriculum is underdeveloped in some subjects. Pupils do not learn well enough. Curriculum leaders need to develop their plans, so that pupils' learning is well sequenced in every subject. Leaders should ensure that teachers know how to teach the curriculum successfully.

And the relative inexperience of primary teachers in placing subject-related issues at the fore of their thinking is underlined by the second (of three) recommendations, which reads:

> Many subject leaders are developing their role. They have not developed the skills they need to evaluate their areas of responsibility.

They do not understand how well pupils are learning by achieving the planned curricular goals. Leaders should provide time to develop the skills of curriculum leaders so that they contribute effectively to the improvement of the school.

Unsurprisingly, therefore, inspection, and the news that a school is 'in the inspection window' (that is, due for an inspection in the near future), is always a cause for concern, especially given the public declaration of the outcome. But could this be different?

Inspection as a development opportunity

Ofsted's promised change of focus during the fall of 2020, carrying out 'non-judgmental school visits' rather than inspections, might prove to be a turning point in its role in the English education system, shifting as it does the inspectorial lens from judgement to knowledge capture and development.

Inspection frameworks are common in developed education systems the world over, and most would concede that some form of auditing of the performance of large publicly funded services is justified and, probably, necessary. The performance of the English education system is audited, though, in multiple ways, more so than those in some other UK jurisdictions, but the nature of this auditing, in spite of the good intentions of many involved in the inspection of schools, has lacked a sufficient developmental dimension. To think of such auditing as a form of assessment and to use the language of assessment, the practice of the inspectorate and the consequence of other forms of audit (notably performance tables and other data-based methods) has been largely *summative* rather than *formative*. For those readers less familiar with such language, summative assessment tells you where you are at a point in time; in contrast, formative assessment enables you to move forward from this location.

In short, to use the jargon, the emphasis has been on 'performativity' rather than on the further development of pedagogy, or curriculum, or pastoral care or school leadership. As argued elsewhere in these pages, when the education system as a whole is characterised by widespread underperformance, a focus on performativity and improving so-called 'hard' outcomes (exam results, attendance statistics, exclusion rates and other phenomena measurable in quantifiable data) is justified and necessary. However, while a minority of schools, usually those encountering the greatest socio-economic challenges, continue to struggle (Ofsted, 2019), the majority of schools are now deemed to be good or outstanding (Department for Education, 2020b). In a system that is characterised by success rather than failure, the persistence of summative auditing processes that are focused on improving performance risk becoming the medicine that kills the patient – a medicine that manifests its impact in declining teacher well-being, leadership burnout, poor mental health among pupils and parental disillusion, factors that are now generating hard data of their own.

And these processes do not simply exist at the level of the inspectorate; rather, the 'performativity' culture of 'tests, targets and tables' risks infusing the system as a whole: the performance management of heads and principals by school governing boards, local authority school improvement teams, multi-academy trust leadership teams and other 'executive' leaders, the performance management of staff by heads and principals, the observation of classroom teachers by various senior and middle leaders and, in a minority of cases, box-ticking curricular frameworks and rigid behaviour policies for children. Thus, the language of performativity translates, at its worst, into a language of policing in which practices such as classroom observation are framed not as developmental opportunities for mentoring and coaching or peer-to-peer learning, but as *monitoring* visits to assess performance against formalised standards defined by, apparently, key performance indicators. The collaborative endeavours of staff teams during lockdown have begun to reveal what might be achieved in already high-performing schools when this culture is necessarily moved aside.

Ofsted's decision, in light of the pandemic, to, first, suspend inspections and then to devote its activities in the final third of 2020 to a series of school visits reveals the possible turning point alluded to above. In the words of Amanda Spielman:

> Ofsted will be carrying out 'visits' to schools and colleges, not inspections. Our visits will look at how schools and colleges are getting pupils back up to speed after so long at home. And we will help them through collaborative conversations, without passing judgement – this isn't inspection by stealth. We'll use our visits to listen to school leaders' experiences and plans, and to provide constructive challenge.
>
> (Spielman, 2020)

Warming to her theme, Spielman continues:

> The visits will not be graded. We'll publish the outcomes of our discussions with leaders in a short letter so that parents can understand what steps are being taken to help children back into full-time

education. And we will use what we learn from our visits to report on the picture across England. The visits will be piloted with volunteer schools and colleges from September, with the full programme starting from October. We'll be having further conversations with unions and others about how the visits will operate and we'll publish more details as appropriate; but I would stress again that this is about a constructive conversation – we're not trying to catch schools out. After all, we share the same aim: helping this generation of children and young people make up for lost time and get the high-quality education they deserve.

And, as with the non-setting of GCSE and A level papers, and Scottish Highers, which we have discussed in an earlier chapter, here we are offered an enticing glimpse of another way in which UK education systems could look different, post-lockdown: this autumn's change – and many readers in England will know of its impact (or not) by the time this text lands in bookstores and library shelves (and possibly on the desks of policymakers and shapers) in late 2020 or early 2021 – in Ofsted's inspection practice could see the emergence of an inspection system with an overt and public development focus.

This could offer an opportunity for the inspectorate to move away from the current overtly judgmental model, one that is often feared as punitive and lacking empathy for those educators who find themselves in 'career-damagingly difficult' schools. More than that, Ofsted, could begin to reposition itself as an educational researcher, and not just an auditor of practice. It is to the importance of such research that we now turn.

The importance of educational research

This potential shift in the outlook taken by Ofsted – and maybe by school inspectorates across the UK and beyond – points to a further possibility: a *research-informed* education system. For approaching fifty years, the British Educational Research Association (BERA) has been the membership body for those involved in educational research across the UK, and is responsible for a number of journals, a magazine, a range of special interest groups, various conferences and events and an increasingly active online community based around the BERA blog, edited by Gerry Czerniawski. BERA also maintains close relationships with similar organisations in the UK, such as the Sottish Educational Research Association and various partners overseas including the European Educational Research Association, the American

Educational Research Association and the Australian Association for Research in Education.

Unsurprisingly, during lockdown, Gerry Czerniawski's inbox has been rammed full of blogs on one aspect or other of the educational impact of COVID-19, or some educational conundrum arising from the pandemic. As many of these posts have demonstrated, in the quiet (and not so quiet) chaos of lockdown, a range of taken-for-granted assumptions (Courtney et al., 2020), competencies (Zhou and Wolstencroft, 2020) and conceptualisations (Fenshaw-Smith, 2020) are being evaluated as never before: that a particular approach to formal schooling is the sole means of delivering mass education; that teacher assessment is intrinsically less valid and reliable than a conventional unseen written test; that the absence of formal examinations and the postponement of inspections will precipitate system collapse; that the primary purpose of schooling – much as we may fight this – is as much about childcare and servicing economic need as it is about fostering a love of learning; that home-schooling – while isolating for some and a likely driver of inequalities – may be a panacea for others, especially those who have never loved the inevitable institutionalisation of traditional schooling; and that technology can open up new pedagogies – some liberating, others limiting, as we explore in greater depth in Chapter 10. In short, the email titles in Czeniawski's inbox read unnervingly like the contents page for this text.

As I have remarked elsewhere, following Goffman (1956), schools – especially secondary schools – have the habit of maximising the feeling of change while minimising its impact (Breslin, 2008). How else, in the emergent post-modernity of the twenty-first century might we explain the survival of a curriculum largely framed in the early independent schools that preceded the industrial era and extended to all through the mass schooling progressively rolled out in the industrial age? How else might one explain the continued survival of an assessment system built around the presumption that the majority of young people exit education at 16, at least a quarter of a century after this has ceased to be the case? Or the survival of the A level, seventy years after it was introduced to select an elite for progression to university in an age when such progression is closer to the norm than the exception? How else might the modular palaces of New Labour's *Building Schools for the Future* programme have bequeathed us a clutch of secondary schools that, in spite of their shiny exteriors and corporate foyers, are largely built on exactly the same organisational and curricular template as the crumbling buildings of the 1950s, 1960s and 1970s that they largely replaced? Building schools for the past, more like. And all of this – and much, much more – in spite of the relentless constancy of educational reform programmes.

As we have argued throughout this text, herein lies the potential of COVID-19; for all its destructive impact, it is delivering a system shock that may itself produce changes that endure beyond lockdown, albeit ones that may replace old challenges with new ones, or the same ones in a different guise, notably the continuance and possible entrenchment of educational inequalities, as we discuss elsewhere in these pages, and in depth in Chapter 3.

For the educational research community – for BERA, for the National Foundation for Educational Research, for our university schools of education, the wider teacher education community and for the plethora of education think tanks and independent educational researchers – COVID-19, as unwelcome as it has been, represents an opportunity, not just for the researchers (activity on the BERA blog would suggest that they have spotted this) but critically for policy shapers and policymakers to *listen* to the lessons from lockdown articulated through the endeavours of this research community.

Policymakers have always claimed that they are committed to evidence-based policymaking, but the sources of their evidence have often been carefully selected, often from favoured think tanks (Demos and the Institute for Public Policy Research in the New Labour years and Policy Exchange during the Conservative-led governments that have followed) or based on chosen methodologies (the favouring of randomised control trials in educational research has been notable over the past decade or so) or, more particularly, the favouring of specific researchers and their preferences. Thus, of particular note are Michael Barber's promotion of target-driven methodologies during the New Labour years and E.D. Hirsch's particular take on cultural capital during Michael Gove's extended tenure as education secretary (Hirsch, 2016), although Gove may not have been aware of the Marxist origins of the concept (Bourdieu, 1986) or the personal politics of his modern-day champion who has been quoted in the *TES* as claiming that 'I have ended up being a poster boy for the Right and that is worrisome', adding 'I am definitely not saying we should narrow the curriculum in secondary. You get wonderful drama and wonderful music and learn through that' (*TES*, 2015).

Whether or not policy shapers and policymakers choose to listen (and Gove, in particular and setting aside Hirsch, is known for his disdain for 'experts' while being famed for condemning the educational research community for being part of an elitist and disconnected 'blob' at the heart of a claimed educational 'establishment'), educational researchers have both an opportunity and a responsibility here: to be ahead of this particular curve; to capture these multiple and differentially experienced lockdown moments; and specifically to capture the experience of the pupils, students, teachers and families of lockdown. Just as the scientific community is throwing all that it has behind efforts to develop tests and vaccinations, and those involved in manufacturing are throwing their energies into producing ventilators and personal protective equipment (PPE), the energies of educational researchers ought to lie in capturing the experience of these cohorts, not simply in retrospect, but as it is being lived now. Whether, of course, our leaders 'follow the (social) science' generated by educational researchers as tightly as they claim to 'follow the science' in easing or tightening lockdown remains to be seen.

The impact of COVID-19 and the need for longitudinal research

Let us finish by offering just one area that requires urgent exploration by the education research community – the experience of those young people currently enrolled on GCSE or A level courses, or on equivalent courses where the pandemic has caused written examinations to be cancelled or postponed.

The class of 2020 and their successors in 2021, those who have just left Year 6, Year 11 or Year 13 and those who have just entered these year groups – those involved in studying for SATs, GCSEs and A levels in the shadow of the pandemic, those sitting Highers and Advanced Highers in Scotland during the same period and those on apprenticeship and similar vocational programmes will have powerful and unique stories to tell, but these personal stories are more than a set of individual narratives.

There is scope here for a body of comparative, longitudinal work that tracks the children and young people who have had examinations and assessments cancelled or adapted, or their immediate pre-assessment studies significantly interrupted, and those who were examined or otherwise assessed under the 'old' normalities in 2019. How, comparatively, will these groups fare as apprentices and undergraduates? How, again comparatively, will they fare in future employment markets and in income profile? And are there other, specific ways in which they might thrive or struggle because of their experience of lockdown, notably in terms of well-being and outlook?

Of course, there are multiple other research opportunities and needs, far more than one could identify in a section (or book) of this size, but the point is to identify and capture these. To fail to collate, curate and share educational lessons from the lockdown would be a missed opportunity to stress how important the contribution of educational research can be at this time; it would also be a dereliction of our duty and our purpose as researchers during a period when the foundations of an education system fit for the twenty-first century, not the nineteenth, might just be being laid. Let's make sure that we play our part in the construction of education's new normal, one that addresses at the outset the pervasive failings of that which it replaces.

Inspection and research: a time for a meeting of minds?

Perhaps the repurposing of the Ofsted workforce for the autumn term 2020 offers an opportunity to reposition the English inspectorate for a longer-term post-lockdown landscape: as a research agency rather than one primarily concerned with monitoring, as the publisher of reports that share intelligence rather than simply pass judgement. How about a world in which the much trumpeted notion of a 'system-led, self-improving' education system is informed in its system leadership and the self-improvement steps that it takes by an agency, or perhaps an *authority*, that helps gather evidence from which parents, governors, teachers, schools and other professionals and organisations can themselves make judgements, rather than be guided by the fading 'good' and 'outstanding' barriers on the school fence?

In such a model – a name change might be apposite – this repositioned inspectorate (or 'developmentorate') would set out the evidence that might enable informed decisions to be taken by both parents and educational professionals, for instance about school choice or whether or not to apple for an advertised post. Those seeking membership of a school community, in these or other ways, would be encouraged to surmise the evidence and read the reports, rather than take headline judgements at face value.

In this kind of school inspection (or school *development*) culture, the conclusions reached in reports would amount to the form of formative assessment argued for at the start of this chapter, not a summative judgement; the language used, in both the title of the recast organisation and its practice, would reflect this, with the language of monitoring and policing departing the stage of school improvement, a stage it should never have occupied, never mind dominated. There are many very skilled and dedicated educational professionals at Ofsted (some of whom have spoken to us in the process of researching this book) and in equivalent agencies, across the UK and beyond, but this has been the reality, at least in England, these past three decades.

Summary and key messages

If educational policy interventions are to be appropriate, timely and effective, they need to be informed by the evidence generated by a vibrant educational research community. Such a community exists in the UK but, too often, the messages that emerge from its work are ignored or misrepresented by policymakers of all persuasions. Further, on some occasions, school leaders, teachers and others in the educational landscape are insufficiently engaged in the research process or informed of its outcomes. It is urgent that, as policymakers and professionals, we address these failings and place research-informed practice at the heart of all that we do.

It is right that publicly funded education and schooling systems are open to public scrutiny and that the performance of schools is not shrouded in mystery. However, in leading to the suspension of a number of the means through which schools are held to account (notably, the inspectorate and performance tables), lockdown has enabled us to see how the system, and individual schools, perform in the absence of these measures.

And, it has enabled us to begin to consider what kind of measures we might need to guide and inform the decisions of parents, professionals and policymakers in a post-lockdown landscape.

Recommendations

9.1 Any reinstatement of inspection and accountability measures should take account of the context and consequences of lockdown and retain this approach in the event of any future periods of suspension.

9.2 Building on the principles underpinning the visits programme to English schools in autumn 2020, consideration ought to be given to the pivoting of school inspection away from a judgemental and towards a developmental ethos.

9.3 Consideration should be given to the prospect of reconstituting and rebranding school inspectorates across the UK in light of this proposed change in ethos.

9.4 The Department for Education should work in partnership BERA, university schools of education and similar bodies and a range of philanthropic foundations to fund and deliver a range of studies designed to capture the many and varied lessons from lockdown, including the major longitudinal study proposed in Recommendation 5.4.

9.5 This body of investigative work should enable the engagement of school leaders, teachers and other frontline educational professionals in the research process.

Recasting the learning blend   **10**

Technology and pedagogy

As we have already argued in previous chapters, and we shall reassert in the pages that follow, when it comes to digital technology, *access* is *everything*: access for teachers to the best available equipment; access to comparable equipment in the home for both pupils and their parents or carers; access to universal, high-quality internet connectivity; and access to training for all parties, coupled with the ability to affirmatively target this training at those in the greatest need. As Kate Green, appointed midway through lockdown as the UK Labour Party's shadow education secretary in the Westminster Parliament and a former director of the Child Poverty Action Group, puts it:

> We know that some children have been able to undertake much more home-based learning because they've had access to the resources to do so. Other children have been able to have very little home learning at all. The government needs to look at what sort of digital access funding it's going to put in place.
>
> (Green, cited in Weale, 2020c)

We have already explored the issues relating to 'catch-up' strategies and the concept of a 'recovery' curriculum in Chapter 6, so let's not revisit those points here. Ultimately, Green's argument is more profound than that. Why? Because, even if inequality and catch-up were not significant concerns – and, *of course*, they are – the virus has exposed an education system, at least in state schools, which the overwhelming majority of young people attend, that is woefully ill-equipped to shift towards a focus on blended learning and a *connected* curriculum that, in the best examples, COVID-19 has opened up the *possibility* of. This is *not* the fault of the schools, given that it is a switch that was barely on the horizon when news of the virus first emerged in China, but it does show a lack of scenario planning and future-focused thinking by system leaders since the millennium.

Given this background, one of our focus group participants, an experienced school governor and governor trainer, reflecting on the experience of lockdown, offered this thought: 'Look, most of us haven't had blended learning, we've had emergency, technologically enabled learning' (Philip Preston, governance trainer, Herts for Learning, focus group – school governors and trustees, 21 July 2020). Shifting from 'emergency, technologically enabled learning' to genuinely blended learning, and becoming comfortable as education professions with the pedagogical shift that this involves, could be one of the enduring legacies of lockdown, but this is only likely to be successful if this shift challenges the educational achievement gaps that characterised the UK's pre-lockdown education systems and developed education systems the world over.

The new digital learning age: a new horizon or the entrenchment of old divides?

It is far from a foregone conclusion that innovations in digital learning will benefit all. The risk is not just that we inflict on children and young people, and their teachers, an austere diet of passive screen watching, without the creative licence of the author to make it both bearable and worthwhile, but that technology reinforces rather than challenges existing hierarchies of power and opportunity. We have seen during the pandemic the success with which middle-class professionals – typically in more spacious homes and sometimes with garden offices – have prospered, commute-free, during the lockdown, largely because of the connectivity offered and facilitated by digital technologies. Indeed, their success has been sufficient to question the future viability of the city centre business districts into which, pre-lockdown, they crammed, supporting flourishing lunchtime and early evening economies in the coffee shops, bars and boutique micro-stores that straddled the short walk from office to tube or metro station in London, Birmingham, Edinburgh, Manchester, Leeds and elsewhere.

Yet this new economy of affluent, often young(-ish), technologically enabled and technologically *confident* homeworkers is mirrored by a shadow economy of disadvantaged communities, crammed into overcrowded housing, possibly with some access to the Internet through a smartphone or shared laptop and employed, often casually, in the kind of labour-intensive workplaces where, on too many occasions, the failure to implement social distancing sits alongside sub-minimum wage remuneration, barely existent health and safety regulations and job insecurity. This is the digital divide – and the home–working divide – writ large, and these were the communities (often minority ethnic communities) in which local lockdowns first re-emerged in mid-summer and early autumn 2020. Access to technology in comfortable homes helps the better off to *de-risk* COVID-19, especially where parents can or do work from home and are experienced in using blended strategies in their daily lives; the inability to access such technology in cramped homes coupled with the need and requirement to work on-site puts disadvantaged communities at greater risk.

Technology, against the background of such inequality of opportunity, is a double-edged sword – great if you have access to it but part of the problem if you do not. As Anthony Painter and Louise Bamfield remark in their RSA Power to Create paper, *The New Digital Learning Age: How We Can Enable Social Mobility Through Technology*:

> New technology is not a force of nature. Its impacts and who gets to share in its potential benefits are grounded in the choices we make as a society. The question is what are the right policy choices to enhance life opportunities for the greatest number as we experience widespread technological change?
>
> (Painter and Bamfield, 2015, p. 7)

To reiterate, the challenge, therefore, is not just for schools to play their part in ensuring that our most disadvantaged young people get access to the technology that, pre-pandemic, they did not have; it is to ensure more broadly that the impact of their access is *affirmative*. In short, the potential of the new digital technologies, especially in how they pertain to our schools and other learning settings, needs to be harnessed as a tool to 'close the gap'. Without positive action in this regard, there is the genuine risk that this emergent technology's impact will be to widen educational disparities. To use Painter and Bamfield's phrase, this is about making 'the right policy choices to enhance life opportunities for the greatest number'. But it is not just about policy choices; the challenge, as always, is policy *implementation*, as the experience of one such initiative, the attempt to get laptops into disadvantaged homes during lockdown, demonstrated. But before we explore the lessons to be taken from this well-intended but poorly executed policy choice, let us turn to another political intervention, that of former Labour schools minister, Lord Adonis.

Andrew Adonis and the digital readiness of schools

We have established that the experience of the virus opens up the possibility of digital and blended pedagogies and of radically revised approaches to schooling, but if these are to succeed and become the norm system-wide, we are talking about a significant reshaping and reorientation of our school system. Here, the intervention, via Twitter, and relatively early in lockdown, of UK Labour peer, Andrew Adonis – the original architect of the academies programme in English schools and somebody widely recognised as an educational innovator – in the debate about schools' readiness, in technological terms, for the pandemic was both instructive and provocative: 'Every state school should be providing a full online learning programme during lockdown so that students don't fall behind' (@Andrew_Adonis, 30 April 2020). In another tweet, Adonis added:

> I have written to Amanda Spielman, the chief inspector of schools, to express concern that many schools are not providing adequate online learning & support during the crisis. @Ofstednews has a key role to play in monitoring schools & highlighting good & poor practice.
> (@Andrew_Adonis, 30 April 2020)

The response of the profession was swift and direct, not least from head teachers and those representing them, including this comment from Paul Whiteman, general secretary of NAHT:

> Yesterday, Lord Andrew Adonis tweeted to say he'd written to Ofsted chief, Amanda Spielman, concerned that schools are not providing enough online learning ... Teachers have effectively rebuilt our education system from scratch in a matter of weeks in response to a crisis deeper than has been experienced for generations. They have moved mountains in mere moments to support children, their families and their communities. They have remained open for the most vulnerable children and for children of key workers. For those not at school, they have provided a rich mix of support and materials, both online and off.
> (Whiteman, 2020b)

Warming to his theme, Whiteman continued:

> And providing material is not the whole game. Getting children to interact at a distance is a new discipline. Teaching is hard enough

when a child is with you (as many parents have discovered), but it's a whole other order of complexity when they are not. A 30 per cent take-up of online material in the first five weeks of lockdown should be celebrated, not derided. Let's build on that success, not jump to suggestions that it is failing.

A twitter spat of some days' duration ensued with the evidence for Adonis's claims, his links with a prominent group of independent schools and his role in New Labour's *Building Schools for the Future* programme (and whether they actually were built for the future or a non-digital past) called into question.

His intervention may have been poorly judged and clumsily executed but his central observation that schools were not, for the most part, digitally ready for the pandemic holds true. However, the same might be said about the majority of organisations, whether their focus is business, public service or charitable endeavour. The question for exploration here is how much more technologically adept are schools now, and how ready might they be for future events of a similar scale? But before we explore the matter of digital readiness, the move to get laptops or comparable devices into the hands of disadvantaged secondary school students is worthy of exploration. Not for the first time during lockdown, it provided an object lesson in how not to deliver well-intended policy objectives.

The laptops debacle

The Department for Education's announcement on 19 April 2020 that it would provide laptops or tablets for disadvantaged children in England, together with a wireless router for those who did not have internet access, was widely welcomed by headline writers, by the profession as a whole and by school leaders in particular, but the implementation of the *Get Help with Technology* programme, and the small print relating to it, brought a contrasting reaction. The government had committed to providing such devices for a particular year group and to supporting those in specific settings. Thus, the laptops or tablets, and the related routers, were made available to:

- care leavers;
- children and young people with a social worker;
- disadvantaged pupils who were in Year 10 in the 2019 to 2020 academic year.

(Department for Education, 2020c)

By the time the scheme emerged some heads had taken things into their own hands. London head teacher Daniel Coyle picks up the story:

> There was another problem ... what we call the digital divide ... Obviously we had tried to ensure before the lockdown commenced that all our children had computers ... Maybe we should've done a little bit better, because it was clear by, you know, the second or third week of the lockdown [that] a lot of children were doing homework on phones or, as I recall now, there might be one laptop in the house and four to five siblings ... So, there's not, there's not one laptop left in our school at the moment everything's gone. There's one on the stage, for presentations, and that's it. Nothing in PE, nothing in DT [design technology], nothing in drama, nothing in science. We just gave them out to the kids. The kids came in and signed for them.
>
> (Daniel Coyle, head teacher, Newman Catholic College, research interview, 10 August 2020)

Coyle continues, illustrating how far behind the curve the Department for Education provision was:

> And then we got one or two schemes going ... the government were useless. We filled in some paperwork in April and they gave us fifty [devices] in July ... July! And we picked up one or two others from different organisations that I know ... the church, the temples and the mosques were very supportive.

And Coyle's was not the only school to make such a move. In rural areas, the digital divide was arguably even starker and harder to bridge than in the cities:

> We're the second poorest region in northern Europe overall, I think, and our schools have often gone the extra mile to get equipment out to kids and to families. One academy stripped out all its desktop computers in the offices because they thought that the desktop computers, plugged in, would be more reliable than giving them wireless devices. And I think that was a really inspired decision.
>
> (Graeme Plunkett, school improvement adviser, Cornwall Council, focus group – secondary education, 15 June 2020)

Probably mindful of the reaction of schools to the implementation of the scheme in the previous academic year, new guidance was issued for 2020–2021, with additional devices being made available to:

- pupils in years 3 to 11;
- clinically extremely vulnerable children across all year groups who are shielding or self-isolating on official advice;
- children in all year groups unable to access remote education while attending school on a hospital site.

(Department for Education, 2020d)

And the updated guidance added: 'More laptops have been made available for disadvantaged children in certain year groups who are affected by disruption to face to face education at their school, or have been advised to shield because they are clinically extremely vulnerable', before going on to confirm that device orders could be placed when:

- face-to-face education at a school is disrupted following official advice;
- a school supports a clinically extremely vulnerable child who is shielding or self-isolating following official advice;
- a school is supporting children who live in an area subject to local restrictions, which means they're unable to attend.

Time will tell whether the well-intended *Get Help with Technology* scheme is more effective during the year ahead and whether the Department for Education can deliver on its promise to deliver the devices within forty-eight hours. But, first time around, the laptop debacle had resulted from a style of leadership epitomised by an ethos that we have highlighted several times in these pages, that of announce first and worry about the detail later; in fact, it was more like announce *immediately* and let heads and their colleagues in schools get on with the detail in due course.

Technology and teaching: towards a 'blended' approach

It might reasonably be argued that much of the technology used by schools during lockdown is not especially new but, for many, it is new in being used in the day-to-day delivery of learning. During lockdown, individual schools and teachers have met with varying levels of success in this regard, some excelling, some floundering, some using these technologies to teach old stuff in old ways, others using the same technologies to develop completely new pedagogies and practices and to develop new styles and types of relationship with the pupils or students that they serve, and with their families, to facilitate new communication techniques and to foster new *collaborative* relationships among pupils or students, among teachers and between teachers, pupils and parents. As a parent and education professional who spoke to us put it:

> It struck me how massive a challenge it was for the teachers to all of a sudden shift to this online world and how there was a big skills gap between what they needed in the classroom and what they needed to be [effective] online.
>
> (Manjit Shellis, assistant director for wider learning, Birmingham Education Business Partnership, focus group – parents, guardians and carers, 23 July 2020)

Against this background, we may see a new set of 'outstanding' schools emerge in the wake of COVID-19; these are likely to be the schools who have used the technology of the online world to excel during lockdown, and those who learn from these schools, post-lockdown. These will not necessarily be those who have hitherto been judged 'outstanding', either by the inspectorate or in their communities. Instead, these will be those schools who have mastered the world of online learning – and in particular socially connected online learning – those who can convene groups and facilitate virtual classrooms, those who can host conversations between students, teachers and parents and those who genuinely 'get' the potential and practice of online assessment and parental engagement.

Already established in a range of business settings, beyond COVID-19 the use of digital technology will become increasingly normalised in our schools. Indeed, in the upper-secondary phase and in further and higher education, where childcare is not an issue, this technology might mean that 'working from home' will become as common in our learning organisations as it already, and increasingly, is in our businesses. Moreover, with concerns about the potential of university campuses to become hotbeds for virus transmission, a number of higher education institutions – including, to considerable media interest, the University of Cambridge – have already announced plans to move away from an emphasis on lecture-based delivery and towards a blend of online and small-group- (or bubble-) based delivery, at least for the 2020–2021 academic year.

This is not, though, about online activity, or on-screen passivity as it is sometimes experienced, *replacing* face-to-face 'in-the-room' learning and collaboration. Although there will be activities that do switch completely from offline to online, the post-virus world is more likely to commonly involve online strategies and techniques augmenting or complementing 'in-the-room' learning, creating a school environment characterised by blended learning and blended working. And, of course, this is the type of blending that is taking place in other spheres – in how we shop, work and engage in leisure. In short, schools are preparing young people for a blended world; modelling that blending in how schools work is a contribution to such an education – not so much a 'click and collect' experience of schooling as a 'click and engage' approach to learning, and one that, a decade from now, is likely to be as embedded in our practice as the use of email and smartphones are now.

Summary and key messages

Many schools have transformed, or have begun to transform, their online practice during lockdown. The challenge now is to sustain this practice, rather than 'putting it back in the cupboard until we need it again', as one conservative head teacher remarked to us. Teachers' often newfound willingness to engage with technology needs to be harnessed through a national continuing professional development strategy that enables teachers to build on the skill set and the confidence that many have begun to develop during lockdown.

The willingness of these schools and teachers during lockdown to embrace digital technologies has been impressive but there is now a need for a much more systematic approach to the development of educators' and education leaders' digital literacy (Zhou and Wolstencroft, 2020).

Recommendations

10.1 Unilaterally raising the capacity and quality of digital and online provision to that of the best schools needs to be a national policy priority and a priority within every local authority, every multi-academy trust and among comparable bodies in the independent sector.

10.2 In due course, and within an agreed time frame, schools should be required to develop and periodically update a blended learning strategy that clearly outlines how digital and online technologies support learning in and beyond the classroom, assessment and liaison with parents.

10.3 It should be recognised as a priority by policymakers that closing the digital divide is key to closing the attainment gap between advantaged and disadvantaged children.

10.4 Forthcoming inspections should capture the use of digital technologies in schools and their impact on learner outcomes.

10.5 Consideration should be given to the development and funding of dedicated adult and family learning programmes for parents and professional development programmes for school staff, so as to build digital literacy, capacity and confidence system-wide.

Next steps

In the Preface, I outlined just how fast-changing the lockdown landscape is, not just in schools but in almost every aspect of our lives, and especially in our workplaces (Naseer, 2020) and our communities (Lawrence, 2020). In terms of schooling, this landscape has changed on an almost daily basis throughout the period of our research and writing. This makes the offering of recommendations and the drawing of conclusions a challenging task, albeit a necessary one if the lockdown-inspired *aspirations* set out in this book are to translate into *post-lockdown* realities.

Thus, in this closing section I draw six headline conclusions, each relating to one of the following themes, which are likely to endure, however the months and years ahead shape up:

1. Putting well-being first.
2. Closing the achievement gap.
3. Rethinking the curriculum and its assessment.
4. Growing digital connectivity and digital literacy.
5. Building a new relationship between schools, families and communities.
6. Creating a teaching profession and schooling system prepared for tomorrow, and for a world as yet unknown.

Our fifty end-of-chapter recommendations, set out together in Appendix C, are largely focused on the detail of schooling practice on the ground; they are recommendations that are likely to impact directly (and positively) on the many stakeholders in our schooling systems: children and young people; parents and carers; teachers and the wider school workforce; those involved in school management, leadership and governance; and the system leaders these stakeholders work with. They are not seeking to place new burdens on these stakeholders, but rather to nudge practice in particular directions, directions captured in these headlines.

Thus, these conclusions are targeted at policymakers and policy shapers and are intended to have applicability, whether these influencers and decision takers are based in England, the UK or in other countries. They are made alongside one plea: continue to capture the story of lockdown, wherever in this power elite you sit. We need to do more than identify and apply 'solutions'; we need to listen to, and trust, the various professionals active in the educational landscape and we need to continue to capture the stories of those who have lived through lockdown, especially the children and young people who must always remain the reason for our shared enterprise.

In this last regard, we must do one more thing, as set out towards the close of both Chapter 5 and Chapter 9: we must track, through one or more large-scale longitudinal studies and a multitude of other research endeavours, the experience of those cohorts of children and young people who have felt a particularly acute impact during the lockdown months or who are likely to feel such an impact because of the lockdown in the years to come, for instance:

- those starting school or in the earliest years of schooling;
- those who are passing through key educational transition points, perhaps progressing into junior or secondary school or setting off for college or university;
- those who will miss landmark events, such as the sitting of written papers as part of their public examinations;
- those who have faced particular struggles during the lockdown, possibly because of bereavement, domestic disharmony, violence, abuse or poverty;
- the parents, guardians and carers of these children and young people.

And we must also continue to capture the experience and career trajectories of the support staff, teachers and school leaders who have guided us through lockdown, for instance:

- those embarking on initial teacher education programmes and gaining their first posts in 2020 and 2021;
- those in leadership positions during the crisis, notably heads, principals, executive leaders and those in senior school governance roles;
- those professionals working in the well-being sphere and related areas, such as student counsellors, educational psychologists, social workers and youth workers.

As the shadow education secretary, Kate Green puts it:

> We have to make good the damage that has been done [in] the last few months and we need to have a plan [for] how we're going to continue to protect those children over the next couple of years as the virus clearly hasn't gone away.
>
> (Green, cited in Weale, 2020c)

But this must be about more than making good the *damage* of lockdown and our interventions will need to endure beyond two years; these interventions must also be about capturing the *impetus* and *opportunity* created by lockdown (Lawrence, 2020) to not just rebuild but *recast* and *reset* our schooling system.

Towards the close of lockdown, BERA (the UK's membership body for educational researchers that we drew attention to in Chapter 9), set up a small grants fund to support COVID-19-related research projects, envisaging supporting three or four proposals to the tune of £4,000 each, a timely but brave move by an organisation that is effectively self-funded through a modest menu of membership fees and events; it received more than eighty applications. Herein lies the hunger of the educational community to explore, capture and share the lessons from lockdown, but we must be much more ambitious if we are to be cognisant of the lessons from lockdown in all their richness and complexity.

At the very least, national departments of education and networks of the biggest philanthropic foundations ought to be supporting one of the biggest international research efforts in educational history, akin to exactly the efforts that are being (rightly) extended in pursuit of a vaccine, and for treatments that address the symptoms of the disease, so as to track the impact of the lockdown and its fall-out on the learner groups identified above.

Our education departments might not have the wealth of 'big pharma' to support such an effort, but a body of research that will tell us, a decade from now and at several intervals along the way, how what Green calls the 'COVID generation' have fared, and the importance of all of those things that lockdown has forced the suspension of – not least the high-stakes assessment and inspection cultures that have become so central to our educational policy and practice over the past three decades – will be invaluable.

It will surely be more costly to not make such an investment. Perhaps the headline conclusions set out at the start of this chapter might be among those themes that such a body of work might explore. It is to the detailing of these headlines that I now turn.

1. Putting well-being and inclusion first

Well-being and inclusion are often presented as the 'fluffy' stuff to be turned to after achievement (usually measured in specific attainments) has been 'sorted'. Proponents of well-being and inclusion often, unwittingly or otherwise, contribute to this narrative by appearing to champion it *over* attainment and achievement with calls to abolish various forms of testing and the public recording of school performance.

On both sides this is unfortunate and amounts to a false dichotomy; the well-being of children and their families, and the staff who work with them, is not an optional extra and inclusion and attainment are not alternatives. Instead, well-being and inclusion are prerequisites for raising both attainment, as measured by examination grades secured, and achievement, much more broadly. Rebecca Brooks, the author of several reports for the charity Adoption UK, has devoted her career to attending to well-being, especially the well-being of adopted and care-experienced children, children who remain twenty times more likely to be excluded permanently from school and achieve approximately half as well as their non-adopted, non-care-experienced peers in terms of attainment at the close of primary and secondary schooling (Adoption UK, 2018), puts it like this:

> The well-being of students is not an annoying add-on to the proper work of school … it's actually foundational. And the research backs [this] up that when students are feeling safe, and nurtured and the well-being is attended to and the relationships are there … the learning and the attainment will come. And once you can get them on that ladder of attainment and doing well in their education, that increases their well-being and leads to a kind of virtuous spiral of goodness for everybody.
>
> (Rebecca Brooks, education policy adviser, Adoption UK, focus group – special education and alternative provision, 8 July 2020)

Moreover, the point has been made in these pages that the *relentless* and *sole* pursuit of attainment has two negative outcomes: first, it consolidates the exclusion of those who, for whatever, reason, are not achieving; second, it burns out pupils, parents and teachers. It especially burns out those working in the most disadvantaged settings because they find themselves working with young people who feel the system has given up on them, and who, reciprocally, give up on the system. The ever-greater efforts of these teachers and those who support them produce ever-diminishing returns, and risk generating demoralisation and damage to well-being in the process.

As if to add insult to injury, all of the performance measures (the tables, the inspectors, the appraisals) tell them just how badly they are doing.

There are two ways out of this, the *romantic* (but unsustainable) and the *smart* (and sustainable). The romantic approach comes in the form of the appointment of the 'super head'. As I have argued, the problem is that while they exist, there aren't enough to go around, and they can burn-out too, unless they move on to another school to be re-energised by a new challenge.

The smart approach is to turn the attainment–inclusion lens around, adopting a deliberately *inclusion-first* strategy. In this model, as we have rehearsed earlier in these pages, inclusion is not the consolation prize for non-achievers; it is the prerequisite for the achievement of all. The returns may take longer but they are sustainable. When there is mass underachievement in the education system, attainment-first strategies are the only educational and political option, but when everybody in the system is working at capacity, the quick gains secured by following the strategies of the school improvement experts of twenty years ago are no longer there to be made. Diminishing returns have set in, and new strategies are needed. Maybe, just maybe, lockdown has provided the pause for this realisation, so adroitly summarised by Brooks, to emerge. At the margin, this may mean trading the eleventh GCSE of one child for the first of another, but the first child will grow up to live in a better society for the sacrifice made on their behalf and they will be the beneficiary of a much richer, more holistic education in the process. Post-pandemic, it is this better, more balanced, more inclusive society that we should seek to build and this more holistic schooling that we should strive to deliver.

As many of the heads and senior leaders who have spoken to us have acknowledged, well-being will be their first priority on the full reopening of schools; there will be significant gaps in learning to address (and urgently) but psychological recovery is likely to prove even more challenging. Well-being is the right starting point; it also provides the foundation stone for a range of *learning* strategies that are inclusion first at their core. Not just a starting point – more of a lockdown-inspired system reorientation.

2. Closing the achievement gap

The achievement gap wasn't created by COVID-19 – forty years of policy innovation are evidence of this: Educational Priority Areas, Education Action Zones, Excellence in Cities, Sure Start, the Standards Fund, a clutch of City Challenge programmes in London, Birmingham and elsewhere, the Every Child Matters framework, booster classes, pupil premium and a range of widening participation programmes, among many other initiatives, too many to remember, never mind list. And, although some have recorded notable successes (in particular, the late, lamented Sure Start programme), the challenges in closing the gap remain. Indeed, as observed above and at various points throughout these pages, the very success of raising the achievement of the majority of young people has consolidated and confirmed the exclusion of a minority, a minority often marked out by the intersectionalities of class, ethnicity and residence. COVID-19 has both rendered explicit and exacerbated this exclusion, confirming that a society divided in this way is neither healthy nor sustainable.

The danger, as we have acknowledged, is that lockdown has exacerbated these gaps and that the greater ability of those already advantaged to support learning at home, to offer additional novel learning opportunities to their children when school set activities have been completed or when these have proved in some way insufficient, and to access equipment and resources, will leave others even further behind.

In the short term, this reality will only be successfully challenged if post-pandemic interventions are deliberately targeted at those for whom lockdown has had the greatest negative impact. In the longer term, serious thought needs to be given to the remodelling of schooling systems that, generation after generation, reproduce and entrench inequalities.

Piecemeal widening participation and raising achievement initiatives may impact on the lives of some children and young people, and the efforts of those involved in crafting these is not to be decried, but providing a few ladders up and out of disadvantaged circumstances – a grant here, a bursary there – serves only to shine a light on the structural inequalities with which too many are forced to contend. The challenge is to design education systems that do not reproduce such inequalities in the first place and, in the effort to do so, there can be no sacred cows, nothing that is 'off the table' in the quest to deliver education excellence as an entitlement, not a prize.

And if we are to achieve this objective, the nature and content of the curriculum, and the assessment frameworks that record the success of children and young people in making their way through it, have to be part of the discussion.

3. Rethinking the curriculum, its purpose and its assessment

Both at the level of the individual school and as a society, the curriculum stands as a testament to that knowledge and those values and skills that we believe are sufficiently important to pass on to the next generation.

Post-lockdown, and in the wake of the movements of our age – Extinction Rebellion, Black Lives Matter, Me Too, Pride and more – we need to take a long, hard look at the curriculum and how it is assessed, to recognise that it is more than a list of subjects, that it is, inevitably, shot through with values and beliefs and that it involves the total learned experience of the child, day in and day out, at school.

In particular, we need to take a look at the concept of curriculum breadth: What do we mean by it and how do we operationalise it? Can a curriculum consisting of *only* academic subjects, and fairly traditional ones at that, be considered broad? And can we expect a single form of examination to have the flexibility and dexterity to assess attainment in *all* subjects, and all *types* of subject? And must access to the domain of so-called 'vocational' education be limited to those who 'fail' in the (singular) academic route? How about a vocational and work-related learning offer that students positively *choose*, rather than one that they *fall* in to? How about a curriculum that reframes vocational and technical learning as professional learning, undertaken alongside programmes of learning in areas like entrepreneurship and active citizenship? Post-lockdown, we need to have the courage to think differently about curriculum, because, as those involved in curriculum studies are not shy in reminding us: *curriculum is what schools do.*

4. Growing digital connectivity, digital literacy and digital pedagogy

For many schools and many families, the quality of digital access during lockdown has been central to their perceived success in responding to the pandemic; most that we engaged with during the research for this book feel that the growth in teachers', pupils' and parents' digital literacy over a period of six months or so has been striking and ought not to be lost as we move forward.

Key to this is maintaining a mindset that sees digital solutions as more than a quick and temporary fix. Thus, while digitisation may have been introduced or enhanced because of lockdown, its greater and more sophisticated use ought to be a longer-term legacy of COVID-19. But mindset and aspiration alone are not enough.

We need to think of digitisation across three dimensions: first, ensuring that homes are connected to schools and that children and young people are connected with each other through safe, secure networks; second, that there is a strategic and system-wide attempt to develop digital literacy among the *adults* who support children's learning. As one of our research participants, the digital lead in a primary school who also works across the multi-academy trust within which the school sits, puts it:

> I think there's this myth that tech is hard, but it isn't that it's hard. It's just that we get a bit afraid of trying it, and children learn so quickly language or tech because they just try it. They just press buttons and they see what happens. And what [the pandemic] has moved forward, perhaps two years forward, for my school and the network of schools I am working in, is that teachers have [begun to do the same]; they've just tried to use these tools and have seen [that] they're not as difficult as they may have seemed.
>
> (Nick Jacobs, lead practitioner for computing, Hillingdon Primary School, focus group – special education and alternative provision, 8 July 2020)

Third, that we need to bring together the best minds in our teacher education and professional development communities to develop new digital pedagogies that maximise the impact of these technologies. Writing for the web is different to writing for the page. Likewise, using the full capability of an electronic whiteboard requires a very different skill set than its chalkboard predecessor; so it is with digital pedagogy. Utilising the potential of online connectivity and digitisation involves more than simply 'putting lessons online'. That has been the perfectly reasonable and commendable response of some schools and some individual teachers during the lockdown, but in terms of *fully* exploiting the potential of digital technology to enhance and open up learning, it only begins to scratch the surface. The challenge is to develop new pedagogies that utilise this potential. As Jacobs puts it:

> The [teachers] that don't like tech are the ones that I want to speak to the most right now, because often they have some wonderful insights [to offer] … a lot of tech can be just substituting and okay, let's have a worksheet online and send it out at the same time, great! But how can we really [re]define learning from tech? That's what excites me the most … it's not enough [to do] the old stuff in new ways.

And, if doing 'the old stuff in new ways' is one risk in the post-lockdown landscape, another is that the technology 'just goes back in the cupboard', so that 'we're already to go next time'. And yet, in the classroom, staffroom and leadership team, the new ways of working that have emerged during lockdown have the potential to augment and complement, rather than displace and replace, existing practice.

For the geographer, historian or linguist (or the young person), the virtual school trip may never replace the real thing, but it does offer the capacity to be in several locations during each lesson, rather than once a year (if your parents or carers can afford the cost). Likewise, for the chair of governors or the head, the prospect of calling a 'pop-up' board meeting may mean that an authorisation can be granted, an appeal initiated or a budget signed off weeks earlier than might have been the case in a world of on-site only meetings. And attendance at network meetings and professional association gatherings by heads and their deputies and assistants – vital if senior leaders are to remain refreshed and updated through exchanging lessons learned (not least about lockdown) with their peers – can mean an hour or two away from the frontline, not a(nother) day out of school.

And these basic examples barely make an impression on the potential of what the new technologies might be able to achieve in this 'new digital learning age' (Painter and Bamfield, 2015). Whatever, they will surely offer us what Matthew Taylor at the Royal Society for the Arts (RSA) describes as 'opportunities to remodel and widen access to education in a host of ways, most of which we have yet to imagine' (cited in Breslin, 2016, p. 4). Critically, Taylor goes on to caution: 'But we will only be able to imagine these possibilities if we are willing to unlearn much of what we know about learning first'.

None of this means an end to face-to-face, in-the-room contact, socially distanced or not. It does mean a future in which we meet, communicate and teach in a much richer range of ways. The challenge, in this regard, post-lockdown, will be to resist simply dashing back to the old normal, before we've had a chance to embed some of the lessons from lockdown in the post-lockdown, landscape as part of a new mixed economy, one in which schools are not the only setting one in which blended learning approaches are a normal part of everyday life and in which how we learn has to itself be *unlearnt* and *relearnt*.

5. Building a new relationship between schools, families and communities

The experience of lockdown has made the relationship between the home and the school much more transparent and has begun to develop the foundations for an approach to learning that is much more bespoke and much more personalised. The inclusion leader at a large, successful London primary school with a diverse intake sums up the potential legacy on offer and her determination to build on this:

> I think for me, [my objective, post-COVID-19], would be … to continue with this depth of personalisation, bearing in mind that I come from a mainstream primary school that is absolutely massive with so many competing priorities, the depth for which I've gotten to know my families and our community, and our children as human beings, and finding out what they are passionately enthusiastic about. That has been the little golden nugget from all of this for me.
>
> (Cara Townsend, inclusion leader, Hillingdon Primary School, focus group – special education and alternative provision, 8 July 2020)

Of course, this has not been the case in every school. We learned of schools that had made calls to parents running into the tens of thousands, and others where there had been little or no contact, but the shared lesson is that the potential of strong parental contact is underused system-wide. We need to remember the old adage that it takes a village to educate a child, but also to understand that not every child in the village has access to anything like the same level of family or financial support.

Unmediated parental access to school is likely to widen the attainment gap between rich and poor, because middle-class parents are more likely to take advantage of the opportunities for access that are presented. However, the pandemic has necessarily (and helpfully) swung the parental engagement pendulum from 'you come to us' to 'we'll come to you'.

This focus on outreach methodologies facilitates exactly the sort of affirmative action that enables schools to better target their parental engagement energies towards those most in need, but such engagement requires those reaching out to be non-judgemental, sensitive and empathetic in their approach.

Developing the skills and confidence of teachers and the wider school workforce, and the associated safeguarding mechanisms, to manage what will sometimes prove to be intrinsically complex relationships with vulnerable families must become a continuing professional development priority, not just for schools, but for system leaders and the wider profession, for those involved in initial teacher education and, *of course*, for policymakers.

6. Creating a teaching profession and schooling system prepared for tomorrow, and for a world as yet unknown

Those children entering nursery groups or reception classes in the wake of lockdown, however long it endures, will, for the most part, find their futures in a world as yet unknown.

Many of these children will find their careers in industries that do not yet exist, making things that have not yet been invented or providing services that have yet to be thought of, meeting needs that we do not yet know we have. And the concept of a career as a singular, linear ladder, already in decline, is likely to have virtually disappeared, at least in the majority of working areas, to be replaced by a more intricate and messy scaffolding that individuals clamber across, building and rebuilding portfolios of activity as they go.

And, as Matthew Taylor observes, this gives us a particular challenge, to educate for a world in which employment is still key but in which it may well have a much reduced place:

> Learning will need to continue to prepare individuals for employment in whatever form it takes – and support individuals and families as they navigate the multiple career transitions of 21st-century working life – but it must also enable individuals to strive and thrive in every aspect of their life beyond the workplace: as citizens, as local residents, and as family and community members.
>
> (Taylor, cited in Breslin, 2016, p. 4)

A parent who works professionally with traumatised children and their families goes further:

> I would like to see a wider systemic shift [in how we do schooling] from the top down … a cultural shift around how all schools help all children to be free, to learn and to access education and to do that in a way that takes into account children's emotional well-being and where children are 'at' emotionally. And I know that's a big ask of a system. That's huge. But the purpose of our education system, when it was first developed, was to prepare children for the workforce, you know, and, and we're not there anymore. We're in a different society, different family compositions and different needs of our children [as they] go out into adulthood.
>
> (Liz Stirrat, co-founder, Families Empowered, focus group – parents, guardians and carers, 23 July 2020)

Another parent concurs:

> I wish that, I don't know how schools would do this, but I do wish that they could reward and recognise children for their own individual achievements and personalities. You know, my son has a very wriggly bottom and I'm sure he's very challenging in school, but he just does some absolutely brilliant things that I'm sure will get him a long way in life. But I do feel, at times, that because they're dealing with thirty children, and that is a massive challenge, isn't it? That those things are not rewarded at school [and] that they're seen as difficulties. And I think that is really sad for him. And I think that possibly, I don't know … we'll see what happens in September.
>
> (Participant, focus group – parents, guardians and carers, 23 July 2020)

In such a setting, the task for educators is a constantly moving feast, or at least a moving challenge, and that of building a system and profession for the purpose is even tougher. The scale of the change that we might now require will need detailed exploration, as we have suggested through, perhaps, a National Commission on Education, and probably the enactment of legislation.

Beyond Baker?

Just over thirty years ago, in pre-devolution Britain, Kenneth Baker's Education Reform Act ushered in much of the apparatus of current schooling UK-wide: performance tables, the national curriculum, a greater variety of school types, local management of schools. In the devolved administrations, subsequent practice has varied but much of the imprint remains and in England its footprint continues to be pervasive. It had begun its passage through Parliament as I attended seminars and participated in teaching practice placements organised by Barry Dufour, Doug Holly and others at the University of Leicester School of Education, and it pretty much dominated our discussions. Love it, or lament what it shoved aside, Baker's Act has been transformative, setting a template for the organisation of schooling on which others – David Blunkett, Estelle Morris and Michael Gove most prominent among them – have built. They have, of course, added transformative innovations of their own: Blunkett's drive to establish citizenship education and embed a culture of widening participation, Morris's innovative and enduring remodelling of the school workforce, and

Gove's 'Back to the Future' qualification reforms have all left their mark, but on a landscape still dominated by Baker's legislative monolith.

It may require legislation as bold and as reforming to usher in a new post-lockdown education era, possibly one with very different priorities and giving rise to a very different infrastructure, preparing young people for the multiple and diverse roles and responsibilities that Taylor points to and capturing the insights and addressing the concerns of the pupils, parents and professionals cited in these pages. Yes, offering a broad and balanced academic education, appropriately assessed, but most of all, providing an *experience* of schooling far better at supporting, holistically, the needs and capturing the talents of every child, wriggly bottoms and all, and using the emergent and exciting digitally enabled apparatus of the twenty-first century to do so.

As I worked through the final draft of what has gone on to become the book that you have just read, on a dull bank holiday Monday in August 2020, the UK radio station LBC, having got wind of my efforts, invited me to comment on arrangements for education after lockdown. In the preceding phone-in conversation, and as she introduced me, the experienced and insightful broadcaster, Shelagh Fogarty, mused: 'It's hard to get a universal education system that works for everybody' (LBC, 31 August 2020). Such wonderful understatement; it just got a whole lot harder, but it would be a good idea, wouldn't it?

Appendix A
Research methodology

This book is part ethnography (albeit in a constantly changing landscape), part quasi-journalistic account of the experience of lockdown and the telling and retelling of COVID-19 stories and part research study. For purists of one parish or another it may, therefore, fail on all three counts, but the attempt has been to write a text that does two things that otherwise excellent and rigorous 'academic' texts sometimes fail at: first, to give voice to those at the heart of these stories: pupils, parents, teachers, support staff, teacher educators, school leaders, school governors and system leaders; second, to cross over to those beyond what we sometimes think of as a 'target audience'. Of course, publishers require prospective authors to identify such target audiences, and they are right to, for a book written for everybody risks appealing to nobody. But my ambition here is that we might meet the aspirations of our target market – education professionals, those preparing to enter the education professions or to progress further within these professions and those enabling them to do so, school and system leaders and those who aspire to these roles, school governors and trustees, policy shapers and policymakers – and go a little further and reach parents, community leaders and those in other professions with no more than an interest in education. After all, an education is for nothing if it is not for sharing, and sharing beyond our own particular ghetto.

And so our methodology has sought to be inclusive and investigative, systematic rather than strictly 'scientific', whatever that now means, and inquisitive and questioning but without anything as constraining as a questionnaire, hoping that in the process we might 'find the answers to questions, we might not have thought to ask' (Foote-Whyte, 1943). Against this background, we have hosted ten focus groups, each of approximately ninety minutes in length, involving between five and fifteen participants. We have also held sixteen face-to-face interviews, each lasting about an hour, and we have taken part in a number of extended telephone conversations, typically of up to an hour in length. In each of these conversations we have sought to capture the essence of schooling during lockdown.

Each of these recorded and subsequently transcribed Zoom discussions were structured around three deliberately broad questions:

1. What were your thoughts as lockdown emerged on the horizon, and how did you initially respond once the closure of schools had been announced?
2. What has the experience of lockdown been like for you and what opportunities and challenges has it presented?
3. What lessons do you draw from lockdown, as we seek to re-establish schooling in the wake of it?

In respect of the third question, we wanted to know what our research participants couldn't wait to get back to, what they couldn't wait to leave behind and, thus, how lockdown might reshape schooling for the future.

In addition, we were invited to a series of additional online discussions and meetings concerned, at least in part, with similar themes hosted by organisations as diverse as the professional development portal Leadership Lemonade, the Fabian Society Education Group, the CollectivED group (the Centre for Mentoring, Coaching and Professional Learning) based at Leeds Beckett University, the journal *Governance* and the membership association and charity Adoption UK. Finally, in terms of primary research, we have taken a small number of written submissions, notably from those who have wanted but not been able to take part in the group or interview sessions.

Throughout, the relationship between research and writing has been iterative rather than sequential. It could not be otherwise for a book commissioned on 1 June 2020 and submitted to the publisher exactly three months later, on 1 September. This has brought benefits in that the focus groups, research interviews and written submissions have been carried out, or accepted, throughout the writing period, spurring an ongoing reflective process that has also proved energising. The final focus groups and research interviews took place in the final full week of August, and, of course, the story kept changing right up to that point. And it continues to do so.

We have also attempted to capture media coverage across a range of newspapers, magazines and broadcast networks, and been asked to contribute to this coverage on various occasions, in particular to pieces carried by LBC, BBC Radio 4, BBC Radio 5 Live, Sky News, Times Radio, the *Daily Telegraph* and *The Times*. We have also sought to capture debates in the educational press and on social media, notably Twitter and a range of blogging spaces, in particular, the British Educational Research Association (BERA) blog.

Throughout the process, we have drawn on a range of educational literatures. As well as the emergent educational literature on lockdown, of which this book forms a part, we have drawn on those literatures concerned with attachment and trauma, assessment and qualifications, curriculum studies, governance, inspection, school leadership and educational technology.

Finally, as a parent of two boys, one at the start of his secondary schooling and one embarking on his GCSE courses, as a chair of governors and a trustee of a charity with a significant stake in the educational landscape, and as somebody married to a head teacher, I have exploited the networks and knowledge that these roles have presented and I have drawn on my own experience as a (sometimes reluctant) participant observer in these landscapes, conscious that my own experience might not be representative or typical, but that it does offer several perspectives from which lockdown might be assessed.

Appendix B
Research participants

We are grateful to each of the 108 participants who have taken part in the range of research activities carried out during June, July and August 2020 – including focus groups, one-to-one research interviews, extended telephone conversations and written submissions – that have informed the analysis offered in this book, and list each of the participants, alphabetically, below.

Whether we have directly cited the contribution they have made in the text or not, those listed below have played a vital role in informing our thinking and the analysis that we offer:

Gemma Absalom, assistant head teacher, Parmiter's School, Hertfordshire

Jill Allen, head teacher, St Wilfrid's Catholic Primary School, Ripon

Glen Amoah, teacher of secondary English, Ministry of Education, Dubai, United Arab Emirates

Peter Barnard, independent education consultant, former head teacher and adviser on vertical tutoring

Alex Bell, co-founder, Leadership Lemonade

Emma Bidston, head of economics, Wellington School, Somerset

Ann Bowen-Breslin, head teacher, Hillingdon Primary School, Hillingdon

Rebecca Brooks, education policy adviser, Adoption UK

Helen Broughman, professional tutor, University of Manchester

Sean Buckley, principal, LSI Independent Sixth-Form College, Hampstead

Michael Callanan, delivery director, Orwell Youth Prize, and teacher of English, Parmiter's School, Hertfordshire

Ella Colley, knowledge centre manager, National Governance Association

Jane Collings, independent consultant, charity and social enterprise sector

Victoria Collis, managing director, River Path Associates

Mary Ann Cooper, federation head teacher, Bushey Primary Education Federation, Hertfordshire

Kim Cowie, lecturer in education, University of Newcastle

Daniel Coyle, head teacher, Newman Catholic College, Brent

Victoria Crooks, assistant professor in history education, University of Nottingham

Stephanie Cubbin, head of art, St Marylebone's School for Girls, Westminster

Caroline Daly, professor of teacher education, University College London

Kate Dixon, school governor, Wimbledon College, London

Allyson Dobson, head teacher, Dalkeith High School, Dalkeith

Ruth Dwight, independent consultant, charity and social enterprise sector

Fiona Ellis, education consultant, Surrey

Mark Ellis, board member, Kite Academy Trust, Surrey

Karen Eyres, Head of Religious Studies, St Margaret's School, Bushey, Hertfordshire

Lesley Ford, school governor, Arbury Primary School, Cambridge and chair of trustees for the Red Hen Project

Karine George, co-founder, Leadership Lemonade

Marios Georgiou, co-founder, Step Teachers

Julie Greer, head teacher, Cherbourg Primary School, Eastleigh

Tim Griffiths, teacher of economics, Regent Independent College, London

Dan Hall, Director of Information Technology Services, Girls' Day School Trust

Haydn Hanna, newly qualified teacher, Hillingdon Primary School, Hillingdon

Ted Hartley, independent consultant, adult and community learning and citizenship education

Georgia Holloran, Independent SEND Consultant

Richard Holme, lecturer in education, University of Dundee

Campbell Hornell, head teacher, Lasswade High School, Edinburgh

Rosemary Hoyle, chair of governors, Wrawby St Mary's Church of England Primary School, Lincolnshire

Donna Hubbard-Young, senior deputy head, Chesterton Community College, Cambridge

Ted Huddleston, consultant in civic and citizenship education, Young Citizens (formerly the Citizenship Foundation)

Sophie Igo, assistant head and initial teacher training lead, Chesterton Community College, Cambridge

Nick Jacobs, lead practitioner for computing, Hillingdon Primary School, Hillingdon

Zak Jalil, head of sixth form, Newman Catholic College, Brent

Nick Johnson, chief executive, British Educational Research Association

Daniel Kerbel, head teacher, Grange Primary, Harrow

David Kerr, head of initial teacher training, University of Reading

Naureen Khalid, chair of governors, Newstead Wood School, Orpington

Sally Knighton, assistant head, Pebble Brook School, Buckinghamshire

Emma Knights, chief executive, National Governance Association

Helen Lewis, education programme director, Swansea University

Rachel Lofthouse, professor of teacher education, Leeds Beckett University

Jane Lovis, deputy head, Pebble Brook School, Buckinghamshire

Nikki Lye, counsellor, Bushey Primary Education Federation

Suzy Marston, head of drama, Chesterton Community College, Cambridge

Loic Menzies, founder and chief executive, Centre for Education and Youth

David Miller, head teacher, Pebble Brook School, Buckinghamshire

Sarah Morgan, governor, Bushey Primary Education Federation, Hertfordshire

Jackie Moses, policy advisor, Universities Council For the Education of Teachers

Margaret Mullholland, SEND and inclusion specialist, Association of School and College Leaders

Sarah Murray, head of English, Parmiter's School, Hertfordshire

Paddy O'Leary, site manager, Bushey Primary Education Federation, Hertfordshire

Deborah Outhwaite, director, Derby Teaching Schools Alliance

Jane Owens, director, Purple Governance

Caroline Pearson, chair, parent council, Dalkeith High School, Dalkeith

Simon Peyton Jones, school governor, Chesterton Community College, Cambridge

Colin Platt, chair of governors, Monks Risborough Church of England Primary School, Buckinghamshire

Graeme Plunkett, senior school improvement adviser, Cornwall Council

Philip Preston, governance trainer, Herts for Learning

Anwara Rasul, Year 1 group lead and early years lead, Hillingdon Primary School, Hillingdon

Diane Rawlins, senior deputy, Arbury Primary School, Cambridge

Cosette Reczek, director, Permuto Consulting and co-founder, Transform Governance

Amy Robinson, head teacher, Monks Risborough Church of England Primary School, Buckinghamshire

Samina Saidiya, assistant head teacher, Hillingdon Primary School, Hillingdon

Wendi Sands, higher-level teaching assistant, Hillingdon Primary School, Hillingdon

Manjit Shellis, assistant director of wider learning, Digital Education Partnership

Nahbila Sher, business leader, Hillingdon Primary School, Hillingdon

Helen Shirley, pastoral lead and staff governor, Bushey Primary Education Federation

Claire Smart, head teacher, PACE Centre, Aylesbury

Julia Skinner, founding fellow, Chartered College of Teaching

Kevin Stannard, director – innovation and learning, Girls' Day School Trust

Liz Stirrat, Dyadic Developmental Psychotherapy (DDP) Practitioner and Theraplay Practitioner, Families Empowered

Neil Strain, head teacher, Stony Dean School, Amersham, Bucks

Annette Szymaniak, consultant head teacher, Monks Risborough Church of England Primary School, Buckinghamshire

Drew Thomson, deputy head, St Albans High School for Girls, Hertfordshire

Tony Thorpe, co-founder, Citizenship Foundation

Graeme Tiffany, education consultant, Federation for Detached Youth Work

Cara Townsend, inclusion leader, Hillingdon Primary School, Hillingdon

Graham Tuck, school improvement consultant, Oasis Community Learning

Camilla Turner, education editor, *Daily Telegraph*

Tessa Willard, assistant head, Kite Ridge School, High Wycombe

Alison Woodhead, director of public affairs, Adoption UK

Jenny Wynn, senior lecturer in teacher development, Bishop Grosseteste University

In line with safeguarding guidelines, we are not publishing the full names of the young people who have supported our research, or that of their schools, but their input has been invaluable.

Special thanks are due to the child or children of every parent and the pupils of every teacher that has spoken with us in the course of the research for this book; they are the inspiration behind these contributions. In addition, we would like to offer particular thanks to Adam, Amy, Ben, Benjamin, Danni, David, Ed, Frankie, Jack, Lewis, Orlando, Rachel, Rhys, Tom and Verity. Their insights have been especially appreciated.

Appendix C
Recommendations

Chapter 1

1.1 There needs to be greater cooperation between policymakers, system leaders and schools to collectively respond to the multiple impacts of COVID-19.

1.2 The Department for Education should urgently provide legal advice on the respective responsibilities of heads, governing boards, trustee boards and local authorities in the event of a future suspension of schooling.

1.3 Plans should be put in place for the possibility of future local lockdowns or school closures at the earliest opportunity.

1.4 There must be much greater recognition of, and sensitivity to, how policy announcements impact on capacity and confidence across the education sector.

1.5 Policymakers must find far more effective ways to directly engage with, and respond to, the experiences of practitioners.

Chapter 2

2.1 Schools ought to be encouraged to periodically reassess the multiple ways in which they can build parental engagement.

2.2 Engagement with parents on pupil progress and attainment should go beyond parents' evenings and attainment updates.

2.3 Schools should endeavour to place the principles of family learning at the heart of their work with parents.

2.4 Online engagement ought to be a part of the parental engagement mix.

2.5 Schools should endeavour to facilitate and improve vehicles for parental voice.

Chapter 3

3.1 Closing the gap must remain a driving principle of educational provision.

3.2 Funding streams and mechanisms should reflect this priority.

3.3 The practicality of remodelling school campuses as multi-service community hubs should be explored, with the community hub model informing new build projects wherever practical.

3.4 The scorecard on which schools are judged needs to be much broader, taking into account contextual factors and issues such as well-being, learner experience and inclusion.

3.5 The Department for Education ought to establish a Standing Commission on Education to map out what a post-lockdown education system could and should look like.

Chapter 4

4.1 The return of the curriculum to inspection frameworks is welcome and long overdue but the inspectorate needs to conceptualise the curriculum as more than a list of subjects.

4.2 Future reforms to the curriculum need to critically examine how breadth and balance are achieved, not just across the range of subjects offered but in the variety of types of learning that learners are exposed to.

4.3 Schools should be encouraged to develop practice beyond the specifically academic, such that there is a stronger focus on the development of character, resilience and the whole child.

4.4 Policymakers should urgently address the neglect of the social curriculum, notably in areas like citizenship education, economic and financial literacy and personal, social and health education.

4.5 The Department for Education ought to give serious consideration to reintroducing an expert advisory body with qualifications and the curriculum as its central concern.

Chapter 5

5.1   Future reforms to the qualifications structure across the UK ought to seek to reintroduce elements of teacher assessment and coursework alongside external assessment and marking.

5.2   The Department for Education and its agencies, awarding organisations and the profession need to work together to produce an agreed model to be implemented in the event of the cancellation of timetabled exams.

5.3   Decisions about whether and when to stage written examinations in 2021 should be made and announced without delay.

5.4   The government ought to commission a major longitudinal study tracking those who would have sat SATs and written GCSE and A level papers in 2020, tracking well-being, academic success and early career progress.

5.5   It is vital that there is a full and transparent enquiry into the 2020 examination grading crisis in each of the UK jurisdictions.

Chapter 6

6.1   Schools ought to be encouraged to take a diagnostic approach to ensure that both the learning losses and the learning gains of lockdown are captured.

6.2   Catch-up programmes need to be tailored to the needs of specific cohorts and individual students.

6.3   Funding streams need to be affirmatively structured so that provision is targeted at those with the greatest need.

6.4   External interventions, such as mentoring programmes, should complement the work of schools in addressing identified gaps in learning.

6.5   School-level practitioners need to be enabled to work with those providing tutoring services, to deliver bespoke solutions in a cohesive manner.

Chapter 7

7.1   It is vital that the emotional, psychological and attachment needs of children and young people are not ignored in the pursuit of academic catch-up.

7.2 Schools, system leaders and policymakers should pivot their efforts towards inclusion-first and well-being focused strategies, both in the immediate aftermath of the pandemic and in the longer term.

7.3 Schools must be enabled to better develop an understanding of trauma and attachment and how vulnerabilities in these areas might be addressed, an understanding that is likely to be vital in supporting the needs of children returning to school.

7.4 Education professionals must recognise that some students have thrived during lockdown and therefore develop strategies that sustain their flourishing in a school setting.

7.5 System-wide, there needs to be a much stronger focus on matters of staff well-being, including the well-being of heads and senior leaders, if schools are to retain the capacity to enable the children and young people in their care to thrive.

Chapter 8

8.1 The positive profile of the teaching profession as it emerges from lockdown ought to be used as the foundation for future recruitment and retention campaigns.

8.2 Initial and continuing teacher education providers need to be enabled to capture the lessons from lockdown for teachers' initial training and professional development, and enabled to innovate in so doing.

8.3 Access routes to the teaching profession should reflect the needs of potential teachers, teachers and schools in a digitally enabled, post-lockdown age.

8.4 System-wide, the well-being of school leaders ought to be an absolute priority, guiding the approaches of school governors, system leaders and policymakers alike.

8.5 System leaders ought to commission a study of the role and effectiveness of different school governance frameworks and strategies in independent, maintained and non-maintained schools during lockdown.

Chapter 9

9.1 Any reinstatement of inspection and accountability measures should take account of the context and consequences of lockdown and retain this approach in the event of any future periods of suspension.

9.2 Building on the principles underpinning the visits programme to English schools in autumn 2020, consideration ought to be given to the pivoting of school inspection away from a judgemental focus and towards a developmental ethos.

9.3 Consideration should be given to the prospect of reconstituting and rebranding school inspectorates across the UK in light of this proposed change in ethos.

9.4 The Department for Education should work in partnership with BERA, university schools of education and similar bodies and a range of philanthropic foundations to fund and deliver a range of studies designed to capture the many and varied lessons from lockdown, including the major longitudinal study proposed in Recommendation 5.4.

9.5 This body of investigative work should enable the engagement of school leaders, teachers and other frontline educational professionals in the research process.

Chapter 10

10.1 Unilaterally raising the capacity and quality of digital and online provision to that of the best schools needs to be a national policy priority and a priority within every local authority, every multi-academy trust and among comparable bodies in the independent sector.

10.2 In due course, and within an agreed time frame, schools should be required to develop and periodically update a blended learning strategy that clearly outlines how digital and online technologies support learning in and beyond the classroom, assessment and liaison with parents.

10.3 It should be recognised as a priority by policymakers that closing the digital divide is key to closing the attainment gap between advantaged and disadvantaged children.

10.4 Forthcoming inspections should capture the use of digital technologies in schools and their impact on learner outcomes.

10.5 Consideration should be given to the development and funding of dedicated adult and family learning programmes for parents and professional development programmes for school staff, so as to build digital literacy, capacity and confidence system-wide.

References

Adams, R. (2020a). Nearly 40% of A level result predictions to be downgraded in England. *The Guardian*, 8 August. Retrieved from www.theguardian.com/education/2020/aug/07/a-level-result-predictions-to-be-downgraded-england.

Adams, R. (2020b). Primary schools in England could reopen on 1 June, reports say. *The Guardian*, 3 May. Retrieved from www.theguardian.com/education/2020/may/03/primary-schools-england-could-reopen-june-boris-johnson-coronavirus.

Adoption UK (2018). *Bridging the gap: giving adopted children an equal chance in school*. Banbury: Adoption UK.

Allen, R. and Sims, S. (2020). *The teacher gap*. London: Routledge.

Alexander, O. (2020). Letter to the editor: GCSEs won't prepare me for the real world. *TES*, 10 April. Retrieved from www.tes.com/news/dear-madam-letters-editor-10420.

Andrews, J., Robinson, D. and Hutchinson J. (2017) *Closing the gap? Trends in educational attainment and disadvantage*. London: Education Policy Institute.

Astle, J. (2019). Education versus poverty. RSA blog, 8 January. Retrieved from www.thersa.org/error.html?aspxerrorpath=/discover/publications-and-articles/rsa-blogs/2019/01/education-versus-poverty.

Attachment Research Community (2020). Attachment theory. Retrieved from https://the-arc.org.uk.

Barnard, P. (2010). *Vertical tutoring: notes on school management, learning relationships and school improvement*. London: Grosvenor House.

Barton, G. (2020). ASCL responds to one billion pound catch-up plan. ASCL, 19 June. Retrieved from www.ascl.org.uk/News/Our-news-and-press-releases/ASCL-responds-to-one-billion-pound-catch-up-plan.

BBC News (2020a). Coronavirus: teens' anxiety levels dropped during pandemic, study finds, 24 August. Retrieved from www.bbc.co.uk/news/uk-53884401.

BBC News (2020b). Marcus Rashford calls for government free school meals U-turn, 15 June. Retrieved from www.bbc.co.uk/sport/football/53042684.

BBC News (2020c). Scottish school pupils have results upgraded, 11 August. Retrieved from www.bbc.co.uk/news/uk-scotland-53740588.

Bernstein, B. (1970). Education cannot compensate for society. *New Society*, 26 February, pp. 344–351.

Boxer, A. (2020). School reopenings: teachers want to go back, but we need to know it's safe. Teachwire blog, 22 June. Retrieved from www.teachwire.net/news/school-reopenings-teachers-want-to-go-back-but-we-need-to-know-its-safe.

Bourdieu, P. (1986). The forms of capital, in J.G. Richardson (ed.) *Handbook of theory and research for the sociology of education*. New York: Greenwood Press, pp. 241–258.

Breslin, T. (2008). *Teachers, schools and change: lessons from Curriculum 2000 for education policymakers* (unpublished doctoral thesis). London: UCL Institute of Education.

Breslin, T. (2015a). A candidate's lessons from Hemel Hempstead. *New Statesman*, 19 May. Retrieved from www.newstatesman.com/politics/2015/05/candidates-lessons-hemel-hempstead.

Breslin, T. (2015b). Time for an arts-friendly E-Bac Plus? RSA blog, 20 October. Retrieved from www.thersa.org/discover/publications-and-articles/rsa-blogs/2015/10/time-for-an-arts-friendly-e-bacc-plus.

Breslin, T. (2016). *A place for learning: putting learning at the heart of citizenship, civic identity and community life*. London: RSA.

Breslin, T. (2017). *Who governs our schools? Trends, tensions and opportunities*. London: RSA.

Breslin, T. (2018). The curriculum and beyond: what every governor needs to know. *Modern Governor*, launch blog, September 2018.

Breslin, T. (2020). Governance during lockdown: can we go governance-light without going governance-free? Breslin Public Policy, 10 April. Retrieved from www.breslinpublicpolicy.com/uncategorized/governance-during-lockdown-governance-light-but-not-governance-free.

Breslin, T. and Moores, M. (2014). *40@40: a portrait of 40 years of educational research through 40 studies*. London: British Educational Research Association. Retrieved from www.breslinpublicpolicy.com/wp-content/uploads/40@40-Online-Version-Tony-Breslin-and-Mike-Moores-BERA-BPP.pdf.

Breslin, T. and Moores, M. (2015). *Curriculum 2015: your guide to the new qualifications framework*. Cambridge: Cambridge University Press.

Brooks, R. (2020a). *Home learning during the COVID-19 lockdown: the impact of school closures on care-experienced children*. Oxford: Adoption UK. Retrieved from www.adoptionuk.org/Handlers/Download.ashx?IDMF=b3326f3b-4cdf-46fe-94e1-8724bbb75475.

Brooks, R. (2020b). The myth of 'catching up' after COVID-19. Adoption UK education blog, 12 June. Retrieved from www.adoptionuk.org/Blog/the-myth-of-catching-up-after-covid-19.

Cann, W. (2020). Letters: children's mental health is paramount. *The Observer*, 26 July. Retrieved from www.theguardian.com/commentisfree/2020/jul/26/childrens-mental-health-is-paramount-letters.

Carter, D. with McInerney, L. (2020). *Leading academy trusts: why some fail but most don't*. Woodbridge: John Catt.

Claughton, M. (2020). Letters to the editor: plan for full return to school in September. *The Times*, 4 July. Retrieved from www.thetimes.co.uk/article/time-letters-plan-for-full-return-to-school-in-september-xsxsxn8bh.

Courtney, S., Armstrong, P., Gardner-McTaggart, A., Gunter, H., Hughes, B., Innes. M. and Rayner. S. (2020). Five educational myths that COVID-19 shatters. BERA blog, 14 April. Retrieved from www.bera.ac.uk/blog/five-education-myths-that-covid-19-shatters.

de Botton, A. and Armstrong, J. (2013). *Art as therapy*. London: Phaidon.

Department for Education (2019). *Governance handbook: for academies, multi-academy trusts and maintained schools*. London: Department for Education.

Department for Education (2020a). Academic year 2018/19: permanent and fixed period exclusion rates in England. Retrieved from https://explore-education-statistics.service.gov.uk/find-statistics/permanent-and-fixed-period-exclusions-in-england.

Department for Education (2020b). *Attendance in education and early years setting during the coronavirus (COVID-19) outbreak: summary of returns to 11 June 2020*. London: Department for Education.

Department for Education (2020c). Guidance: get help with technology during coronavirus (COVID-19), 19 April. Retrieved from www.gov.uk/guidance/get-help-with-technology-for-remote-education-during-coronavirus-covid-19.

Department for Education (2020d). Guidance: get laptops and tablets for children who cannot attend school due to coronavirus (COVID-19), 7 August. Retrieved from www.gov.uk/guidance/get-laptops-and-tablets-for-children-who-cannot-attend-school-due-to-coronavirus-covid-19.

Department for Education (2020e). School governance update, 25 March 2020. Retrieved from www.gov.uk/government/publications/school-governance-update/school-governance-update-march-2020.

Department for Education and Williams, G. (2020). Press release: triple lock for students ahead of A level and GCSE results, 12 August. Retrieved from www.gov.uk/government/news/triple-lock-for-students-ahead-of-a-level-and-gcse-results.

Department of Health and Social Care (2020a). Coronavirus (COVID-19) in the UK, cases by specimen date, by nation, 31 August. Retrieved from https://coronavirus.data.gov.uk/cases.

Department of Health and Social Care (2020b). Coronavirus (COVID-19) in the UK, deaths within 28 days of positive test by date of death, by nation, 31 August. Retrieved from https://coronavirus.data.gov.uk/deaths.

Department of Health and Social Care (2020c). Coronavirus (COVID-19) in the UK, patients admitted to hospital, 31 August. Retrieved from https://coronavirus.data.gov.uk/healthcare.

Department of Health and Social Care (2020d). Statement from the UK chief medical officers on schools and childcare reopening, 23 August. Retrieved from www.gov.uk/government/news/statement-from-the-uk-chief-medical-officers-on-schools-and-childcare-reopening.

Dufour, B. (1990). *The new social curriculum: a guide to cross-curricular issues.* Cambridge: Cambridge University Press.

Education Endowment Foundation (2020a). Frequently asked questions, 23 July. Retrieved from https://nationaltutoring.org.uk/faqs.

Education Endowment Foundation (2020b). National tutoring programme, 22 July 2020. Retrieved from https://educationendowmentfoundation.org.uk/covid-19-resources/national-tutoring-programme/.

Ellis, B. (2020). How will we look back on the coronavirus pandemic? *Watford Observer*, 25 July. Retrieved from www.watfordobserver.co.uk/news/18606454.will-look-back-coronavirus-pandemic.

Fenshaw-Smith, A. (2020). Should we really call this home schooling? Reflections from the research field. BERA blog, 6 May. Retrieved from www.bera.ac.uk/blog/should-we-really-call-this-home-schooling-reflections-from-the-research-field.

Fiorillo, C. and Fuller, A. (2020). Down town UK local lockdown list: latest as Lancashire and London on brink of coronavirus restrictions. *The Sun*, 19 September. Retrieved from www.thesun.co.uk/news/12362875/local-lockdown-watchlist-uk-towns-cities-restrictions-bolton.

Foote-Whyte, W. (1943). *Street corner society: the social structure of an Italian slum.* Chicago: University of Chicago Press.

Gamble, L. (2020). National tutoring programme: how to make it work. *TES*, 24 June. Retrieved from www.tes.com/news/national-tutoring-programme-how-make-it-work.

Gardner, B. (2020). Head teachers may refuse to fine parents who keep children at home in September. *Daily Telegraph*, 29 June. Retrieved from www.telegraph.co.uk/news/2020/06/28/headteachers-may-refuse-fine-parents-keep-children-home-september.

Goffman, E. (1956). *The presentation of self in everyday life.* New York: Doubleday.

Goldthorpe, J., Lockwood, D., Bechhofer, F. and Platt, J. (1969). *The affluent worker in the class structure*. Cambridge: Cambridge University Press.

Griffiths, S. (2020a). Pupils may sit only five GCSEs as state schools play catch-up. *Sunday Times*, 5 July. Retrieved from www.thetimes.co.uk/article/schools-reopening-pupils-may-sit-only-five-gcses-as-state-classes-play-catch-up-qhcjmbjbk.

Griffiths, S. (2020b). Schools reopening: pupils ay sit only five GCSEs as state classes play catch-up. *Sunday Times*, 5 July. Retrieved from www.thetimes.co.uk/article/schools-reopening-pupils-may-sit-only-five-gcses-as-state-classes-play-catch-up-qhcjmbjbk.

Henry, J. (2020). Missing out on school is disaster that lasts forever. *Mail on Sunday*, 8 August. Retrieved from www.dailymail.co.uk/news/article-8607983/Missing-school-disaster-lasts-forever.html.

Heren, K. (2020). Gavin Williamson apologises to A level students for 'distress' caused by results chaos. *Evening Standard*, 17 August. Retrieved from www.standard.co.uk/news/education/gavin-williamson-apology-a-level-results-students-distress-a4526906.html.

Hirsch, E.D. (2016). *Why knowledge matters: rescuing our children from failed educational theories*. Cambridge, MA: Harvard Education Press.

Hodges, D. (2020). For Boris Johnson's new working-class voters, getting schools back is now as vital as Brexit once was. *Mail on Sunday*, 9 August. Retrieved from www.dailymail.co.uk/debate/article-8608301/DAN-HODGES-new-working-class-voters-getting-schools-vital-Brexit.html.

Hutchinson, J., Reader, M. and Akhal, A. (2020). *Education in England: annual report 2020*. London: Education Policy Institute.

Johnson, B. (2020). Keeping our schools closed a moment longer than is absolutely necessary is socially intolerable, economically unsustainable and morally indefensible. *Mail on Sunday*, 8 August. Retrieved from www.dailymail.co.uk/debate/article-8607987/BORIS-JOHNSON-Keeping-schools-closed-longer-necessary-intolerable.html.

Jolly, J. (2020). Coronavirus parent survey 3. Parentkind, 16 July. Retrieved from www.parentkind.org.uk/Research--Policy/Research/Coronavirus-Parent-Survey-3.

Knights, E. (2020). Planning for a year of liberation. National Governance Association blog, 17 July. Retrieved from www.nga.org.uk/News/Blog/July-2020/Planning-for-a-year-of-liberation.aspx.

Lawrence, M. (2020). Impetus: the times are a-changing, but will they change us? Transform Communities blog, Breslin Public Policy, 21 May. Retrieved from www.breslinpublicpolicy.com/transform-communities/impetus-the-times-are-a-changing-but-will-they-change-us/.

Lawton, D. and Dufour, B. (1973). *The new social studies: a handbook for teachers in primary, secondary and further education.* London: Heinemann.

Lightfoot, L. (2020). 'I'm going round in circles': parents in England still undecided about return to school. *The Guardian,* 29 August. Retrieved from www.theguardian.com/education/2020/aug/29/coronavirus-parents-undecided-children-return-to-school.

Local Government Association (2019). *Improving school improvement* [unpublished research report based on a series of focus groups with school leaders]. London: LGA.

McCrone, T., Southcott, C. and George, N. (2011). *Governance models in schools: local government education and children's services research programme.* Slough: National Foundation for Educational Research.

Naseer, N. (2020). Leading like never before: power relationships, post-lockdown. Transform Organisations blog, Breslin Public Policy, 2 June. Retrieved from www.breslinpublicpolicy.com/transform-organisations/leading-like-never-before-power-relationships-post-lockdown/.

Ofqual (2020a). Awarding qualifications in summer 2020: information for schools, students and parents on how GCSE, AS, A level, vocational and technical qualifications will be graded and awarded in summer 2020, 3 April. Retrieved from www.gov.uk/government/publications/awarding-qualifications-in-summer-2020.

Ofqual (2020b). Making grades as fair as they can be: advice for schools and colleges. Ofqual blog, 15 May. Retrieved from https://ofqual.blog.gov.uk/2020/05/15/making-grades-as-fair-as-they-can-be-advice-for-schools-and-colleges/.

Ofqual (2020c). News story: appeals based on mock exams Ofqual sets out the criteria for what will determine a 'valid' mock for appeals of GCSE, AS and A levels in England, summer 2020, 15 August. Retrieved from www.gov.uk/government/news/appeals-based-on-mock-exams.

Ofsted (2019). *The education inspection framework.* Manchester: Ofsted.

Ofsted (2020). *Fight or flight? How 'stuck' schools are overcoming isolation: evaluation report.* London: Ofsted.

Painter, A. and Bamfield, L. (2015). *The new digital learning age: how we can enable social mobility through technology.* London: RSA.

Proctor, K. and Adams, R. (2020). Johnson pledges £1bn school rebuilding programme for England. *The Guardian,* 28 June. Retrieved from www.theguardian.com/education/2020/jun/28/johnson-pledges-1bn-over-10-years-for-school-rebuilding-in-england.

Putnam, R.D. (2015). *Our kids: the American dream in crisis.* New York: Simon and Schuster.

Ridler, F. (2020). Every child below 11 and teenagers with exams will return to school for a month before the summer holidays under Boris plan. *Daily Mail,*

11 May. Retrieved from www.dailymail.co.uk/news/article-8306735/School-union-bosses-hit-Boris-Johnsons-irresponsible-plan.html.

Robinson, K. (2001). *All our futures: creativity, culture and education: report of the National Advisory Committee on Creative and Cultural Education to the Department for Education and Employment and the Department for Culture, Media and Sport.* Nottingham: DfEE Publications.

School Curriculum and Assessment Authority (SCAA) (1994). *The national curriculum and its assessment: final report* [usually referred to as the first Dearing Report, the first of three reports by Sir Ron Dearing]. London: SCAA.

School Curriculum and Assessment Authority (SCAA) (1996). *Review of qualifications for 16–19-year-olds: full report* [usually referred to as the second Dearing Report, the second of three reports by Sir Ron Dearing]. London: SCAA.

Seldon, A. (2010). *An end to factory schools: an education manifesto 2010–2020.* London: Centre for Policy Studies.

Seldon, A. and Abidoye, O. (2018). *The fourth industrial revolution: will artificial intelligence liberate or infantilise humanity?* Buckingham: University of Buckingham Press.

Sharp, C., Julius, J., Lucas, M., McCrone, T., Nelson, J. and Sims, D. (2020). *Schools' responses to COVID-19: the challenges facing schools and pupils in September 2020.* Slough: National Foundation for Educational Research.

Shipman, T., Griffiths, S. and Wheeler, C. (2020). Boris Johnson: children suffer more by staying home. *Sunday Times*, 9 August. Retrieved from www.thetimes.co.uk/article/boris-johnson-children-suffer-more-by-staying-home-2bxk9mgsf.

Spielman, A. (2019). Keynote speech at the National Governance Association, 8 June. www.gov.uk/government/speeches/national-governance-association-speech.

Spielman, A. (2020). HMCI commentary: our plans for the autumn, 6 July. Retrieved from www.gov.uk/government/speeches/hmci-commentary-our-plans-for-the-autumn.

Steward, R. (2020). *The gradual art of school improvement: a practical guide.* Abingdon: Routledge.

Teach First (2020). Let's do better: children aren't getting the education they deserve. Retrieved from www.teachfirst.org.uk/inequality-education.

TES (2015). Five quotes from E.D. Hirsch that you wouldn't expect, 8 November. Retrieved from www.tes.com/news/five-quotes-ed-hirsch-you-wouldnt-expect.

Tiffany, G. (2020). Algorithmic grading is not an answer to the challenges of the pandemic. *Algorithm Watch*, 12 August. Retrieved from https://algorithmwatch.org/en/story/uk-algorithmic-grading-gcse/.

Turner, C. (2020a). Exams U-turn as pupils win reprieve over A level and GCSE grade appeals. *Daily Telegraph*, 6 August. Retrieved from www.telegraph.co.uk/news/2020/08/06/exams-u-turn-pupils-win-reprieve-a-level-gcse-grade-appeals.

Turner, C. (2020b). Extended Easter school holidays on the agenda as heads meet ministers. *Daily Telegraph*, 14 March 2020.

Turner, C. (2020c). GCSE fears as Scottish exam results are downgraded. *Daily Telegraph*, 5 August.

Turner, C. (2020d). Speaking tests scrapped for GCSE languages, *Daily Telegraph*, 3 July 2020.

Weale, S. (2020a). Fines for school non-attendance in England to resume from autumn. *The Guardian*, 29 June. Retrieved from www.theguardian.com/education/2020/jun/29/fines-for-school-non-attendance-in-england-to-resume-from-autumn.

Weale, S. (2020b). Government's catch-up fund for English school pupils comes under fire. *The Guardian*, 20 June. Retrieved from www.theguardian.com/politics/2020/jul/20/governments-catch-up-fund-for-english-school-pupils-comes-under-fire.

Weale, S. (2020c). Labour decries 'wasted summer' of inadequate support for pupils in England. *The Guardian*, 23 July. Retrieved from www.theguardian.com/education/2020/jul/23/labour-slams-wasted-summer-of-inadequate-support-for-pupils-in-england.

Weale, S. and Adams, R. (2020). Government to fund private tutors for English schools. *The Guardian*, 17 June. Retrieved from www.theguardian.com/education/2020/jun/17/government-to-fund-private-tutors-for-english-schools.

Whiteman, P. (2020a). The government announces £1 billion investment to support schools over the next two years. NAHT, 19 June. Retrieved from www.naht.org.uk/news-and-opinion/news/leadership-news/the-government-announces-1billion-investment-to-support-schools-over-the-next-two-years.

Whiteman, P. (2020b). Keyboard commentators should think before they type. *Schools Week*, 1 May. Retrieved from https://schoolsweek.co.uk/keyboard-commentators-should-think-before-they-type/.

Woolcock, N. (2020a). Coronavirus: one in four parents to keep children at home. *The Times*, 8 July. Retrieved from www.thetimes.co.uk/article/coronavirus-one-in-four-parents-to-keep-children-at-home-3239b6sjn.

Woolcock, N. (2020b). Ofqual allow thousands more appeals against A level grads. *The Times*, 7 August. Retrieved from www.thetimes.co.uk/article/ofqual-allows-thousands-more-appeals-against-a-level-grades-9bdvvq9cw.

Zhou, X. and Wolstencroft, P. (2020). Digital masters? Reflecting on the readiness of students and staff for digital learning. BERA blog, 9 April. Retrieved from www.bera.ac.uk/blog/digital-masters-reflecting-on-the-readiness-of-students-and-staff-for-digital-learning.

Index

Note: Page numbers in *italic* denote figures.